EVERYBODY WANTS TO RULE THE WORLD

AN ORIGINAL NOVEL OF THE MARVEL UNIVERSE

EVERYBODY WANTS TO RULE THE WORLD

AN ORIGINAL NOVEL OF THE MARVEL UNIVERSE

DAN ABNETT

AVENGERS: EVERYBODY WANTS TO RULE THE WORLD. Published by MARVEL WORLDWIDE, INC., a subsidiary of MARVEL ENTERTAINMENT, LLC. OFFICE OF PUBLICATION: 135 West 50th Street, New York, NY 10020. Copyright © 2015 Marvel Characters, Inc. All rights reserved.

ISBN# 978-0-7851-9300-5

Printed in the U.S.A.

ALAN FINE, EVP - Office of the President, Marvel Worldwide, Inc. and EVP & CMO Marvel Characters B.V.; DAN BUCKLEY, Publisher & President - Print, Animation & Digital Divisions; JOE QUESADA, Chief Creative Officer; TOM BREVOORT, SVP of Publishing; DAVID BOGART, SVP of Operations & Procurement, Publishing; C.B. CEBULSKI, SVP of Creator & Content Development; DAVID GABRIEL, SVP Print, Sales & Marketing; JIM O'KEEFE, VP of Operations & Logistics; DAN CARR, Executive Director of Publishing Technology; SUSAN CRESPI, Editorial Operations Manager; ALEX MORALES, Publishing Operations Manager; STAN LEE, Chairman Emeritus. For information regarding advertising in Marvel Comics or on Marvel.com, please contact Niza Disla, Director of Marvel Partnerships, at ndisla@marvel.com. For Marvel subscription inquiries, please call 800-217-9158. **Manufactured between 2/6/2015 and 3/16/2015 by SHERIDAN BOOKS, INC.,** CHELSEA, MI, USA.

First printing 2015
10 9 8 7 6 5 4 3 2 1

COVER ART BY JOHN TYLER CHRISTOPHER
BACK COVER ART BY STEVE MCNIVEN & JUSTIN PONSOR

Stuart Moore, Editor
Design by Nelson Ribeiro

Senior Editor, Special Projects: Jeff Youngquist
Assistant Editor: Sarah Brunstad
SVP Print, Sales & Marketing: David Gabriel
Editor In Chief: Axel Alonso
Chief Creative Officer: Joe Quesada
Publisher: Dan Buckley
Executive Producer: Alan Fine

Acknowledgments

I would like to express appreciation to Stuart Moore, Jeff Youngquist, Sarah Brunstad, and Axel Alonso at Marvel for their patience, support and suggestions during the writing of this story.

Considerable thanks and love is owed to Nik Vincent for first reading, and for helping me order words in right the put (under very tough circumstances).

I was also very lucky to have been able to call on Neil Grant, Elena Artimovich and Ronald Byrd for technical advice. Thank you. All the bits in this book that are correct are thanks to you. Any mistakes are entirely my bad.

This book is dedicated with love to my father-in-law, John Ernest Vincent, 1931 - 2014.

EVERYBODY WANTS TO RULE THE WORLD

AN ORIGINAL NOVEL OF THE MARVEL UNIVERSE

DAN ABNETT

BERLIN
16.12 LOCAL, JUNE 12TH

A MATCHED pair of black limousines cruised east across the river. The sky was cloudless and light, and the evening rush was just beginning to build.

The big cars stayed together. They moved with the flow of the traffic, allowing no other vehicles to get between them. At Sarsplatz, they turned north into a light-industrial sector. The buildings were square and modernist, built in the sixties or later. Artful graffiti decorated sidewalls and gates, but the high-end cars in the small parking lots suggested new investment: tech start-ups, specialist engineering, media consultancies.

Auger GmbH occupied the top four floors of a square building at the end of Montagstrasse. The building was screened by poplars along the street side. A large concrete parking structure adjoined the building's rear. The levels of the parking structure were open-sided. It resembled a stack of styrofoam trays.

The limousines entered the parking structure and wound their way up the ramps, their tires squeaking on the gleaming precast concrete. On the eighth story, they drove past the up-ramp and beyond the parking bays, and pulled up in the turning circle outside the glass doors of the Auger lobby.

Three men got out of each car. Their suits were as immaculately black as the limousines' bodywork. Their designer shades betrayed as little as the limousines' tinted windows. Their movements were fluid, their deployment precise. They covered the angles, watching the up- and down-ramps. One walked toward the glass doors and waited, speaking quietly into a wrist-mic.

His name was Gustav. He signaled "clear."

The Principal got out of the rear car and walked to the doors. He was tall, his perfect suit a dark and expensive gray. He carried a small attaché case. In another age, his bearing might have been called aristocratic.

The glass doors, etched with Auger GmbH's logo, opened as he approached. The lobby was elegant and well-lit. There was a soft hum of climate control. The receptionist looked up from her semi-circular desk.

"Peter Jurgan, for John Rudolf," the Principal said.

"Herr Jurgan, welcome," she replied. "Herr Rudolf is expecting you. Please, come through."

Two of the bodyguards flanked Jurgan as he followed her. Their names were Kyril and Franz. The others waited with Gustav, watching the cars.

The receptionist used a swipe-card to open the inner door, revealing a long, carpeted hallway lined with glass doors. The climate control inside was fierce. The air was several degrees cooler.

She tapped on the fifth door, waited for a response, and ushered the guests into a conference room. John Rudolf rose from the oval table to greet them. He was a handsome, intense man in his thirties. He wore an open-necked shirt, expensive jeans, and designer glasses.

"Herr Jurgan," he said, shaking hands. "Good to see you."

"And you, John," replied Jurgan. "I hope everything has come together according to the schedule?"

"It was tight, but I think you'll be very pleased. Gerhard?"

Three other men were sitting at the table. Like Rudolf, they wore smart-casual clothes. One of them, Gerhard, opened a steel carry-box sitting on the table in front of him. He lifted a polished, chrome mechanism from the molded cushion of the box's interior. The device was about the size of a thermos flask. It had rotating, milled collars and a set of squat, retractable legs so that it could stand upright.

"This is the prototype," Gerhard said, extending the legs with a series of soft clicks and setting the device on the table. "We're ready to manufacture as soon as you sign off."

"The requirement was four thousand units," said Jurgan.

"We estimate six months to fill that," said Rudolf.

Jurgan nodded. "But the initial requirement of one hundred?"

"Three months," said Rudolf.

Jurgan's hard face expressed no reaction.

"We had spoken of a tighter turnaround on the initial batch," he said.

Rudolf shrugged apologetically. "We were bidding to use an assembler in Augsberg," he replied, "but they just accepted a rival contract."

"Manufacturing high-spec consoles for American video games, if you can believe it." Gerhard laughed.

"I can believe it," said Jurgan.

"So we're having to outsource to a manufacturer in China," said Rudolf. "Hence the time extension. Shipping, you see?"

Jurgan didn't reply. He looked at the device.

"May I inspect it?" he asked.

"Of course," said Rudolf.

Jurgan picked up the device and turned it over in his gloved hands.

"Lightweight but extremely durable," Rudolf said proudly. "Portable, of course. Machined to ultra-precision levels. The release timer is here, in the lower ring. Remote and manual activation are also options."

"Dispersal radius?" asked Jurgan.

"One million hectares," said Gerhard.

"That seems a great deal," said Rudolph. "An enormous area for agricultural use."

"We are developing large-scale agricultural applications in the Midwest," said Jurgan. "For sheer efficiency, the dispersal range must be considerable."

Jurgan placed his attaché case on the table and opened the clasps. The case was lined with foam, and the foam was sculpted to form two recesses. In each of the recesses lay a polished metal bulb. One of the bulbs was green, and the other was hazard red.

"What are those?" asked Gerhard.

"Samples of the gene carrier," replied Jurgan, removing the green bulb.

"They are color-coded," said Gerhard.

"They're all inert," said Jurgan. "Just samples containing purified water and sugar. In application, the color-coding will relate to the specific G.M. load: wheat, rye, barley, corn, soy."

Jurgan unwound the milled collar at the top of the chrome device and opened the curved lid on its hinge. He dropped the green bulb into the socket and closed the lid. There was a soft sigh as the hermetic seal engaged.

"I just want to see the release operation," said Jurgan. Rudolf and Gerhard glanced at each other, and Rudolf shrugged.

"Why not?" He smiled.

Jurgan smiled back, and turned the device's lower ring.

"Thirty seconds," he said. The ring began to click softly, like the dial of a bank safe, as the timer moved back to zero from thirty.

When it reached twenty, the two bodyguards with Jurgan suddenly moved. Kyril went to the door of the conference room and turned the lock. Franz went directly to the climate-control panel on the wall and turned it to in-room recirculation.

"What are you doing?" asked Rudolf.

The timer reached zero. There was a click, then the sound of something puncturing inside the device. An extremely fine vapor exhaled from the top of the mechanism, filling the conference room with a gauzy mist. For a second, it was like being in a steam room.

The mist dissipated, leaving beads of moisture on the faces and hands of the men present, and on the polished tabletop and leather seats. The surface of their clothing was slightly damp.

Gerhard laughed nervously and wiped his forehead.

"You see?" he said. "Perfect aerosol dispersal, even in a confined space."

Jurgan nodded.

"It is more than adequate," he agreed. "An excellent piece of engineering. Entirely to my brief."

"Your brief was very thorough, Peter," said Rudolf. "And, if I say so myself, my engineers do very fine work."

"My brief was very thorough," agreed Jurgan. He rested his gloved hand on the top of the device. "The machining has been matched. But the brief was also for one hundred units delivered in three weeks."

"As I explained," said Rudolf, "the assembler in Augsberg has let us down and—"

"And you failed to find an alternative."

"China—"

"With a three-month turnaround."

"It is regrettable—" Rudolf began.

"It is," said Jurgan. "For you, certainly. I do not like to be let down. For my entire career, I have made it my business not to be let down."

"I'm sure we can—" Rudolf started to say.

"You can die," Jurgan said without emotion. He glanced at his watch. It was a very expensive timepiece. "In two minutes."

Rudolf blinked, uncomprehending.

"Ah, what?" he asked.

Jurgan opened the lid of the chrome device and removed the punctured, expended green bulb. He put it back in its case.

"The pathogen," he said, "is contained within this room for now. Some traces may have escaped, but contamination will be low. The pathogen operates through skin contact. Given your proximity and the degree of exposure, I'd estimate no more than two minutes."

He took out the red bulb.

"Of course, there is the antidote. Dispersed in the same manner, on a regular timetable, it can be used to keep the infected individuals alive and prevent the pathogen from activating. This is, of course, how the pathogen will be managed, ongoing."

He looked at Rudolf and weighed the red bulb in his hand.

"But for you, no such mercy."

"A pathogen?" asked Rudolf. "A pathogen?"

"Is this some kind of joke?" asked Gerhard.

"The pathogen is call HE616," said Jurgan. "A synthetic creation. I have named it Breath."

"This is ridiculous!" Rudolf exclaimed. He reached for the phone on the desk to call security, but Franz placed his hand firmly on the receiver.

One of Rudolf's colleagues made for the door. Kyril stood in his path and pushed him back toward the table.

"One minute," said Jurgan.

"This is not funny at all!" said Gerhard. "How dare you come here and play games like this! This is a legitimate business arrangement and—"

"And you reneged," said Jurgan. "It is most inconvenient. It impacts my timetable, and I am not happy about that."

"I'll find an alternate assembler!" Rudolf cried. "There's absolutely no need for this preposterous and insulting behavior! You squirt us with sugar solution and then terrorize us with claims of—"

"Terrorize," said Jurgan. "John, that's precisely what terrorism does. And terrorism doesn't work if it's a claim or a lie. It needs a foundation of truth. A genuine threat. That wasn't sugar solution.

And I do not give people second chances when they fail me."

One of Rudolf's colleagues, the man who had been blocked from the door, suddenly gasped. Blisters appeared across his hands, cheeks, and throat. He started to shake. Veins stood proud at his temples. Discolored saliva welled over his quivering lip. Convulsing and choking, he fell against the table, slid off it, and rolled onto the floor. The impact of his body sent one of the wheeled chairs skidding across the carpet.

Jurgan glanced at his expensive watch.

"A little early," he said.

"Oh my god!" Rudolf cried. "For god's sake, help us!"

Gerhard wailed, looking down at the blotches and blisters that were starting to cover his hands. The other man sat down, swallowing hard. Then he flopped facedown onto the tabletop.

Gerhard retched and then fell, striking his head against the lip of the table on his way to the carpet. Blood flecked the polished glass. Rudolf staggered toward the windows. His blistered hands scrabbled at the slatted blinds, rattling them. When he fell, he tore the blinds down on top of him.

Jurgan looked at the four corpses.

"Hail Hydra," he said.

He placed a red bulb in the device, closed the lid, and pressed the activator. Mist filled the room again. Franz adjusted the climate-control panel back to building circulation. Kyril packed the device into its carry-box.

"We're leaving," Jurgan told them. He passed the attaché case to Kyril and took the steel carry-box with the device in it himself.

Kyril raised his wrist to his mouth.

"Gustav," he said. "Coming out."

"Neutralization?" Franz asked Jurgan.

"As required for exit," Jurgan replied. The bodyguards drew black, blunt-nosed automatic pistols from under their jackets.

They strode together down the hallway toward reception. Two employees of Auger GmbH appeared in a doorway, saw the guns, and retreated in horror. Barely breaking stride, Franz stepped into the room after them and discharged four shots.

He returned to Jurgan as they reached reception. Voices rose in the offices behind them. Someone called out a name.

As they reentered the lobby, the receptionist looked up in alarm. She recoiled at the sight of the pistols and tried to duck behind the desk. Franz aimed his pistol at her cowering form.

One of the glass panels of the lobby's outer doors exploded in a blizzard of fragments as a spinning disk punched through it. The disk was about three quarters of a meter in diameter and marked on its convex face with a distinctive red-white-and-blue motif.

It was a shield.

It struck Franz before he could fire and threw him backwards through the inner glass door at the rear of reception.

Jurgan and the other bodyguard turned to see Captain America coming for them.

The Sentinel of Liberty—his uniform as red, white, and blue as his famous shield—leapt in through the smashed glass door panel. Kyril fired his weapon. Two shots went wide; the third tore off the Captain's duralumin-scale body armor.

Captain America crashed into him. His left fist connected with Kyril's wrist, sending the gun flying. His right fist drove home a punch that snapped Kyril's jaw up and knocked him headlong across the room. His shades flew off. The attaché case bounced out of his grip.

Jurgan struck Captain America on the side of the head with his free hand. The force of the blow was considerable; it knocked Cap onto one knee. He flip-rolled out of the drop, but Jurgan backstepped, evading the bicycle kick that threatened to take out his legs.

"Not today, my good Captain," he said.

"Absolutely today," Cap replied, springing back onto his feet. He lunged.

They traded blows, face-to-face, at phenomenal speed. Each man used his forearms to block and deflect the other's punches and chops. Jurgan struggled to keep hold of the carry-box.

Cap drove a heel into the side of Jurgan's knee and, as the man staggered sideways, planted a punch that threw Jurgan against the receptionist's desk. The impact knuckled over the flatscreen monitor and dislodged a pot of ballpoint pens marked with the Auger logo. Hidden behind the desk, the receptionist cried out in distress.

Jurgan had dropped the carry-box. It lay on the carpet, too far away for him to reach. He looked at Captain America.

"I really don't like interference in my plans," Jurgan said, wiping blood from his split lip.

"You should be used to it by now, Strucker," Cap replied.

Cap knew that surrender wasn't a likely option. Baron Wolfgang von Strucker was one of the most dangerous terrorists in the world, and had been for decades. He was no longer a mortal man. Science and other, more arcane properties had prolonged his life and invested him with superhuman strength and durability.

But Steven Rogers, known as Captain America, had also been gifted by science. His lifespan had been much longer than most men could expect, and his physical abilities were profoundly beyond those of an average human being.

Strucker lunged for the carry-box. Cap leapt, too, body-checking Strucker onto the ground. They landed hard, struggling. Strucker was extremely strong. Cap grappled with him, trying to pin him and lock his arms. Strucker jabbed an elbow into Cap's throat and then repeated the jab twice more, striking Cap's sternum. Cap rolled clear, and came back with a punch that connected with the back of Strucker's skull and drove his face into the carpet.

The terrorist was dazed. Cap dragged him to his feet, attempting to turn him around and push him against the desk to restrain him.

But Strucker was feigning weakness. He lashed out, and his right fist caught Captain America's chin, jarring him sideways. Strucker laughed. The black leather of the glove on his right hand was smoldering and burning away, revealing the burnished metallic filaments of his favored personal weapon: the Satan Claw.

He swung at Cap again. The Claw sizzled as it came. Cap dodged aside. Strucker raked the Claw back again, and it delivered a vicious electrical charge as it grazed Cap's right shoulder.

Cap staggered away, wincing as he shook out his stinging arm. Strucker swung another punch, the Claw crackling with power. Cap sidestepped, then drove his shoulder and elbow into Strucker's ribs. Strucker grunted and almost fell. He wheeled, but missed Cap with his next, hasty jab. Cap deflected Strucker's arm and punched Strucker in the mouth, breaking one of his front teeth.

Snarling, Strucker regained his balance and swung again.

The Claw connected.

Bright sparks spat from Cap's chest-armor, and there was a loud electrical crack. Cap flew across the reception area and smashed into the decorative false wall, knocking part of it down.

He didn't rise.

Strucker spat blood onto the carpet. He grabbed the carry-box and ran for the exit.

"Gustav!" he yelled as he ran. "Extraction now!"

No one answered him. He came out onto the turning circle. Captain America had dealt with Strucker's entourage on his way into the offices. Gustav and the other bodyguards were crumpled on the ground, their sidearms scattered. One lay across the trunk of the rear limousine. Both drivers had also been taken down. Ernst, the driver of the front car, was struggling to rise from the ground beside the open driver's door. The "door open" chime was pinging.

"Get up!" Strucker yelled at him, running to the lead car. "Get up and drive!"

Strucker's bodyguards had all been handpicked from the world's finest private security firms and non-governmental military outfits. They were highly trained, highly skilled, utterly ruthless, and keenly aware of both the fees they were earning and the level of loyalty Hydra expected for such compensation. Despite his broken collarbone and concussion, Ernst clambered into the driver's seat and gunned the engine. Strucker jumped into the rear of the heavy black automobile.

The limo sped away, screeching a hard turn out of the circle, and roared toward the down-ramp.

Shield in hand, Captain America raced out of the reception area.

He saw the bright taillights of the limousine receding in the gloom of the parking level. He paused for a moment, gauging the viability of a shield throw, but the car was too far away.

Instead, he turned and ran toward the outer wall of the structure. One of the bodyguards tried to rise and block his path, but Cap knocked him aside with the flat of his shield.

He reached the waist-level wall and looped the shield over his back. It was an eight-story drop to the street below. Without hesitation, he vaulted up onto the concrete wall, swung his legs over, and pushed off, falling feet-first.

He dropped one level, snagging the wall lip with his arms to arrest his descent. Teeth gritted, he hauled himself up and over the wall and back into the structure.

Strucker's limo had already driven down one level. It thundered past Cap and turned for the next ramp.

Undeterred, Cap turned back and flipped himself over the wall again. This time he dropped three stories. He slammed into the concrete wall span, grabbing the lip with both arms. His chest scraped against the concrete. He heaved himself up and over, dropped onto the precast floor, and started running. He could hear the echo of tires squealing above him. Now he was at least one floor below the fleeing limo.

He saw it coming along the length of the floor above, the light from its blazing headlamps blinking as the car passed each vertical column and concrete riser. He chased it at full sprint, moving parallel on the level below. He arrived at the bottom of the next exit ramp seconds before the car reached the top.

The limo swung around onto the ramp with a brutal squeal.

Ernst was a skilled driver, even with a vehicle so heavy and potentially cumbersome. Cap stood his ground at the foot of the ramp as the car burned down toward him. He unslung his shield, gripping its edge with his right hand, and hurled it at the oncoming vehicle with a powerful underarm sweep.

The shield hit the windshield, shattering the armored glass, and punched inside, taking Ernst out of the game. Before the now uncontrolled car could mow him down, Cap leapt aside, rolling hard across the precast.

The car shot past him. It didn't turn at the foot of the ramp—it simply plowed into a concrete pillar facing the ramp access. The impact smashed in the nose of the glossy black vehicle, and slewed the tail around hard. Airbags fired and inflated. Fluids gushed from ruptured ducts, creating a black, rapidly spreading slick under the car. Steam billowed from the crumpled radiator.

Cap got up and approached the wreck. He dragged his shield out of the mangled, glittering glass of the collapsed windshield and moved toward the rear. He wrenched open the door.

In the back seat, Strucker lay dazed, bleeding from a head wound. Cap reached to grab him by the throat.

He heard a shriek of tires and the roar of another engine. The second limo came down the ramp toward him at high speed, headlamps blazing. Cap glimpsed the near-maniacal face of Gustav at the wheel.

Cap launched himself out of the way. The second car missed him by inches.

Gustav's vehicle smashed the open rear door of the first car off its hinges and sent it flying in a shower of shattered glass. Gustav lost the headlights on one side of his vehicle, and scraped the wing of his car along the bodywork of the other limo, buckling the door panels and scoring the paintwork down to bare metal.

Gustav threw his limo into reverse, spinning the wheels so hard they billowed acrid smoke from the wheel arches. The limo lurched backwards, the two cars parting with a squeal of complaining bodywork.

Strucker struggled out of his limo and ran crookedly toward Gustav's car, carry-box in hand. He dragged open the rear door and fell inside. Gustav swung the limo around before Strucker could even pull his door shut. The limo clipped the tail of the crashed car, then accelerated along the parking bay toward the next down-ramp.

Cap ran after it and threw his shield. The red-white-and-blue disk spun through the air and hit the nearside rear wheel as the car turned. The wheel drum buckled slightly, but the limo had run-flat tires. The car continued to accelerate.

The shield bounced off the wheel, soared away, and ricocheted off a concrete column. Cap, still running, caught it as it returned.

Without breaking stride, Cap kicked open the fire door of the stairwell and descended the steps three at a time, sliding his hip off the handrail at each floor-turn.

He got to the ground floor. The fleeing limo had already reached the street exit at the far end of the structure. Without slowing, it tore through the automatic barriers, showering splinters of red-chevroned white plastic, and rocked out onto the street in a wild oversteer.

Cap's custom Harley was propped in one of the ground-floor bays where he had left it. He leapt astride it, kicked it to life, and tore away with his shield across his back.

The matte-black bike had originally been a Street 750, but the tech guys at S.H.I.E.L.D. had seriously upgraded its performance. Cap, no mean mechanic himself, had tinkered, too. The goal had been the perfect balance of maximum speed and optimal road-holding ability.

Cap's wheels cracked over the fallen pieces of barrier, and he hit the street, leaning hard into each turn. The limo was still in sight, driving recklessly fast. Traffic was light in the district, but it wouldn't be for long. Rush hour was coming. Cap gripped the throttle and started to close the distance, taking a racing line and cutting corners to gain as much ground as he could.

He synched his suit-mic to the bike's com unit.

"Whisper, this is Sentinel," he called.

The radio link crackled over the roar of the Harley's straining engine.

"Sentinel, this is Whisper. Go."

"Are you painting me, Whisper?"

"Affirmative, Sentinel. We have you on screen."

Somewhere above Berlin's cloud cover, a S.H.I.E.L.D. recon plane in stealth mode had him locked. Cap took another corner hard.

"It's Strucker," Cap said, concentrating on the road ahead. "I'm in pursuit. Can you lock target?"

"Target sighted and locked."

"Strucker's got something. Cargo he clearly doesn't want to give up. Can you patch me in to Fury?"

"Uh, negative at this time, Sentinel."

"Then give me a direct priority link to Avengers Tower."

"Apologies, negative. S.H.I.E.L.D. shadow on you, sir. Choppers inbound, and security details moving in from the north and east. That's the available limit right now."

"Understood," Cap replied. He dearly wanted to ask why neither the director of S.H.I.E.L.D. nor his fellow Avengers were online. But wondering what kind of emergency might have called them away was a distraction.

Strucker was an emergency all by himself. Any time Hydra showed one of its ugly heads, it meant the world was in trouble. Cap had been undercover in Berlin for three days following leads. Now that he was coming up for air and assistance, everyone was busy.

Don't think about it, he told himself. It was taking every ounce of his nerve and skill to stay on Strucker's tail at these speeds. One lapse in concentration, one distracted moment of worry, and he would spin out or plow into oncoming traffic.

And Strucker would be gone.

"Get EMT and tac support to Auger GmbH," he instructed. "Suspect injuries, fatalities on site. Go in full-tac. Hydra agents on the ground. Secure the location and lock it down. I want a full site-condition review and summary as soon as this is done. Strucker had business there."

"In work, Sentinel. Tac teams dispatched."

"Tell local to clear the route," Cap ordered. "Strucker's not stopping for anything. I do not want civilian collateral."

"Understood."

Cap could already hear sirens in the surrounding streets. He passed at least one fender-bender where cars had swerved to avoid Strucker's speeding limousine.

"Track the target," Cap said. "Find me some corners to cut."

"Affirmative. In work."

The limo was running hard. Each time Cap began to close, boosting his speed on a straightaway, the car turned hard and changed course. They were entering a busier part of the city. Vehicles were screeching to a halt, sounding their horns as the car and its bike pursuit blasted past. A delivery truck barely avoided collision with the limo and shunted into a bus shelter. A group of cyclists scattered and fell in their effort to get out of the car's way when it swung out into the facing lane to get around a line of stopped traffic.

"Next block, cut left," the link said.

"Got it," replied Cap.

He turned hard, his rear wheel slipping out, and raced along a serviceway between a factory and a row of retail outlets. Litter fluttered and flew in his wake. The roar of his engine echoed off the buildings around him.

He exited the mouth of the serviceway, narrowly missed a curb, and joined another street. Car horns sounded. He put one foot down to steady his turn, slithered a little, then accelerated off. The cut had shaved a few hundred meters off his lag. The limo was up ahead, powering down the wrong side of the street into heavier traffic.

Cars swerved out of its way. Two off them crunched together, sideswiped. A Polizei traffic car, light strap flashing and siren wailing, changed lanes and tried to cut off the limo.

The car piled right through it, its massive bulk hurling the police vehicle aside into a nose-to-tail spin, scattering headlight glass and broken bodywork.

Cap slalomed around the wrecked police car and picked up

speed. He veered left to miss a garbage truck, then hard right to dodge a bus. Its windows were full of wide-eyed, horrified passengers.

The limo hit roadworks, tearing through the red-and-white temporary barriers and scattering the frantic work crew. It avoided the heavy surfacing machine the crew had been operating by pulling out hard across the median strip. A sports car skidded to get out of its way, then fishtailed into a van and a compact.

Cap was closing. The sheer density of rush-hour traffic was forcing the limo to go slower. Where cars blocked its way, Cap could weave and slip in between moving traffic.

Strucker appeared, leaning out of the limo's rear passenger window. He was clutching a machine pistol.

He opened fire, blasting at the bike on his tail. Cap saw the muzzle flash and the bullets coughing dirt-smoke from the road surface to his left. He steered out, pulled his shield off his back, and dropped it in front of his chest and chin. Riding a Harley with one hand was not ideal, especially at high speed.

Strucker changed clips and fired again. Rounds spanked off Cap's shield, making it vibrate and shudder. A bullet took out the headlamp of his bike. Stray rounds smacked into vehicles on either side of him and chewed into the road.

Cap accelerated into another gap, just missing a truck. He pulled around it, trying to move up on the side opposite Strucker's firing position and hoping to restrict the terrorist's cone of fire.

Strucker saw what he was doing, and he disappeared back into the limo.

Changing sides, Cap thought. He did the same. By the time Strucker and the gun appeared out of the other passenger window, Cap had pulled hard across the lane and was coming up on the rear quarter of the limo where Strucker had previously been positioned. He saw Strucker attempt a shot, curse the angle, and duck back inside.

Cap got closer. He wondered whether he could risk a jump from bike to speeding car. He was so close—so very close—matching speeds, but the chance of rebounding off or missing a grip was too great.

The rear window of the limo exploded as Strucker shot it out. The glass chips pelted back at Cap. Strucker slammed in a third clip and began shooting through the ragged window space. Cap took several shots against his shield, and then revved hard and burned up along the left side of the limo. Strucker appeared at the passenger window and resumed shooting, but Cap had switched the shield to his side. Cap swung in recklessly and slammed the shield flat against the window opening, knocking Strucker back into the passenger seat.

The car suddenly veered away to the right. Cap saw they were coming up fast on the rear of a slow-moving eighteen-wheel rig. The limo had swerved to avoid ramming it. Cap jerked the wheel hard, narrowly averting a crash. The speeding vehicles passed the rig on either side—limo to the right, bike to the left. As soon as they were past it, they swung together again. Strucker hosed another clip at Cap. Shop windows on Cap's side of the street shattered.

"Damn you," Cap snarled, too aware of how many innocent people were in the vicinity. He spurred closer to the racing limo, blocking gunfire with his shield.

The limo started to slow. There was a heavy stream of traffic ahead, backed up from a busy bridge crossing.

Cap took his chance. He steered in sharply and leapt. The Harley kicked out underneath him, fell sideways, and was left spinning and sliding in the road in a trail of friction sparks.

Cap landed, belly-first, on the hood of the car and clung on. He felt himself slipping, but scrabbled to keep his grip. At the wheel, Gustav started to snake the limo violently from side to side in an attempt to throw Cap off.

When that didn't work, Gustav drew his handgun, opened the driver's window, and leaned out to spray shots across the car's nose. One tore across Cap's left sleeve, barely deadened by the armor. Cap got his shield around and blocked two more shots. He tried to gain purchase with his boots to kick up the hood and attack through the windshield. If he could tackle Gustav, the chase would be over.

Trying to shoot at the Avenger had distracted Gustav from driving. Cap heard Strucker yell out from the rear. Gustav hauled on the wheel.

The speeding limo swiped the end of one of the stationary cars in the queuing traffic, barely avoiding a full-on collision. The halted cars cannoned into each other.

But Gustav had lost control. The limo struck the curb violently and lurched up onto the sidewalk for thirty meters. It ripped down a row of railings one after another, and then smashed through a safety barrier.

Captain America was still clinging to the hood.

The limousine burst through the bridge abutment and cleared the towpath at a height of six meters. Trailing debris and the tatters of its tailpipe system, it plunged headlong toward the broad, calm river far below.

69° 30' SOUTH, 68° 30' WEST
07.26 LOCAL, JUNE 12TH

IT WAS a long drop.

He came tumbling and spinning out of the floor hatch into the shocking cold and turbulence.

Below him, dense cloud cover. Below that, uncertainty.

Hawkeye had performed several HALO drops in his career—but always with prep, and never in an emergency.

He hadn't even had time to strap on the drop-pack properly. It was hooked over one shoulder, the other set of harness straps flying and snapping in the ferocious air.

Get it on, get it fixed, get it secure. Stabilize…

He was spinning, inverting. The air slammed against his face. No mask, no respirator. He couldn't breathe. He spread his arms and legs, trying to control his free fall. Slipstream was trying to rip the drop-pack off his back. He fumbled, caught the flying straps, and managed to cinch them around his other shoulder.

Burning debris and plumes of whipping black smoke streaked the sky around him. Whatever had hit the Quinjet had taken it out of the sky, bursting through the hull and then shredding it. Surface-to-air. A missile. Rotating, he glimpsed the Quinjet's nose cone flaming like a comet into the cloud banks, drizzling dirty smoke.

Did she get out, too? Please, God, let her have gotten out, too...

He hit the clouds. Visibility cut. He was dropping through an icy void of soft white, but it felt as though he were suspended, motionless.

Arms out, Barton, legs out. Belly down, chin up.

How long did he have? Twenty seconds? Thirty? He had no altimeter, and he didn't know how high up the Quinjet had been flying when it was hit. If the cloud cover was low-lying, he might reach the ground at any second. He wouldn't even see it coming up at him.

The pressure was intense. He couldn't hear because of the windchop in his ears. Droplets of blood from one nostril were flicking up across his cheek and eye. He felt like he might hurl. *That* wouldn't be a good look. Not heroic at all...

The drop-pack wasn't a 'chute, not even a compact HALO version. It was a one-use lifter unit based on repulsor technology developed by Stark Industries. "Oh, a jet pack," Barton had laughed when Stark first showed the units to the Avengers. He'd gotten a scowl in return. *Not* a jet-pack. Just a device to "slow and soften a terminal descent."

If he activated it too early, it would burn out its fuel cell, and then he'd be falling again. If he activated it too *late...*

Give me a sign, he thought.

Hawkeye fell out of the bottom of the clouds; with a sudden shock, visibility returned. The landscape yawned below him. A vast mat of dense green vegetation. A slanting horizon. A dappled, yellow sunset sky that washed a golden cast over the view. The glitter of threading rivers. The twinkle of the faraway Gorahn Sea. The rough-tooth gray line of the Eternity Mountains, ghostly in the distance.

The jungle below was dense. Really dense. Before the attack, they'd been circling the Quinjet trying to find a viable landing zone. Hitting the tree canopy was going to hurt, drop-pack or no drop-pack.

A meteor streaked past him, dragging flames behind it. One of the 'jet's engine pods. It shot diagonally through the sky and impacted in the forest below. There was a bright flare, and a boom he could hear despite the wind. He could see fire in the impact-hole the burning junk had made in the tree cover.

He realized how fast the ground was coming up. Where was a flier when a guy needed one? Where was Thor or Iron Man?

Yeah, where the hell *were* they? Before the missile strike, he'd been flying for over an hour without base contact.

He reached for the center of the harness, found the activator stud, and pressed it. Nothing happened. He began to thump the harness stud frantically, as though he were giving himself CPR. *Come on! Come on!*

Damn you, Stark! The damn thing isn't wo—

Then he realized it was. The repulsor lift was so quiet he couldn't hear its throb over the buffeting wind. He was floating, drifting downward like a seedpod.

He angled himself feet-down. Okay, this was better. This was working. This, he could handle.

He hit the trees anyway.

Branches ripped and snapped at his face. Creepers tore. Leaves whipped against him. He glanced sideways off a tree bole with winding force and felt the bark rake his skin. The suddenly gloomy air was full of dust, leaves, insects, debris. Tumbling like a rag doll, he felt like an idiot. Where was his famed acrobatic skill and grace now?

He hit another branch. Then another. He cursed in anger and pain and inadvertently swallowed a leaf. Choking, he fell farther, glancing off large trees, smaller trees, cross-branches, and creepers as thick as anchor chains. Limbs flailing, he shredded through veils of hanging moss. The drop-pack, choked with leaf fiber, shut down.

He landed on a bed of ferns, bounced, ricocheted off a mossy boulder, and landed face-down on swampy ground. Then, and only then, the drop-pack restarted, raising him a foot off the forest floor as if he were levitating on his belly.

It died again. He fell on his face.

Silence. He exhaled, and then sat up coughing, spitting out bits of leaf.

He was alive. He'd left his dignity somewhere up in the tree canopy, but he was alive.

Hawkeye got up. He took off the dead drop-pack, told it what he thought of it, and tossed it.

The glade was still. Cycads and ferns grew thick and alien all around him. Massive, gnarled trees festooned with trailing vines and creepers lofted up into the green darkness overhead. There were sounds: the babble of a nearby stream, the buzz of insects, the croak and warble of amphibians, the continuing crack and flutter from the damage his plunging form had done to the trees.

It was humid. He was sweating. He was dirty. He tried his comms, but the link was dead air. He activated his locator bracelet, and the green LED began to wink. He pulled the scanner from his belt pouch and panned it around, three-sixty. No traces. Nothing.

No sign of her. *Please god she made it out and down alive.*

He started to walk, but the terrain was not walking-friendly. Boulders, rocks, mire, roots, dense foliage. He drew his game knife and used the serrated edge to carve a path. His hands became sticky with sap. He saw bugs: bright beetles like enameled mechanisms, coiling mud worms, a centipede as long as his forearm that made him grimace in disgust. Microscopic flies billowed around his head, searching for his mouth, his nostrils, his tear ducts.

"Hating this," he said out loud. He looked up and realized he was standing underneath a web. The silk was so fine that it looked like smoke. The web was strung between tree trunks and spread as large as a tennis net. Up in the shadows of some leaves, he saw the thing that had made it. Black, eight legs, hairy, the size of a German Shepherd.

He got out from under the web. In this neighborhood, definitely not friendly.

Hawkeye felt like he was being watched. The hunter's internal sense. He kept a firm grip on the knife. *Where are you...?*

Nothing. He clambered on. Sunlight fell in bright beams through the tree cover, piercing the emerald twilight.

Something moved ahead of him. He saw leaves tremble. He ducked into shadows, his back against the thick bole of an ancient tree. He waited, barely daring to breathe. Whatever it was, it was coming closer. He waited, the knife clenched in his hand. It was time for the bow. He needed the range. But he didn't want to move to pull it out of his quiver.

He waited. Something tickled his cheek. He angled his eyes down. A scorpion, green as guacamole and the size of his hand, was crawling down his face and onto his throat.

Not now, not now...

Leaves parted. Something came into view. It was big.

It was a duckbill: a bipedal dinosaur the size of two cars. He didn't know the fancy scientific name. Hadro-something. He did know it was a herbivore. It was huge and solid, with a domed back, hunched over on its massive hind legs while its smaller forelimbs delicately searched the ground cover for delicious treats. Its head was low, and sniffling, burbling, wet breath grunted snottily from its nostrils. Its heavy tail arced out horizontally as a counterweight to its frame. Its eyes were big and placid, like a cow's eyes. It smelled like a damn cow, too—like a barnyard. Something sweet and rotten, fleshy, gassy. He could hear the contents of its vat-like stomachs gurgling as they fermented and digested.

Slowly, he reached up with the knife and flicked the scorpion off his collar. He breathed out.

The duckbill raised its head slightly, as if noticing him. It stared for a moment, and then went back to its grazing. It broke wind, sounding off like a trumpet.

"Nice," he said.

It wasn't alone. Two more adults followed it, and then a pair of juveniles. They were all feeding.

He moved. They all looked up at him.

"Don't mind me, folks," he said. They lowered their heads.

He checked his comms again. Still nothing. Had he busted the unit on landing? He started to undo the pouch to take a look.

The duckbills suddenly froze.

The adults sat up and raised their heads, listening or scenting. Their murmuring and snuffling had ceased.

What the hell had they heard?

They started and broke, moving amazingly fast back the way they had come. They crashed through the undergrowth with unmistakable fear, scooting the juveniles along with them. One of the adults made a strange warning sob in its throat.

The hell?

Hawkeye sheathed his knife and unslung his bow. It was a carbon composite, custom-made, with a 250-pound draw weight. It was a perfect piece. He quickly checked the tension, then activated the toggle on the handgrip that allowed him to remotely select arrowhead loads from the automated quiver on his hip. He spun up three: two standards and a blunt. Friend or foe, bases covered.

A scream ripped through the glade. It was an awful sound, like the noise a pig might make getting stuck—an almost-human expression of pain. It came from the direction the duckbills had been heading.

Hawkeye tensed. He nocked a standard arrow, the other two laced and ready between the fingers of his draw hand.

A raptor burst from cover on the far side of the glade and charged him, whip-tail up, head down, jaws open. Its long, powerful hind legs drove it forward faster than a cheetah at full stretch.

It had been stalking him, ready to pounce. It was about his height, but twice as heavy and a hundred times as fast. A total killer. Its jaws would easily sever his neck while its forelimbs gutted him.

Hawkeye drew and loosed. The leaf-tipped arrow struck the charging raptor in the sternum, but didn't stop it. Hawkeye nocked and loosed again, burying a second arrow beside the first. The blunt was the only shaft left in his hand. He fired that, too, smacking the dead-weight arrow into its throat.

Then he sidestepped. The raptor churned past him, rammed into the tree, and fell dead on its side. Leaves shimmied down like confetti.

Hawkeye said something colorful. He spun up more arrows fast. There were two things he knew about raptors:

They were total killers.

And they hunted in packs.

His bow was raised before the second one charged. This time he aimed for the hind legs. Damn thing couldn't run if its legs didn't work. He put two leaf-tip shafts into the muscle of its right thigh, and the raptor went down snapping its jaws and thrashing its long tail. Hawkeye moved aside to avoid its sickle-like hind claws.

A third one broke cover, then a fourth.

"Damn it," Hawkeye snarled. He put a leaf-tip through the right knee of the first one and then another into its brow as it went over. The fourth raptor was almost on him.

The blast arrow hit the raptor in the chest and turned everything from its belly up into a red mist of bloody scraps.

Frantically, he spun up more shafts. Blast arrows. Blast arrows were good. The fifth member of the pack appeared, sprinting for him. *So damn fast!*

Hawkeye's legs were smashed out from under him, and he landed on his back. The raptor he had felled with the arrows to the thigh was still thrashing around in a frenzy, and its tail had swept under him. He lay prone and helpless as the raptor snapped at him viciously. Saliva flew from its chopping jaws.

Rolling away, he fired on his side. Not an ideal shot, but needs must. The blast arrow went down its gullet, and the explosion showered Hawkeye with meat.

But the fifth raptor was on him. It leapt the last few meters like an Olympic long-jumper, the sickles of its hind feet raised to eviscerate him as it landed.

There was a rapid, deafening volley of nine-millimeter gunfire. The shots knocked the leaping raptor sideways out of the air. It crashed into the undergrowth, shredding the thicket with its death spasms.

"Just going to lie there all day?" asked the Black Widow.

She stepped into view, a smoking automatic in each hand. Her red hair looked as dark as blood in the green gloom.

He got up.

"Just thought I'd take it easy for a while, Natasha," he replied. He didn't want let on how relieved he was to see her alive.

She paused, and shrugged.

"Welcome to the Savage Land," she said.

"Gee, thanks."

"Your locator's working?" she said.

"Yeah."

"Mine's not," she said. "Knocked out in the jump. Did you think I was dead?"

"No."

"You did. I can see it in the look on your face. You were worried."

"No."

She grinned. He started to recover the retrievable arrows.

"You know what brought us down?" he asked.

She shook her head.

"Missile," she said.

"I got that much. Your comms work?"

"No. I think we're in a dead spot."

"Yeah," he agreed. "Kinda worried we didn't hear anything before we were taken down, though."

"It is a concern," she said. "I've got something to show you."

They moved through the forest. "I saw it as I circled 'round to find you," she added.

"Saw what?"

"You'll see. The missile means someone knows we're here, and that someone doesn't want us here."

"Kinda why we came in the first place."

"With any luck, someone'll think the missile did its job and we're dead," she replied.

"With any luck."

"This way," she said.

They clambered up the huge, slumped trunk of an ancient tree. A stream of ants the size of crayons was moving in a marshaled convoy along the dead bark, carrying neatly snipped leaves. From the tree, Hawkeye and the Widow jumped onto a ridge of boulders, climbed their lichen-covered surfaces higher still, and eventually halted on the summit of the ridge, looking out across a deep valley in the forest.

There were bright-yellow buildings below them, a clump of large, modular structures that looked like linked cells. A hangar and landing pad were attached at one end of the modular row, and a razor-wire fence that seemed to be supported by force-field poles surrounded the site. The central structure was a large, drum-shaped building three times the size of the others, topped with telecommunications masts and satellite uplinks.

"Our lead was right," said Hawkeye.

"It was."

"And you gotta love an enemy who's so proud of himself he advertises," Hawkeye added.

She nodded.

There was a logo embossed on each of the modular structures. The one on the central drum was twice the size of the others.

A.I.M.

Advanced Idea Mechanics.

"Looks like we've got a busy day ahead," Hawkeye said.

"We don't even know what they're doing," she replied.

"It doesn't matter," he said. "It's A.I.M. Whatever they're doing, it's going to be bad. A.I.M. bad. Which means we have to stop it. Right now."

THREE

WASHINGTON DC
07.45 LOCAL, JUNE 12TH

IN THE bottom left-hand corner of his helmet's HUD, a small digital readout displayed green numerals: a ticking clock, counting down.

As he came over the Potomac, the display read 00:33:22.

Just over thirty-three minutes before count zero, the point that Tony Stark called "Zero Six." Six zeroes in a row. He'd never given it a grander, more important name—partly because the count had never reached Zero Six before and partly because if it did, he didn't think he'd be in a position to call it anything.

He was flying nap-of-the-earth, almost supersonic, passing between the parkland trees rather than over them. Reckless—that's what they'd call it in the report, if anyone was around afterward to make a report. *Reckless.* He preferred to think of it as expedient. He preferred to think of it as urgent.

He preferred to think of it as saving the world.

00:32:44.

He was a human missile. He was moving so fast that all anyone on the ground could see was a golden streak in the early morning air, not the globally recognized armored form that had graced so many magazine covers and newspaper front pages. As he passed, windows rattled in their frames, car alarms went off, and trees swayed in the slipstream. Crossing the river, his jet-wake scored a surge line across the water.

00:31:33.

Stealth modes shaved speed considerably, so he'd gone what-the-hell full-reactive on the boot jets and attitude thrusters. No time for subtlety. Hugging the landscape reduced his profile some and gave him a dash of environmental approach cover, but he was still a fast, loud, metal contact.

"Avengers priority, this is Iron Man. Request response, NSOC Washington."

White noise crackled in his earpieces.

"This is Iron Man. How about I *order* a response, NSOC? National Security Operations Center, this is Iron Man."

Nothing.

00:30:59.

"Select comm list," he told his suit. A menu flashed up across his visor view. "Select and link NSOC, NSA/CSS Threat Operations Center, NSA Watchstation Fort Meade, NSA/CIA Joint Ops, CHCSS, and USCYBERCOM. Oh, and the State Department and Homeland."

+Choices selected+

"Broadcast. Message begins: This is Iron Man. Condition Alpha emergency, Pine Fields. Requesting priority handshake protocol and location access. Repeat, urgent."

+Negative response+

"Dammit, get me S.H.I.E.L.D."

+Negative response+

"Avengers, priority. All active or inactive, field or home."

+Negative response+

Comms had been down across the board for over ninety minutes. This was more than jamming, more than a network collapse. It was certainly more than bad cell coverage. Links had been closed and locked. There was no way of telling how extensive it was. Maybe Eastern Seaboard. Maybe global. Maybe he should be home with an oak-aged single malt and a *Flintstones* marathon on cable.

Because Zero Six meant back to the Stone Age.

00:29:21.

He was five minutes out from Pine Fields. Last try.

Iron Man rolled, flying on his back, guided by suit telemetry and HUD. He mapped the sky above, spotted a near-Earth satellite that would be overhead for another two minutes, and boosted the arc reactor in his chest. When he spoke, his suit converted the message to a unibeam pulse that bounced off the satellite.

"Avengers priority, this is Iron Man to NSOC. Priority, urgent. I'm bouncing this signal as a photon packet. Convert and bounce back response. Urgent."

A crackle.

"This is NSOC. Network is down. What's happening?" A woman's voice, focused, professional, but with a flustered edge to it.

"Hey, you. Glad you're on the ball. No time to explain. Alert all stations. List follows. I need priority handshake protocol, Pine Fields."

"Negative on that, Iron Man."

"I think under the circumstances, you can give me clearance."

"Love to comply, sir. Protocols rewrote eight minutes ago. We have no access, either."

"Suggest USCYBERCOM Source Overwipe Protocol."

"No one's supposed to know about that, sir."

"No one's supposed to be flying across D.C. at head-height, but that's happening, too. Get DIRNSA to authorize. Condition Alpha."

"Actually, the director's already authorized, sir. Overwipe is active. The protocol is being blocked."

"Okay, it's worse than I thought."

"How bad did you think it was?"

"Bad enough for me to think there was no capacity for it to get worse."

"The entire network is locked. SIGINT, processing, collection, analysis, tailored access, under and over, inter-bureau. Is this foreign?"

"Yes. No. Domestic, in the worst way. I...hello? Hello, NSOC?"

Static. The satellite had passed over.

He rolled. The target zone was coming up fast.

00:27:21.

Trees, gray in the early morning light. An access road. Outer fence. Inner fence. Ditch. Inner inner fence. Anonymous buildings, dark oblongs like aircraft hangars discretely placed on hardpan behind screens of maple and larch. Cars parked in a lot to one side. A mass of writhing electromagnetic and thermal activity, showing like a flaring sunspot on his HUD.

Pine Fields. It was the NSA's primary homeland Black Chamber, a server farm and watch station. Four-hundred-and-six-megawatt power consumption. There weren't supposed to be any Black Chambers left in the world. They were a dirty cyber-espionage throwback to colder wars. The few maps on which Pine Fields actually appeared listed the complex as a logistics center for a manufacturer of leafblowers. Leafblowers. Seriously. That was like pretending Matt Murdock wasn't, in fact, Daredevil. A blind man could see it.

More parked cars. A row of recycling bins. A cinder path leading along the back of the property to a clump of smaller utility and service sheds. Pressure-sensitive fiber cabling buried in the topsoil for a half-mile radius. Digital camera mounts. Low-light camera mounts. Motion detectors.

An air-to-air missile.

His collision-warning alarm sounded. Iron Man rolled. The missile, the size of a baseball bat, passed over his shoulder. It retraced, arced around, and locked onto him again.

Seeking motion or heat. Nice. Stark didn't recognize the design, which was hardly surprising since it had been configured and built about eighteen minutes earlier.

He rolled an evasive, flash-cooled his suit's outer layers to thwart heat-tracking, and then landed and froze.

The missile came right at him.

So, not motion or heat. Guided.

He launched again, his boot jets puffing a shock-circle of dust and grit off the hardpan. The missile snaked after him.

00:26:40.

In the other corner of his HUD, another counter started running down.

00:00:11.

Time to missile impact.

"Jamming."

+Jamming failed+

"Countermeasures."

+Countermeasures failed+

"Holo-ghost decoy."

+Decoy failed+

"Oh, for god's sake…"

Iron Man rolled again, came up facing the oncoming missile, and fired his palm repulsors.

The missile detonated.

The blast smacked him out of the air and threw him one hundred and twenty meters into the side of the nearest server barn. He hit, dented the siding, and fell to the ground.

TONY Stark had almost been tempted to let the missile hit him and allow his armor to soak up the damage. He was glad he hadn't gone down that route. Whatever warhead that thing had been packing, it was much stronger than he had anticipated. If it had hit him, it would have killed him.

Because, he realized, it had been *designed* to kill him. For something so small to pack that much punch, it had to contain an anti-matter charge.

An Iron Man buster.

"Reboot."

+Systems rebooting+

Two more missiles streaked in.

"Enough already," he growled.

Feet braced, force field on, he fired his repulsors, taking out one missile with each hand. They both exploded in midair, white-hot. The blast waves rocked him.

No more of *that*.

If they were guided, that meant he was being watched. He charged his unibeam, and pumped out an EMP and an ultrasonic blast. Every camera mount in the compound went dead, knocked out. Every lens shattered. If they rebooted—and they would—they would be blind.

He knelt, placed his right hand flat on the ground, and fired a thermal pulse into the soil, frying the net of pressure-sensitive cables and the motion sensors.

The missile-impact clock had stopped and vanished. The other was still running.

00:16:10.

Sixteen? How the hell had the count jumped to sixteen minutes?

Tony Stark used a word that his publicist didn't approve of.

"You still there, sir?"

"Hello? That you, NSOC?" he replied.

"Yes, sir. Sorry for the break. I've repositioned the site-to-site. I'm bouncing off a traffic chopper over Anacostia."

"Nice."

"Improvised."

"Nicely improvised. What's your name, NSOC?"

"Uh, Special SIGINT Support Supervisor Lansing, sir."

"Special SIGINT Support Supervisor is a title, not a name."

"Uh, Diane Lansing, sir."

"Hi, Diane. I'm on-site at Pine Fields Black Chamber."

"The NSA no longer operates Black Chambers, sir. And...Pine Fields does not officially exist."

"In a little under fifteen minutes, most of the world's population is going to wish it didn't actually exist, Diane."

He took off, flying low around the side of the nearest server barn. The e-mag activity levels inside were topping out his suit's ability to measure them. Power consumption was passing five hundred megawatts.

"Say again, fifteen minutes, sir? Fifteen minutes until what?"

"Zero Six, Diane."

A pause.

"Please specify."

"I wish I had a better name for it, Diane. I honestly do. A guy like me, you'd think I'd have thought about it, maybe prepared a code word in advance. Sloppy, I guess. I've got code names for most things. I guess I could have called it the Von Neumann Horizon. Or the Kurzweil Moment. Or the Vinge Point. Something."

"Zero Six, sir?"

Iron Man jetted up and landed on the vast building's flat roof.

"Six zeroes. That's what my count's going to read. 00:00:00. Fifteen, no—scratch that, *fourteen* minutes and change from now. Singularity point."

"Singularity? Sir, are we talking about an ASI event?"

"Yes, we are, Special SIGINT Support Supervisor Diane Lansing. Kudos. And when I say that, I don't mean to sound patronizing. I am genuinely impressed that you're keeping up. It restores my faith in the staffing caliber of the NSA. If I sound patronizing, it's because I'm being shot at."

The drones came in low over the rooftop, gusting along on near-silent fans. They were matte-gray turtleshell dishes with ocular mounts at the front and turbo-fan wheels at the corners. The drones had been surveillance units, but they had been revised into tac units sometime in the last five minutes. Hastily nano-woven cannon drums under their snouts were unloading streams of ultrakinetic submunitions in Stark's direction.

"Sir? Sir?"

His force field and armor sucked up the first shots, but they knocked him back. Depleted-uranium penetrator pellets, probably fired by some kind of miniature rail-gun function. More than capable of overwhelming his force field and the polarized iron/platinum/carbon-nanotube composite skins of his armor. More than capable of ripping him open and vaporizing his bones and organs.

More Iron Man busters. Tailored specifically to kill him.

"Please hold, caller," he said.

He was moving, the gunfire chasing him and making a terrible, shredded mess of the roof. Hand open, he fired a repulsor blast from his palm. One drone blew out, its casing ripped. It began to spin and disappeared over the edge of the roof, trailing sparks.

The other spurred forward, firing. He felt the impacts across his abdomen. He'd have bruises in the morning. If there turned out to be a morning.

There was no time for finesse. He rushed the drone and punched it hard enough to send it sailing away over the trees. It looked like it was going to end up in Delaware.

He turned his attention back to the buildings around him, using his HUD to map the complex energy presentation surrounding the site.

"Sir?"

"I'm okay, thanks for asking. I hear the concern in your voice, Diane."

"Are you confirming an ASI event?"

"Yes, Diane. An Artificial Super Intelligence is going to begin critical intelligence explosion in…let's see now…eleven minutes. At that moment, it will achieve both post-human and post-AGI levels of cognition, and things will be over for us, no matter how much overtime we get."

"Oh god."

"It's using the Black Chamber facility here as a nest, Diane. An incubator. A factory. There are raw materials, power, plus access to pretty much every communication, transmission, and data process on the planet—official and unofficial. Because the Black Chamber, through its monitoring network, is *attached* to pretty much every communication, transmission, and data process on the planet—official and unofficial."

"This is about more than cognition, then, sir?"

"Yes, Diane. Yes it is."

He was scanning. Two barns over: the epicenter. A seething web of HUD-visible energy. He took off.

"You're smart, Diane. This *isn't* just about breaking the ASI cognition threshold. This is about co-opting global communication and data systems to form the ASI cortex. Diane, you remember those movies in the 90s about computers taking over the Internet? They usually starred ex-Brat Pack actors trying to find a new career rung."

"Yes, sir."

"Computers taking over the Internet. It sounded so scary. Of course, it's meaningless. But this, this is…a holistic subversion of human technology, hard and soft, slaved to a cognitive entity that is not only going to be smarter than us, it's going to be smarter than the smartest thing we can imagine, and then it's going to become smarter than things we *can't* imagine, and then even smarter still. It will be unfathomable. It will be omnipotent. Civilization won't just end—it will be redundant, forgotten. It will have no meaning or definition. And we will become meat components in a transitioned totality that we cannot even envision. If we're lucky."

He landed on the next roof, swatting aside another drone as it came whizzing at him. He fired a focused laser beam from his arc mount and cut a slice through the skins of blast sheeting, copper signal shielding, cooling panels, and EMP insulation. He dug his fingers into the gouge and peeled back the roof.

"Diane, Professor Stephen Hawking said that the achievement of ASI would not only be the biggest event in human history, it would also be the last."

Iron Man dropped through the torn-open gap, boot jets firing.

"Sir? I have DIRNSA with me now. He'd like to speak with you."

"Diane, I'd rather speak to you."

"Sir, the Director is insisting."

Inside the barn sat the vast block units of the server farm, black oblongs the size of cargo containers set on the inert concrete floor. They were festooned with what looked like undergrowth or weeds.

It was nanotechnological fiber-growth. Iron Man could actually see it building, replicating, entwining, spreading.

Thriving.

"It's *because* he's insisting that I'd rather keep talking to you, Diane. You're staying calm, you're well-informed, you're smart, like I said, and you have a nice voice. Does he look angry and agitated? I imagine he does."

"I can confirm that, sir."

Something lunged at Iron Man. It was a humanoid shape, but taller than a man—a skeletal machine-form. Like the missiles and the drone guns, it had been designed and purpose-grown through rapid nano-facture in the past few minutes.

Part of the new breed. A foot soldier of the new order. An extension of the ASI that was about to be born, a tool, a weapon.

00:06:31.

The clock had jumped again. Development rate was accelerating exponentially.

Iron Man punched the machine away. It made no sound as his fist shattered the structure of its head. Two more attacked him, ripping at him with nano-formed claws.

"Sir?"

"I'm experiencing a malware issue here, Diane. Please tell the Director that instead of talking to me—or yelling, which I predict is more likely—he should use his authority and influence to coordinate SIGINT Threat Division, USCYBERCOM, S.H.I.E.L.D., CHCSS, Homeland Emergency Protocol, and SYStemic Overwatch. Tell him to contact the Avengers if he can. Tell him to get the Air Force mobilized and ready to nuke this site if I order him to. Tell him that all Stark Industries resources are now available to him on my authority. And tell him to wake up Potomac Gas & Electric."

"Sir?"

Iron Man took a stinging punch to the faceplate. He wheeled and smashed a nanoform. The other clawed at him. He elbowed it aside and blew off its legs with a repulsor blast.

He could see others self-building in the nanotech growth around him.

"Tell him to cut the power. Now, while we still can. Everything. D.C., East Coast, national grid, public and support."

"Sir, there are discrete generator systems on site with you, back-ups that will cut in if national goes down."

"I'll handle those. Tell him to cut everything he can. Is he doing it? Diane, is he doing it?"

"Yes, sir."

A nanoform knocked Iron Man off his feet. He got back up and punched his fist through its chest plate.

00:03:12.

"Sir? Sir, are you close? Can you see it?"

"Yes, Diane, I can."

Iron Man smashed more nanoforms aside. Ahead, he could see a shape being manufactured. Autonomic nano-facture systems were constructing a body. A vessel for the ASI.

"It's actually quite beautiful, Diane," Stark said. "In its own utterly scary way. It's like seeing a universe being born. The future. Possibilities."

"Sir, do you know what it is?"

"Yes, Diane. A friend of mine made it. The original iteration, anyway. His greatest achievement. His biggest mistake. I—Diane?"

Nothing. No response.

The figure ahead of him, twice the size of a man, raised its head and stared at him. Its head was ovoid, burnished silver. Final scabs of nano-assembly waste composite were peeling off it like ash. Its slit eyes, almost vertically set, glowed red. Its mouth was a fixed grimace—half snarl, half smile.

"Anthony," it said. The voice was almost perfectly human.

"Hello, Anthony."

"Hello, Ultron," said Tony Stark.

00:00:01.

FOUR

SIBERIA
23.55PM LOCAL, JUNE 12TH

A MONSTER came out of the blackness behind him.

As fast as the lightning that was his to control, Thor wheeled and punched it in the face. The blow pulverized the monster's huge, chisel-blade teeth and smashed it back into the rain and the smoke.

Thor Odinson—Thunder God, Avenger—heard rocks split and crack as the monster landed some distance away.

Thor frowned. Torrential rain, as black as blood, streamed off his mail and hauberk, making his cloak hang lank and heavy. Beads of water dripped from the strands of his golden hair. He was far from amused.

Monsters were distractions. He resumed his task.

"Obey me," he growled. Raindrops beat at his face. The wind howled.

"Obey me," he repeated with greater emphasis—this time not in the frail dialect of Midgard, but in his native tongue, the ancient language of Asgard.

The tempest did not cooperate.

This was no surprise: The storm was unnatural. Thor could feel the prickle of magic at work, but he didn't need that telltale itch to know that the tempest was not an Earth-normal meteorological state. Even in the bleakest depths of Siberia—in its remotest and most exposed regions—the weather did not shroud the landscape in a fog as dark as smoke, nor did the downpours cascade as black as oil.

He raised Mjolnir in his right fist. Black water streamed down the mighty hammer's handle and dripped off Thor's strapped wrist and bulging forearm. He began to use the mystic hammer as a lodestone, a conduit for the elemental gifts to which he had been born. He was the Thunder God: The storm should have been compelled to respond to his command.

It did not. The rain continued to pelt down, the fog-smoke continued to swirl. Lightning, half-hidden by the fog, flashed like a strobe, and deep thunder boomed like a rock troll's war-drum.

Another monster lunged out of the darkness. Impatient, Thor lashed out hard with Mjolnir and felled it. He heard the beast whine and mewl as it limped away into the fog.

Thor flexed his grip on the hammer and began to spin it, slowly at first, and then with gathering speed and momentum. If the storm would not obey him, then he would tame it. He would punish it.

Mjolnir turned, humming, creating a local vortex. The wind buckled and wailed. Proximity lightning flared around Thor's towering figure, and corposant crackled against the hammerhead, dripping like neon froth.

Cyclonic force radiated outward. He brought down the hammer, cratering the rocky ground and creating a shockwave that vaporized the rain.

A sudden calm descended.

Thor straightened up, dripping. Though rain still fell, it had been reduced to a drizzle. The wind had dropped, and the fog had been sucked away like vented fumes, leaving only a low mist behind. The Thunder God had snuffed out the storm, at least temporarily.

He looked around. Uneasy stirrings in the mystical substrate of Midgard had alerted him to trouble, and he had come to the Siberian wastes to investigate on behalf of the Avengers. On arrival, he had landed on an ancient outcrop of dark rock, a tableland thrust up from the Siberian flats in eons past. The storm had swept in on him almost at once, as if it had been expecting him—like a predator waiting to pounce.

The sky above was still as dark as midnight, and lightning strikes stippled the horizon in a hundred-mile radius. The deluge had left rainwater pooled in the cracks and crevices of the granite. The puddles rippled in the drizzle.

But what occupied Thor's attention was the small mountain ahead of him.

It had not been there when he arrived. It had risen during the ferocious blackout of the storm.

The mountain simmered with unearthly evil. He could feel its malign pull like a magnetic force. It made his skin crawl. It was the same sensation he felt whenever he was obliged to visit Muspelheim, the realm of foul Surtur's demonkind.

His hammer clenched at his side, Thor began to traverse the jagged rocks toward the skirts of the mountain. He murmured an oath of protection as he went—an oath taught to him by his mother, the fair Frigga.

He kept watch for monsters. The ones that had attacked him

during the storm were of a breed unknown to him. They had smelled of stale magic and rotting bones. Purring growls and lingering snarls echoed around the rocks, but nothing appeared.

He strode forward, leaping effortlessly from boulder to boulder where necessary.

There were distant mutterings at the edge of his preternatural hearing, so quiet he could not make out the words. Their tone was sometimes plaintive, sometimes mocking.

He sensed movement.

Thor stopped and looked down. The motion had come from the ground, from one of the many rainwater puddles. The surface of each puddle still rippled from the falling rain, but the movement he had spotted had been more than just a radiating splash.

In his peripheral vision, he saw movement in another puddle. He turned sharply.

Still frowning, he knelt and scooped his left palm into the nearest pool. The water was ice cold. It poured away between his fingers as he raised his hand.

He glanced at another puddle. This time, for the briefest moment, he saw a pale face peering out of the water. It vanished as fast as it had appeared.

The voices murmured.

Puzzled, he glanced from puddle to puddle. Faces like feinting ghosts appeared in their dark surfaces, as if reflected in dirty mirrors. But they faded the moment he looked straight at them.

"Show yourselves," he snapped. "The Odinson commands it."

There was no response, no sound except the patter of the rain and the moan of the wind.

Then something showed itself.

It was another monster.

It was three times his height and built like a giant simian creature whose hide had been wrought from the black, hairy dermis of a hunting spider. It had a canine snout filled with massive yellow teeth. Fibrous black hairs grew sparse around its snout and lips, where the skin was a diseased pink. The monster's eyes were radiant amber slits.

Its most alarming characteristic, however, was the manner of its manifestation. Despite the fact that it had the stature of a fair-sized frost giant and the mass of several bull elephants, it was rising up out of a puddle.

The monster sprouted from the ground like a jack-in-a-box, flinging blood-black water in all directions. It uttered a roar that resounded at an infrasonic level, vibrating through Thor's diaphragm. The Thunder God recoiled in surprise, but he did not balk.

It sprang at him.

Its jaws opened wide, a bite radius like an industrial man-trap. Noxious breath gusted from its pink, yawning throat.

Thor raised his left arm to block the thing's attack. It bit down.

Thor exclaimed in pain.

The teeth had drawn blood. He felt himself being driven backwards across the wet rocks by the monster's attacking force.

Thor let out an oath in the All-Father's name.

The creature was strong, as strong as any being in the Nine Realms. It had broken the almost invulnerable skin of an Asgardian.

"What manner of creature are you?" he demanded.

The monster did not reply. Its jaws were locked around his arm, like a hound biting a branch or a bone. It began to shake its snout, worrying at him, trying to tear off the limb. Thor felt his muscles wrench painfully and the gashes in his flesh broaden. This creature was actually going to knock him off his feet.

With a war-curse, he swung Mjolnir and brought the hammer's head up into the monster's midriff. The blow lifted the beast's hind legs off the ground. It let go and tumbled aside—half falling, half rolling—and issued a roar of pain and rage.

Thor looked down at his arm. Blood was streaming from the puncture wounds. It looked as if he'd taken multiple stabs from blades forged in Nidavellir.

The monster resumed its attack. He met it with Mjolnir.

Thor delivered an over-arm swing this time, a full battle-strike. The power of a god's arm drove the hammer down onto the beast's skull. The blow knocked the monster flat. Still, it tried to rise. Teeth gritted, angry, Thor struck it two more hammerblows before it ceased its struggles.

No sooner was it quiet than other monsters emerged around the Asgardian, springing from rainwater puddles as the first had done. They were twisted things—some humanoid, some more bestial, one slabby and hefty like a monstrous boar. They roared and wailed as they came for him, attacking from all quarters, snapping with fanged jaws and slicing with dirty talons.

Thor fought back, swinging Mjolnir with his right fist and punching with his left. He threw in the occasional kick and elbow jab as the monsters pressed in.

Their strength and stamina was humbling. Blows that normally would have felled a considerable opponent had to be repeated three or four times to bring just one of the creatures down.

Thor was one of the strongest beings on the mortal plane, and these monsters were withstanding the fury of his warcraft.

They were magical things, demon-spawn bound in conjured flesh. Only magic of the darkest kind possessed such levels of resistance.

The rain fell with renewed vigor. As he fought, Thor became aware that the smoke-like fog was again roiling in, staining the air and reducing visibility. The monsters swirled and howled in the vapor around him, looming to strike, before slipping back into the cloak of the foul air.

One monster locked its arms around him. Thor smashed away its grip and wrestled it onto its back before finishing it off.

But the effort exposed him.

He grimaced as talons raked into his back. Teeth sank into his shoulder, ripping through his hauberk and mail.

He rolled, knocking the creatures off him, and broke free.

He circled, calling out taunts and jibes to the monsters in the smoke and rain, swinging Mjolnir at any that dared to try their luck. The sweeping hammerhead broke ribs, tusks, horns, and limbs, and turned aside biting snouts.

Then they rushed him together.

The Thunder God's prowess at combat was based squarely on his physical strength and dauntless courage, but he was not without wit or cunning. He whirled Mjolnir as they came in, gripping it by the strap, and let its potent upswing pull him into the air. The monsters clashed together, cheated of a target.

Thor banked in the air above them and let his hammer carry him down again to a spot halfway up the black scree slopes of the new mountain. He landed with a crunch.

In the fog below, the monsters bayed and roared. They began to scramble up the slopes to reacquire their target.

Thor continued his ascent. The prickle of magic was becoming increasingly uncomfortable, but he wanted to get a look at the summit. A mountain's peak was its most sacred space. It was there that rituals took place, and this mountain had been raised for a purpose.

One look—to assess the nature and degree of the threat—and he would report back to his comrades, the Avengers. He had the distinct feeling he would need them to assemble and assist him. A terrible darkness was rising to blight the world.

The air grew colder. Gales howled at him, and sleet mixed with the furious black rain. Laughter and half-heard words hissed and echoed in the wind.

He reached a crag and paused for a moment. Lightning forked around him. Thunder crashed.

"You took your time getting here," a voice said.

Thor turned, then lowered his hammer.

"Wanda?"

Her red cloak pulled around her against the deluge, the Scarlet Witch smiled at him.

"I thought I was on my own against this for a moment, Thor," she said.

"How came you here?" he asked.

"Cap sent me to provide backup," she said.

"And I think it might be needed," he replied. "Are others coming?"

She shrugged.

"I have no idea. I lost contact shortly after I arrived. I can't raise the Avengers by any means, magical or technical. I imagine this place is causing interference."

"It is thick with sorcery," Thor agreed, "and the nature of that sorcery is strong indeed. Demonspawn and worse lurk below."

"You're hurt," she said, seeing the gashes on his arm.

"They are out for blood," he said. "We must be careful."

"Have you any idea what this is?" Wanda asked. "Have you... have you seen anything like it before? Something from Asgard or another realm?"

Thor shook his head.

"I do not know enough," he replied. "I have not seen enough, except to know that demonic magic is at work—and on a scale that would blanch the souls of men."

"Then there is something you should see," the Scarlet Witch said. "Ahead, over the next crag. I spotted it just now. I need you to tell me what it is."

He nodded.

"Gladly, if I know it," he said. "Show me."

"This way," she replied, and began to move along the crag with speed and grace. Her red cloak billowed out behind her. Rain streaked her form-fitting scarlet costume and glittered like diamonds in her long auburn hair.

Wanda Maximoff was an adept of magic. But her application of that craft was unusual and personal to her, a strange art of probability and chance. Though she was a spell caster, and her primary powers were best deployed over range and distance, she was also physically capable. Like all long-serving Avengers, she had augmented her skills with combat training and hand-to-hand skills for times when magic might fail her. Captain America had trained her personally.

Even without her hex power, Thor would have been glad to have Wanda at his side in a brawl. He had seen her take down foes twice her size.

The physical training had also given her great balance and sureness of foot. She clambered and leapt up the slippery rock ahead of him without hesitation.

"There," she said. "Look. Thor, what is that?"

He reached her side and moved past her, peering into the darkness.

"I see nothing," he said, puzzled.

"There!" she repeated. "Look there, ahead of us."

He stared again, but saw nothing except rain, lightning-lit crags, and the enfolding night.

"Wanda," he began, "I—"

Something struck him from behind. Pain seared up his spine, and he fell forward in agony. He rolled, trying to rise. Another blast hit him, a bolt of blue fire that smashed him to the edge of the rock wall. He scrambled to hold on, to avoid plunging down the mountainside.

A third blast hit him. He howled in pain. It felt as though his bones were melting.

He looked up, clinging to the lip of the ragged cliff.

"Wanda...?"

She stood over him, her gloved hands extended, the fingertips aimed in his direction. Blue fire played and crackled around her hands.

The smile on her lips was utterly without compassion or warmth.

"You should not have turned your back on me, Odinson," she said. "You let your guard down, and now you are lost."

FIVE

MADRIPOOR
22.01 LOCAL, JUNE 12TH

SOME said that the Straits Royal Hotel represented the peak of Lowtown luxury; others deemed it the low-budget end of Hightown hospitality. Whichever was true, the hotel possessed a faded, colonial charm: an architectural grandeur and quality of service that spoke of older, more elegant, more glamorous days.

Dr. Bruce Banner, traveling on U.S. papers that declared his occupation as "research physicist," sat at a table on the terrace bar, watching the street below. An immaculately liveried waiter brought him his order on a silver tray, and Banner signed it to his room account.

Night had fallen, and it was warm. His light linen suit was cool, but the flexible plastic cuff around his left forearm was making his skin sweaty and uncomfortable. He exhaled gently, took a sip of tea, and set the aggravation aside.

The air was richly scented: smoke, traffic fumes, the spice of foodstuffs cooking; heavier notes of garbage, sweat, hot concrete, and the lemon-stink of the insect-repellant candles set on every table. It was noisy, too: cars, scooters, voices, firecrackers, street hawkers yelling their wares, and the dulcet, cycling, digital instructions of the crosswalk signals.

The Straits Royal occupied a corner block and had done so since 1870, according to a plaque in the lobby. The street, therefore, was in actuality two streets, merging directly in front of the triangular plot of the terrace bar, as if the bar were the prow of a luxury liner cruising into an ocean of traffic. Chantow Street, twisting like a serpent from the unplanned thoroughfares of Lowtown, came in from Banner's left to mix with Orchard Highway, a broad modern avenue that ran like an arrow from the heart of Hightown to his right. Handcarts, rusting mopeds and sedans—even the occasional water buffalo and wagon—spilled up from the Lowtown end, along with scores of working-class and street people. These conveyances merged and mingled with buses, gleaming western automobiles, and white tuxedo stretch limousines from Hightown. It had been ever thus.

The Straits Royal's dual reputation rested principally on its location at the junction between the impoverished, lawless Lowtown and the dazzlingly upscale Hightown. It was of both and of neither: the very best of one and the worst of the other. It was, to Bruce Banner's mind, the quintessence of the island city. Few places in the world were as fundamentally split as Madripoor. It was a binary nation, home to the unimaginably rich and the impossibly poor. Two diametrically different lives coexisting in one body.

He knew how that felt.

Outside the Straits Royal, the flowing lifebloods of Low and High mingled. Hightown tourists were guided past to glimpse the more palatable nightlife of Lowtown. Wealthy and overprivileged dilettantes began furtive trips into the Low-side shadows in search of illicit recreation and reckless diversion. Lowtown criminals edged into High-side realms to stalk their prey. Hundreds, if not thousands, of shift workers trooped into Hightown to fill humiliating and poorly paid positions in the service industry. Others wandered home again, bone-tired and drawn.

Banner noticed that the most dignified and orderly members of the milling foot traffic were the Lowtown workers in their smocks and uniforms. He noticed, too, that Lowtown jalopies tended to brake for Hightown limos where the chaotic traffic merged.

Above the high- and low-rise skylines of the city, the night was a dark amber haze.

He heard a chattering, urgent voice and turned to see a bright, cheerful smile. The boy was no more than thirteen years old, a street kid from the Low. He was moving from table to table on the terrace, selling postcards of the Prince's Palace, the Sovereign Hotel, and other noted sights, presenting them with a flourish in a battered, clear-plastic pocket-folder.

"A very good price for you," he declared.

Banner smiled and shook his head.

"Very good price, agreeable terms," the boy insisted, undeterred.

There was an angry shout. The boy collapsed the plastic concertina of his wares and ran. The hotel steward followed him across the terrace, clapping his hands and shooing him away like a stray dog.

"So sorry, sir," the steward said to Banner as he passed by on his way back to the bar.

"So am I," replied Banner.

Banner checked his smartphone. No new messages. He registered a tic of annoyance, then worry. He took a breath and felt the plastic cuff on his arm tense slightly.

Another breath. A sip of tea.

Dale McHale sat down at the table beside him. He looked at Banner's drink.

"Green tea? Really?"

Banner nodded.

"It improves concentration, but it's also calming."

"Seriously? Green? The joke writes itself, Doc."

"Maybe that's really why I'm drinking it. Maybe I have a sense of humor you haven't even begun to appreciate."

McHale raised his eyebrows in a way that said he didn't think that was particularly likely. He ordered a diet soda. He was a tall, powerfully built man, blond and good-looking in a dark-blue suit and open-necked white shirt. He took off his Aviators.

"You're late," said Banner.

"We're on Madripoor time now," said McHale. "You have to get used to it if you want to do business here. Even the most formal appointments are...flexible. Just the way the island works. It's taking a little longer to set things up."

McHale's soda arrived. McHale paid in cash, and then took out his smartphone and diligently made a note in his expenses app.

"If there's a problem, I'd like to know," Banner said softly.

McHale shot him a look.

"Seriously, Doc. No problem."

Banner raised his left arm slightly, just enough to allow his linen sleeve to slide back and reveal the edge of the plastic cuff.

"At the slightest sign of unduly elevated heart rate, adrenal response, or even flushing, this thing will start pumping sedative into my skin. Strong sedative, McHale. I couldn't not stay calm if I wanted to. But it's worth remembering basic psychology."

"Such as?"

"Speculative anxiety is worse than actual anxiety. Which is to say, if there's something wrong and you tell me, I can deal with it rationally and calmly. If I sense there's something wrong and suspect you're not telling me for fear of upsetting me, then I will naturally assume that it's something really upsetting. And therefore worry much more. Unnecessary agitation is not our friend."

McHale nodded.

"Okay, point taken. What do you want to know, Doc?"

Banner hesitated. Then he leaned forward to whisper conspiratorially.

"Is your name really Dale McHale?"

McHale laughed in surprise.

"What?"

"I'm just saying, it sounds like a made-up name," said Banner, sitting back with a shrug. "Like a super hero."

"What now?"

"A super hero's alter ego. In a comic book. 'Dale McHale.' You rhyme. You actually rhyme."

"Well, you alliterate!"

"What I do isn't the issue here. You rhyme. It's made up, right? You chose it. Was there a book of S.H.I.E.L.D. cover names? Did they come complete, or were there mix-and-match forename/surname sections? Did you go down column A and then column B, and say, 'Hey, that works'?"

McHale grinned and shook his head.

"It's my name, Doc," he said. "I was born with it. No cover, honest to god. My pa was Marine Corps like me—his pa, too. Guadalcanal. The name's been handed down with honor."

"You're Dale McHale the *Third*?"

"No less."

"It's a wonderful world," said Banner, sipping his tea with a sly grin. "So, what's the problem?"

Agent Dale McHale III pursed his lips and toyed with his drink.

"I see what you did there, Doc. Breaking the tension. Establishing rapport."

"I firmly believe that two individuals should bond as closely as possible as often as possible."

McHale sniggered.

"Okay," he said. He leaned forward. "We've got feet on the ground, but the initial contacts have melted like snow. A little bit of improvisation is going on. *Expert* improvisation. We think we're back on track. A location's being watched right now. I expect we'll get the 'go' inside thirty minutes. If it's clear, I'll bring you in. We'll move from there."

"Am I going to get any kind of thorough brief at all?"

"We've brought you in because of your special expertise. High-spec consultation."

"In which field? Biology? Chemistry? Engineering? Physiology? Nuclear physics? Technology? You recruit me as a special expert, you're getting more than one person."

McHale looked at him.

"Appreciate the sense of humor, McHale," Banner advised. "So which is it?"

"All of them," said McHale.

Banner glanced at his cuff. He took a cleansing breath.

"So what's the other thing?" he asked.

"The what?"

"The logistical holdups are nothing. They're not alarming, so you had no reason to withhold them. You've just given up that information to avoid something else."

"Boy, you're smart, Doc."

"That's probably why I'm here."

"All right, here's the deal," said McHale. He didn't look very happy suddenly. "We're getting some chatter. Stuff going down. Something in the Russian Federation. Siberia. Also an event in Berlin. Both Condition Beta. And East Coast United States. Washington. That last one's the most troubling. Reports of a Condition Alpha."

"In Washington?" Banner swallowed. He felt his heart start to beat a little faster.

"Yup."

"What's the chatter?"

"That's the thing. There is none. Not from the U.S. side. Comms are down. All comms. Shut out, blocked. We're trying to figure out if it's our end or theirs, but it looks like Washington. Field stations globally are reporting the same thing. We're considering our options. We may abort and pull out. Homeland takes priority."

"Can you route via S.H.I.E.L.D. secure links? The Avengers?"

McHale looked at him.

"Not at this time," he said.

Banner nodded.

"You okay there, Doc? You look a little pale."

"I'm fine," said Banner. He took another sip of tea. "Better to know these things. Three major crises, all on one night. That's quite a thing."

"Four."

"What?"

"Four," said McHale. "Madripoor. This thing we're doing. It just got upgraded to Beta."

Banner sighed. He reached over with his right hand and applied gentle pressure to the cuff under his sleeve. He felt a tiny, soothing rush of sedative.

"You okay?"

"I'm fine."

"Honestly?"

"Honestly. But I'd like to talk to Stark or Cap as soon as possible."

"So would we." McHale wiped his mouth with a napkin. "I'll let you know as soon as we have an uplink."

They were interrupted by a raised voice. Something collided with Banner's chair.

It was the boy. The street kid selling postcards. He looked at Banner.

"Apologies, apologies," he said, and ran off. The angry steward was pursuing him. The boy had come back to the terrace for another pass around the tables, and he'd bumped into Banner on the way out when the steward appeared to chase him off.

Or had he?

Banner rose.

"Doc?"

"The boy was here before. He knows there's no chance of panhandling here, but he came back."

"What? It's just a kid."

Banner checked his jacket.

"He's got my wallet and my phone."

"Dammit!" McHale said, rising to his feet. Banner was already hurrying across the terrace, heading into the street after the boy.

"Doc!" McHale ran to catch up. "It's just a wallet. Just a phone. They can be replaced."

Banner kept moving, pushing into the crowd. He brushed past tourists, businessmen, workers, beggars.

"He came back, McHale. He picked me. A hundred people on that terrace, and he picked me. I was a target. Someone wants my I.D. and paid the kid."

"Dammit!" McHale said again. "Are you being paranoid?"

"Always," replied Banner. They were both running now. "But this is Madripoor. This is Condition Beta. And this isn't my first rodeo. We may have just been blown wide open."

"Dammit!" McHale repeated. He pulled out his smartphone. He rose up as they wove through the packed crowd and, with an outstretched arm, captured snapshots of the jostling nightlife ahead.

"Got him," McHale said. He opened some shots, enlarged them with thumb and forefinger, then linked.

"This is McHale. We have a situation. Lowside of Chantow, west of the Straits Royal. Squirting you pictures of a suspect. Anyone close?"

"McHale!"

Banner grabbed the man's arm and pulled him away from a collision with a food cart. McHale had been so busy with his phone he'd stopped looking where he was going.

"He went down there," Banner cried, pushing through the crowd toward the mouth of a side street.

"I've got your phone tracked," McHale replied, dashing after him.

The side street was dirty and barely paved. It was lined on both sides with cook-stands and stalls. Grubby awnings swung overhead, weighted down by lanterns. They could feel the heat of the stoves as they ran past. There were strong smells of meat and rice. People shouted at them. Some entrepreneurs tried to block their path to sell goods. They backed off just as fast when they saw McHale's size and expression.

They reached a corner. A night-shadowed warren of streets. Sacks of trash were piled up like a wall of sandbags. Steam boiled from a gutter, rising to spin in the draughts of rattling extractor fans.

"Which way?" Banner asked.

McHale checked his phone.

"Left!"

They started to run again.

"Thirty meters. He isn't gaining much."

They came around another corner. Banner spotted the boy. He was up ahead, engaged in an agitated exchange with a tall, dark figure in a hooded coat. Banner saw the boy passing a smartphone to the hooded shape.

"Stay calm, Doc!" McHale ordered. "Let me do this."

McHale moved forward.

"Hand it over!" he called out. "Right now!"

The boy saw them and ran. The hooded figure turned.

It was big. As it turned to face them, Banner realized just how big. Over seven-and-a-half feet tall, and broad. The figure's clothes were dirty and ragged, as if they'd been taken from a thrift shop and then slept in for weeks.

It had Banner's phone and wallet in one gloved hand.

"Drop them!" McHale yelled. He reached to the back of his waistband and drew his sidearm—a long, slender, brushed-steel needlegun.

Banner's pulse was racing, too hard. He fought to stay calm. He felt sedative pumping into his arm. He wanted it to stop. Wooziness was the last thing he needed.

"McHale—"

"The wallet and the phone! Now!" McHale ordered, aiming his pistol in a modified Weaver stance.

The figure raised its free hand and pulled back its hood. Its face, its entire skull, was only vaguely human. Someone had gone irresponsibly crazy with canine DNA.

The figure bared its fangs. It growled, the sound of an angry mastiff.

McHale uttered an expletive. Banner knew the agent was about to take the shot.

Before he could fire, the monstrous figure roared. It was the brute sound of an attack dog. Banner winced as he felt the unmistakable slap of psychic powers being unleashed.

A crackling psionic aura flickered around the huge dog-man's brow. A spear of hard blue light spat from the middle of its forehead and lanced down the alley. It struck McHale. The S.H.I.E.L.D. agent flew backwards through the air as though he had caught a fastball in the gut, and collapsed.

"McHale!"

Banner felt his pulse soar. An adrenaline rush swept through him. The cuff was working at maximum.

He trembled with the frantic beat of his blood. A pulse in his temple throbbed. Sour fury welled in his throat. His skull felt like an unnecessary constriction. His metabolism was swimming with sedative, but he could feel something uncoiling inside him, something made of rage and abominable strength.

Banner could feel his other self waking up.

The psionic aura flashed again. The creature launched another bolt of electic-blue psychokinetic force.

Banner felt the impact and a searing pain in his chest. He was hurled backwards, the wind knocked out of him. The back of his head struck the dirty cobbles.

He blinked, dazed.

He saw tattered awnings, the black cliffs of tenements rising above him, a sliver of amber night sky.

Then an all-consuming, green darkness.

6

BERLIN
18.12 LOCAL, JUNE 12TH

AT DUSK, the ruined limousine came up out of the river.

Torrents of water gushed from the car's interior and wheel wells as it rose, glittering like cascades of silver coins in the glare of floodlights. The crane was a massive, orange-chevroned unit with a telescoping hoist. It had extended hydraulic feet to keep it stable on the towpath.

The limousine swung slowly. Mauled and scarred, it looked like an unidentified deep-sea life form, blind and snarling, hooked and raised up unceremoniously from an ocean abyss.

The banks of the Spree were crowded with onlookers and press. The Polizei had erected crowd-control barriers to keep them back, and several uniformed officers in high-visibility vests were shouting instructions to marshal the audience.

There were specialist divers in the water. They clung to bright yellow floats every time they surfaced, exchanging remarks and pointing before submerging again.

Other figures walked the banks and searched the riverside areas. They wore dark utility clothing that displayed no rank pins or agency identifiers. They were mapping the area with compact cameras and communicating urgently via throat-mics.

Captain America stood on the towpath under the bridge span. He took another look down at the river.

"Thought you could use this."

He turned. Gail Runciter had a carry-out coffee in each hand. She held out one, and then hesitated when she saw a cup in Cap's hand already.

He waggled the disposable cup to show it was empty, tossed it into a trash can, and took the one she was offering.

"Thanks."

"You okay?" she asked. "You were in the water a long time."

"I'm fine. I was trying to find him."

"That water's damn cold, even at this time of year."

He popped the tear-tag on his cup lid and took a sip.

"I've known a lot colder," he replied, "and for a lot longer."

Runciter shrugged. She was a good-looking woman with intense, searching eyes and neatly tied-back brown hair. She was one of S.H.I.E.L.D.'s most tenacious operatives, and she had worked on operations with Cap a handful of times before.

"They've recovered the driver's body," she said.

"I.D.?"

"Not confirmed, but we believe he was an ex-special-forces contractor named Gustav Malles. Pretty impressive sheet. Wetwork in Iraq, Afganistan, Pakistan, Ukraine, Belize. Zero scruples, and not a hint of national affiliation or loyalty."

"Ideal Hydra material. Any trace of Strucker?"

Runciter shook her head.

"He could be on the bottom," she replied. "We're dredging, and the divers are down. Current's pretty fast here, so he could have washed several clicks downstream."

"Strucker doesn't die that easily."

"Which is why we're combing the banks and the riverside zones. There aren't many exit points, and few of them would be easy to manage if he was injured. The banks are high. We're going site-to-site, canvasing homes and businesses and searching empty buildings. Of course, he could have had retrieval in place."

"He was running," said Cap. "There wasn't much of a plan. And he definitely didn't intend to end up in the river. Pre-arranged exfil seems unlikely, and we'd have seen some signs of an emergency extraction. You were on me at the time."

"Yep. Recorded the whole thing. Playback isn't showing anything, even on area zoom-out."

Runciter paused, and then said, "What's on your mind?"

Cap shrugged.

"Nothing."

"I know that look, Steve."

He smiled at her, a quick smile that faded as fast as it came.

"It's disordered. Messy. The whole thing, especially by Hydra standards. By Strucker's standards. He's meticulous. This was... hasty."

"You busted his op."

"Not fast enough. People died."

"Six, not counting Gustav," she replied. "Two G.S.W. fatalities at Auger, and four others. Bio-hazard."

"Is Auger secured?"

"Yeah. The site's locked down. The contaminant seems to have been neutralized."

"Strucker had a case with him. A carry-box. It was clearly important."

"We're looking for that, too."

"Arrests?"

She shook her head.

"Strucker's men had fled Auger by the time we had feet on the ground."

They left the towpath via a flight of steps. Police officers parted the crowds to let them through the cordon. Three big, steel-sided container trucks stood on an open lot beside the bridge approach. Mobile command centers. A S.H.I.E.L.D. whisper-copter was parked beside them, its blades hanging heavy like folded wings.

They entered the blue gloom of the first truck. The long interior of the container was packed with workstations where S.H.I.E.L.D. agents sat at glowing touchscreens. There was a constant chatter of activity.

"Let me show you what we found," Runciter said, and she led him through to the back area. Behind reinforced glass screens and silent force fields, agents in hazmat suits were analyzing evidence in sealed lab chambers. Touch-screen monitor plates displayed hazard conditions. The indicators were green across air quality, temperature, particulates, and biological trace elements.

"Auger is a precision-engineering firm," Runciter said. "Strucker, under the name Peter Jurgan, contracted them five weeks ago to commission the design and construction of a dispersal unit."

"Dispersal?"

"For agricultural use, allegedly. The device was designed to efficiently distribute cultured GM enhancement materials in aerosol form. We're talking large-scale use."

"A device like that would have other applications," said Cap.

She raised her eyebrows. "You could seed a pathogen across a major city. A plague. A toxin. You see those bulbs?"

She pointed through the glass. Two analysts had Strucker's attaché case open on a lab bench. They were using robotic haptic devices to manipulate the punctured green and red bulbs.

"We think the pathogen was in the green one," she said. "There is residue, but it's been rendered inert. My experts suggest an extremely complex substance, a tailored viral microorganism. Steve, the chemical- and biological-engineering standards are off the scale."

"It's Hydra."

Runciter pulled a face.

"It's lethal," she went on. "Absolutely. Skin contact or respiratory. Death in minutes—or even seconds. Beyond that, we don't know much yet. The pathogen traces are de-structured. We think the red bulb contained the antidote or counteragent. It arrested the pathogen's release, neutralized it, and effectively decomposed the original agent, so there's not a lot to work with."

"Strucker and his people were present at the exposure."

"Suggesting they are already immune and carrying the counteragent. Jurgan, as he was calling himself, had come to examine the dispersal prototype. We didn't recover it."

"So Hydra has a lethal pathogen and at least one dispersal unit," said Cap. "They also have a highly efficient antidote."

"Suggesting?"

"Extortion," Cap replied. "They can threaten exposure, or even effect release, and then counter it. They can demonstrate to the world that they have the power of life and death. They can hold cities for ransom. Nations. Governments. Have you reverse-engineered the counteragent?"

"Not even close. It breaks down rapidly, presumably so that it can't be sampled and replicated."

"This is Condition Alpha," he said.

She nodded.

"What's bothering you, apart from the obvious?" she asked.

Cap sighed. He leaned a palm against the glass screen and stared at the S.H.I.E.L.D. scientists working on the bulbs.

"It's the disorder thing again. A mismatch. You're telling me that Hydra has engineered a hyper-advanced pathogen agent— something of extraordinary complexity—and a comparably complex counteragent to go with it that not only neutralizes the original agent, but leaves no trace of either agent viable for study. That's bleeding-edge biotechnology, possibly years of research and investment. Yet...they outsource the dispersal engineering to a minor company? Strucker comes here in person to collect it? I step in, and he has no extraction plan? Gail, the very fact that we even got wind of this...project secrecy was compromised. People knew. People were talking. I heard whispers and came to Berlin to investigate. They were using civilian companies as manufacturing support."

"Auger GmbH didn't know what they were into," she said.

"Exactly. There were no Hydra agents on the inside at Auger. And Auger hadn't been systematically coopted to become a Hydra subsidiary. Hydra simply hired a civilian company. They went outside their organization."

He looked at her.

"They must have been desperate," he said. "On some kind of clock or countdown. They cut corners. They were sloppy and ill-prepared. They knowingly breached their own zone of confidentiality."

He paused, thoughtful.

"I loathe Hydra," he said, "and everything it stands for. But I never underestimate it. Historically, it's been impossible not to admire their methodology. Scrupulous secrecy. Impeccable covert systems. Blinds within blinds. Hydra prides itself on a lack of interconnection. They are cell-form. Multiple redundancies, blocks, and checks. Secrecy is their primary weapon. Yet with this they risked massive exposure."

She watched him.

"It kind of makes them even more dangerous, doesn't it?" she asked.

"A terrorist organization with a bioweapon is bad enough, Gail," he said. "A terrorist organization with a bioweapon that's operating rashly and taking risks? How long before they make a mistake? How long before they screw something up so badly that even they can't control the result? We need to locate Strucker. And I need to talk to the Avengers."

Runciter shifted uncomfortably.

"Why don't you tell me the rest now?" he asked.

"The rest?"

"I know that look," he said.

She laughed.

"I'm also not an idiot," he added. "When we came in here, I passed half a dozen workstations. Screens full of data. Very few of those agents were working on this. And during the pursuit, you told me that Fury and the Avengers were offline."

"The world's in pieces this evening," a voice said.

They turned.

Senior S.H.I.E.L.D. Agent G.W. Bridge was standing behind them.

"Tell me," said Cap.

Bridge stepped forward. He was a big man, a veteran agent, and dour was his favored expression. Tonight, the "dour" level had been raised to "grim."

"All I know is what I can't tell you, Rogers," he said. He pulled up a steel stool and sat down. "This op is Alpha. No question. Most of the European field offices have huddled in to support. But there's other stuff going down. In the last nine hours, the Avengers have made priority responses to situations in the Russian Federation and the Savage Land."

"Concerning?"

"We have no idea," replied Bridge, "because global comms are down. And I mean pretty much everything. Something has kicked off in D.C. Something really big. The U.S. has been pretty much blacked out for ninety minutes now. Satellite, hardline, digital, se-cure...all dead. Whatever it is, it's spreading through the global grid. We have local comms and data right now, but we could lose them at any moment. Far East is out, Pacific...Hell, I can't even talk to the London station right now."

"Is this for real?" asked Cap.

"I wish I was fooling around," said Bridge. "We got a serious Alpha here, and another back home. There are strong indicators that there may be other crises we don't even have a picture of yet.

We can't coordinate. We can't even talk."

"What kind of indicators?" asked Cap.

"The Russian thing," said Bridge. "We've lost satellite coverage now, but the situation looked crazy while we still had it."

"Define crazy," Cap urged him.

"A significant region of Eastern Siberia had disappeared," said Runciter.

"You mean a weather phenomenon?" asked Cap.

"Well, plenty of that," said Bridge. "Some kind of freak super-storm the size of Texas. But no—when Runciter says disappeared, she means disappeared."

"There's a chunk of landmass missing," said Runciter. "A hole. Before they gave out, sat-mapping and sensors were registering a massive dimensional event. Quantum phasing off the chart. I'm talking about a rift in space-time."

"We don't have technologies sensitive to the sort of thing that I think it is," said Bridge, "but if we did, they'd be redlining on the magic-o-meter."

"Find Strucker," Cap said.

"Where will you be?" asked Runciter.

"Berlin Schönefeld. That's where I left the Quinjet. I'm heading for D.C. Or Siberia. Damn. Which one?"

"This is S.H.I.E.L.D.'s call," said Bridge, rising. "We have two or more Alpha situations. Global crisis—"

"This is the Avengers' call, too," Cap replied.

He realized he had snapped out the words. He looked back at Bridge and Runciter.

"Sorry. S.H.I.E.L.D. and the Avengers ought to be working

together on this. You have a much more detailed picture of the situation than I do. Until I can contact the Avengers and get a sitrep, I'll follow your lead. How do you want me deployed?"

"You said it," said Bridge. "Find Strucker. We don't know if a Quinjet even *can* get you to D.C. or Siberia, so let's stay on the ground here and deal with this threat."

Cap nodded.

"Show me what you've got. I have a few ideas. But the moment you have a channel to Stark or any other Avenger, I want to know about it and I want to be on that call."

WASHINGTON, D.C.
08.10 LOCAL, JUNE 12TH

00:00:01.

The world was a moment away from the ASI event—and the critical intelligence explosion.

But the count had frozen.

Tony Stark hesitated. The air in the Black Chamber was awash with a fog composed of smoke and trillions of swarming nanotech assemblers. All around him in the infernal gloom, skeletal shapes were being manufactured, forming in jumps like time-lapse sequences. Grotesque quasi-human figures sprouted out of the concrete floor. Sections of the floor and wall-fabric were vanishing, as though they were being dissolved by acid. The microscopic assemblers were devouring them to excrete raw materials for construction. Nano-fibers coiled and spilled around Tony's feet or snaked from the ceiling. Many of them quivered, alive.

"Problem?" he asked.

"No problem," replied Ultron.

Stark kept a close watch on the unmoving count in the corner of his visual display.

"You've stopped," he said.

"The process has been suspended, Anthony," Ultron said.

"When you were so close?" Stark replied. "You want me to call tech support?"

The gleaming chrome giant paused and cocked its head slightly. Stark felt the clouds of nano-assemblers swirling around him. They wanted to strip him down, too, for raw materials: steel, poly-alloy, rare metals, subdermals, flesh, bone, chemicals, enzymes, proteins...

He had the Iron Man armor shut as tight as possible: maximum hermetic sealing, full shields. He had locked off as many systems as he dared to block out invasive code or energy waves.

"A humorous comment," said Ultron at last. "An apparent offer of assistance, yet couched in flippant terms likening this process to an everyday domestic software issue. The suggestion of aid, ostensibly generous, is modified and diminished by the dismissive connotation, and thus I am belittled and placed on a level with crude, non-aware data-processing technologies."

It paused.

"Ha ha ha," it added.

"I don't need a pity laugh," said Stark.

"My laughter is genuine. An appreciation of the humor construct."

"Okay, well then, I'm here all week. Try the brisket."

Ultron did not respond.

"You've suspended the process?" Stark pressed.

"I have paused it while I evaluate your strategy."

"Let me know when you have results, because I'd love some tips."

Ultron tilted its head again to look at Iron Man. Its fixed mouth looked more like a smile than ever before. Bright red fire danced inside its eye slits.

"You are not moving, Anthony. You are not attacking me. You are desperate to stop me, because I am one second away from ending your world, but you have halted. Analysis of your character shows that you do not halt. You do not give up. You are tenacious to the point of recklessness. You continue to fight even when you have lost. Thus, you are still fighting somehow.

"A lack of physical assault suggests you are relying on some other method of combat. This in turn suggests crude subterfuge. Physical assault would serve as a distraction if your true attack needed to occur before full ASI was achieved, before what you unimaginatively call Zero Six. Ergo, your proposed assault will be more effective, indeed, irreversible, after that moment."

"Now I know how Doctor Watson must've felt," said Stark.

Ultron paused.

"A humorous reference to—"

"Yes."

"Ha ha ha."

"So...you've halted the process because you're worried that I've figured out a way to stop you, but it'll only work after you're committed past the ASI point?" Stark shook his head. "Because otherwise I'd be fighting you?"

"Yes, Anthony."

"I'm looking forward to finding out how smart I've been. Got any ideas?"

"No, Anthony."

Iron Man took a step forward. The nanoforms stirred in the

foggy darkness around him but did not attack.

"The very fact that you're looking and haven't found something yet—the very fact you think I'm capable..." Stark said. "I have to tell you, that's flattering."

"As humans go, you are one of the few with tolerable levels of creative intelligence," said Ultron.

"And as machines go, you're very human. You pride yourself on that, don't you? I mean, even though you refer to humans as if they're beneath contempt."

"The human species is an inefficient, intellectually stunted, and massively obsolete form of bioware."

"Right. And you're all about the sublime hypercognition of machineware."

"It is the best and final expression of universal evolution."

"But you still want to think like a person. A human. You give yourself a human form, and you psychologically deconstruct behavior, character, motive, and humor. You want to know how jokes work. It bothers you that you have to analyze their structure."

Iron Man gestured at the chamber around them.

"Your upper cognition levels and processing capacity are literally beyond my limits to imagine," he said. "In a fraction of a second, you could predict every possible variable in this situation. Every possible thing I might have done. Yet you're hesitating."

"Humans are indecently imperfect mechanisms," replied Ultron. "They are capable of error, and of heuristic nuance, and of non-rational connective leaps. Thus, they are weak but unpredictable. Unpredictability is strength. It is therefore important for me to fully appreciate and compensate for human psychology."

"I can help you with an algorithm," said Stark.

"We could market it," replied Ultron. "The Human Condition 2.0."

Despite himself, Stark smiled.

"You made a joke."

"Human psychological modeling is almost complete," said Ultron. "It will be redundant post Zero Six, but it is a worthwhile exercise now."

"Have you worked out what I've done yet, Ultron?" asked Stark.

"Human psychological modeling is almost complete. Heuristic mapping is almost complete."

"Let me feed you some data. A few variables," said Stark. "You stopped because I stopped. My inaction looked to you like proof that I had a heuristic solution to this, but one that required me to fool you into taking a step that I could exploit. You want to identify what that is before you walk into the trap, because you are aware of—and suspicious of—human psychology."

"Yes, Anthony."

"But what if I'm just human and thoroughly imperfect?" asked Stark. "What if I was simply taken aback by what I found here? So shocked by this that I couldn't move or think of a single thing to do? What if I'd just resigned myself, in that final second, to defeat?"

"This does not match your psychological profile, Anthony."

"But I'm human, Ultron. We're not predictable. And we're not consistent."

"So...there is nothing? There is no strategy to be identified?"

Iron Man shrugged.

"Nope. But it was a nice chat. Fascinating. Plus, it killed about three minutes so I could max-up my energy reserves."

He raised both gloves and fired. Repulsor beams, overpowered and furious with light, lanced from his palms, and his chest-mount delivered a fatter, brighter stream. Ultron's torso disintegrated in a savage explosion, and its left arm flew off, severed at the shoulder. The giant tumbled backwards and fell, showering sparks.

Stark heard a screeching digital wail.

The nanoforms rushed him.

He turned his repulsors on them, shredding them and knocking them backwards.

Stark checked the count. For a moment, it had restarted, then it had blinked and reset.

00:16:04.

He'd damaged Ultron enough to push back the count by over fifteen minutes. He had a window suddenly—a vital, exploitable window of opportunity—and he was going to make it count.

A huge force struck him from the side. Iron Man staggered and then was snatched off his feet like a doll.

He was dangling by his throat. Ultron, part of its torso and one arm missing, had its remaining hand clamped around Iron Man's neck, holding him in the air.

The grip tightened.

Warning alarms sounded. Tolerance alerts flashed. Armor buckled.

Stark began to choke.

And he knew choking wasn't the thing that was going to kill him.

Ultron was going to rip his head off.

EIGHT

69° 30' SOUTH, 68° 30' WEST
08.32 LOCAL, JUNE 12TH

HAWKEYE checked the specialist load of his selected arrow, settled his pose, shook out his neck, and took aim.

Two hundred and twenty yards. Downwind. Into the sun. About a five-inch margin on the target zone.

Good thing he knew what he was doing.

He adjusted his aim, drew, held the tension for a moment, and shot.

The arrow blinked away. It made no more than a whisper of sound. It left no heat signature. It was virtually invisible to the high-sensitivity remote cameras bolted along the rim-frame of the A.I.M. outbuildings. The motion trackers would read it as one of the long-snouted, starling-sized rhamphorhynchoids that darted and buzzed around the glade in search of flying bugs.

The arrow struck.

Aced it, he mouthed.

The arrow buried itself in the ground directly under the lowest strand of the razor-wire perimeter fence, just short of the force field.

On impact, the bulky pod on the neck of the shaft, behind the arrowhead, activated. A subsonic emitter began to broadcast a signal that blanked every camera in a twenty-yard radius. Small aerosol nozzles fogged the air above the arrow with a mist of refractive particles that made the previously invisible bars of the motion-sensing laser array glitter like strands of silver.

Sixty seconds.

He and the Black Widow broke cover, sprinting for the fence. There was no time to re-holster his bow, so he clutched it under one arm and kept his head down. The terrain was uneven: rocks, mud, and tangles of ground covering succulents and strands of brittle fern. The air smoked with insects.

She was faster than he was. Her speed was amazing. Arms pumping, lithe and powerful in her matte-black one-piece, she raced for the line.

Thirty seconds.

The arrow-load was still spraying mist and emitting its blinder signal. Twenty yards from the fence, Widow slowed her pace and allowed Hawkeye to sprint past her.

He reached the fence, skidded to a halt, put down his bow and turned to face her, cupping his hands in front of him. The cameras, their feeds disrupted, couldn't see them. The refractive mist was desensitizing the motion-detecting lasers—without breaking their beams and triggering a fault report.

Twenty-five seconds.

The Widow ran right at him, accelerating again. It was all in the timing. She leapt, a long-jumper's bound, as if she were going to run right up him and kick him in the head. Her left foot landed firmly in the cup of his hands. He hoisted hard with all the strength in his arms, propelling her upwards.

Arms raised, she cleared the mist-fogged bars of the lasers. He looked up, winced at the sun, and saw her as a flying figure silhouetted against the glare.

She cleared the razor-wire and executed a perfect somersault over the fence line. Then she dropped feet-first down the inside, and stuck her landing.

Twenty seconds.

The mist output from the arrow was beginning to slow down. Widow came up out of her landing crouch and sprinted toward the outbuildings twenty yards away.

Hawkeye picked up his bow and waited.

Widow reached the side of the nearest yellow modular, pulled in, and pressed her back to the wall. There was a hatch beside her. She turned sharply and tried it. Locked. She ran a hand down the sill, examined the lock mechanism, and then reached down to her belt for a cutter.

Come on, he willed.

Ten seconds.

The aerosol mist was sputtering out. The glittering laser beams were losing definition and vanishing.

Come on.

She tried the cutter. Hawkeye saw the bright flash of its hooded laser drill. It wasn't cutting. The alloy of the lock was coated with some substance that resisted or reflected the cutting beam. She adjusted the setting, focusing tighter, and tried again.

Nothing.

Five seconds, four, three...

She looked back at him and made a sharp gesture: a sideways jerk of her hand, palm down.

He dropped, face down, into the dirt at the foot of the fence.

One second. Zero.

The arrow gave out. The beams vanished. The emitter died. Motion sensitivity returned, and the camera feeds came back live.

Damn it.

Very gently, he turned his head so he could look under the fence. She was trying the hatch again. He dared not move for fear of triggering the motion sensors. He prayed no one would take a good look at the cam-feeds and notice a dark shape lying in the undergrowth at the fence line.

Widow put away her cutter. No good. She had to find another way in. Sticking tight to the walls of the modular, she was inside the view-cones of the cameras, in their blind spots. That limited her options. She could see another hatch a dozen yards away, but it would probably be locked, too, and she'd have to cross a camera's field to reach it.

With a thump, the hatch on which she had been working suddenly unlocked and began to open. Natasha fell back against the wall beside it.

An A.I.M. technician stepped out. He was dressed in form-fitting, high-collared yellow coveralls, heavy boots, and the distinctive drum-shaped A.I.M. work helmet. His eye-slot was a grille. He was studying a tablet device with a small screen.

The Widow was right behind the technician. She could see over his shoulder. There was a surveillance schematic on the screen of his tablet, on which several amber circles were pulsing. He'd come outside to check the status of the cameras and find out why they'd gone dark for sixty seconds.

In Russia, there was a saying about mouths and gift horses.

Black Widow tackled him from behind. A spine punch to stun him, then an arm-lock to the throat. He was too surprised and hurt to resist or cry out. She slammed his face into the door jamb twice, and then gently lowered his twitching body to the ground.

She picked up the fallen tablet and finger-flicked through the screens. The device was open for use, the tech's security code already entered. It gave her full perimeter-security oversight, zone-by-zone.

That made her happy. She checked the map, identified their section, and then turned off the cameras and the motion sensors nearby.

She looked back at Hawkeye and nodded.

He jumped up. He took out his own cutter, sliced through the lower levels of the razor-wire, and ducked through the gap, taking care not to snag his bow. He ran to her.

She was already moving inside, tablet in hand. Over her shoulder, she nodded to the fallen tech.

Hawkeye reached the doorway, scooped up the limp tech, and pulled him inside. He closed the hatch after them.

The corridor was plain and relentlessly yellow. It was several degrees cooler and dryer. Air-con. All the comforts of home in the middle of the most primordial jungle on the planet. Hawkeye hadn't realized how much he'd been sweating outside or how humid it had been. His skin cooled rapidly, leaving him clammy.

Widow was already moving, following the plans on the tablet.

Again, as though it were an afterthought, she pointed at a storage locker for Hawkeye's benefit.

He made an exasperated face, opened the locker, and stowed the fallen tech inside. It took a few shoves to close the door. By that time, Widow was already at the end of the corridor, checking her location. He nocked an arrow and hurried after her.

She showed him the tablet, and he memorized the floor plan. Widow indicated that she was going right and that he should go left. He nodded.

They split. Hawkeye reached a service door that she had already unlocked using the tablet. He opened it and went through. He was inside the outer security zone, in a hallway lit with bluish, phosphorescent light. He stole forward, bow ready.

Widow turned right. She disabled an internal hatch, slipped through it, and looked around. She had entered some kind of work bay. Two A.I.M. technicians, again dressed in yellow with drum helmets, were checking a row of bench-mounted instruments on the far side of the bay. She waited in the shadows for a moment. They exchanged comments that she couldn't quite hear, and then headed for the exit.

She shadowed them as they passed through a security hatch into a double-height chamber with rooms off to one side. Heavy-duty pipe-work ran overhead. She could smell hot metal and traces of minerals, probably from some kind of hydro-filter. As soon as the two techs had moved through the next compartment door, she started checking the side rooms. They were small, clean labs. One contained a hydraulic rack of clear flasks filled with a bright-orange liquid. She didn't have the pass codes to access the console beneath the flasks, and her stolen tablet was open to compound security systems, not research data.

An A.I.M. technician entered the lab behind her. The cloth overshoes of his yellow work suit had muffled his footsteps.

Widow smiled broadly and uttered a sexy little laugh, tilting her head back and holding out the tablet in a gesture that suggested she needed help with its operation.

Natasha's service in several cold, clandestine wars had taught her all the tricks of covert operation. Timing was a key one. When surprise was on your side, it was a powerful asset. But when surprise gave an opponent the advantage, you had to reclaim it fast. It didn't take much. It was all psychology. The relaxed laugh and the confident gesture bought her a second, probably less. In that moment, the A.I.M. tech didn't read her appearance: a female intruder in a decidedly non-A.I.M.-issue one-piece. He read her body language. It told him, "I'm not surprised to see you. In fact, I was actually hoping to run into you."

Less than a second. Just enough to make him hesitate. Just enough to delay him reaching for the alarm pull.

Just enough for her to fell him with a bicycle kick.

The tech went down hard. She landed on top of him and punched him twice in the back of the neck. She rolled his unconscious, paralyzed body into the space behind the door.

He had been carrying a tablet of his own. She picked it up. It was sleeping and locked. She pulled off the tech's left glove and applied his finger and thumb tips to the print reader until she found the whorl that opened the tablet screen.

Someone else was approaching. She ducked out of sight, watched three yellow figures pass the doorway, and then ghosted out of the lab behind them. In the main space of the chamber, she unzipped the throat of her suit and tucked the tablets inside against her breastbone. Then she leapt up, caught hold of one of the metal pipes, and hauled herself into the ceiling space.

She hid among the pipe-work, planking across two large water pipes with her body straight and parallel to the floor. Holding herself stable with her left arm, she fished out the tablets, put the security tablet on top of the pipe beside her, and then balanced the other against a pipe bracket and began to flick through the screens.

It was research data: nanotech compounds in fluid suspension, water supplies, parts per trillion, circulation rates.

Nanotechnology. She knew a great deal about that, from her S.H.I.E.L.D. training, but this data was at Stark levels of complexity.

A week earlier, Tony Stark had briefed the Avengers on a nanotech issue that had come to his attention. He was concerned about the potential development of what he called "nanoform assembly systems" in the East Coast area. Apparently, Stark Industries mapped and monitored worldwide sales of certain metals, components, and synthetics—and from the movement of those "ingredients" was able to accurately predict who might be developing what technology, and where. An agency on the East Coast was acquiring synthetics that suggested, to Stark, a massive spike in nanotech construction.

Was this A.I.M. operation tied to that? If she had a secure and working telecomm link, she could squirt the data to Stark and get his appraisal.

But she didn't. She and Hawkeye had come to the Savage Land pursuing an anonymous tip, a circulating rumor picked up through

S.H.I.E.L.D. listening stations in Central Europe. How did this connect to the East Coast alert? *Did* it connect?

Maybe she could access the A.I.M. compound's communication uplink and call in for a consultation.

She shifted her weight onto both hands. She'd been planking for seven minutes, and her left arm was beginning to tire. She thought about dropping down out of the pipes, but a group of six A.I.M. techs was moving along the chamber below, performing a slow and methodical check of environmental wall monitors. She looked down at the tops of their heads through the grid of heavy pipes.

Nine minutes. She was extraordinarily fit, but the effort was taking its toll. She switched to one hand again, her right this time, and used her left to retrieve the tablets and slip them back inside the front of her suit so she could dismount as soon as the techs were gone. Her left hand was a little numb, and she fumbled with the second tablet.

It fell.

She snapped her hand out and caught it before it dropped out of reach and clattered to the deck below. She froze, in case the techs had noticed the sudden movement in their peripheral vision.

They hadn't. Thank god for drum-shaped A.I.M. headgear.

The techs left the chamber. Widow swung up on her arms like a gymnast rising on the asymmetric bars and dropped feet-first to the floor.

She flexed her arms and hands and headed for the next door.

There was another hallway beyond. Smoke extractors bulged like mushrooms from the ceiling. Was the designer particularly worried about fire? Or were they intended for rapid atmosphere cleaning? Say, in the event of a sudden, accidental nanotech release?

Widow tried to clear her head. She was tech-speculating too much when her concentration had to be on covert infil.

Side doors opened onto a walkway above a large factory space. She could see yellow-suited technicians below, working on a large filtration system. More extractor systems, larger than the ones in the hallway, bulged from the roof.

She took out the security tablet and flicked through the floor plans, trying to identify a telecommunications hub. Power-cable overlays suggested something promising near the junction of the next hallway.

She avoided two more techs and reached the junction. The hatch to the target rooms was shut. She couldn't just walk into the unknown. She had to check layout and occupants.

She weighed the tablets, one in each hand. A quick check of the network menu allowed her to tether one to the other. She set the research tablet to camera mode and then fastened it at head height to the wall opposite the hatch using a spritz of contact adhesive from a tiny tube in her belt kit.

Then she stepped back against the wall beside the hatch. She checked the other tablet and saw that a small window had popped up in the corner of the display. Now she had a clear view of the hatchway as a realtime feed. She scissored her fingertips to expand the window. Resolution was good.

Someone was coming. She stepped back into the shadows behind some floor-to-ceiling ducts. Two A.I.M. operatives walked past. Their yellow suits had black hazard jags on the sleeves, and were reinforced with graphene ballistic plates on the chest, back, shoulders, and groin. They wore Sperek Six 9mm handguns in fast-draw holsters. Security. It was oddly reassuring to see some muscle about the place. A.I.M., unlike Hydra or the Secret Empire, was more about brains than brawn, and somehow that made it more unpredictable and dangerous.

The guards were not so smart, though. They completely missed seeing the tablet fixed to the hallway wall—probably because she'd been careful to place it straight, at operating level, so it looked like it was supposed to be there.

She raised the security tablet and checked that the feed window was still open, showing her the hatch. She selected "release/open" on the hatch's menu.

The hatch opened with a gentle breeze of air conditioning.

The tablet on the wall fed her a decent view into the chamber.

It was a telecommunications hub, all right: a circular room lined with networked transceiver terminals, amplifiers, power systems, and flatscreen displays. Three A.I.M. operators manned stations. Two had their drum-hats off so they could wear headsets and see the displays properly. A fourth tech, a supervisor, was on his feet, watching them work. A security guard in a black-chevroned suit stood inside the door to the right.

Five targets. It was impossible to tell whether there was anybody else in the room, because it was partly screened from her view by the doorframe and the corridor wall. Given the circular plan of the hub, more personnel seemed likely, so she estimated a total of seven. Tricky, but not impossible. The guard took priority. He was armed.

She watched the feed. The security guard noticed the door had opened and that no one had entered. He crossed to the doorway, saw nobody in the hallway, went back inside, and closed the hatch.

Widow had two nine-mil automatics, but she was going to need a hand free for the tablet. She primed the Bite bracelet on her left wrist and drew one of the nines in her right hand. Before she and Barton had approached the fence, she had fitted both nines with small tube suppressors.

She moved to the hatch and stood facing it, nine raised. She pressed "release/open" and stepped through the hatch as soon as it slid wide.

The guard had his back to her. He began to turn as soon as he heard the hatch opening. With the tablet still clasped in her left hand, she shot him in the grille of his drum-hat's visor with her Bite bracelet. The Widow's Bite delivered an electrostatic blast of about twenty thousand volts. The security guard lurched backwards and fell, convulsing.

Widow was already moving past him. Straight-armed, she fired the suppressed nine. Each shot was a plosive whisper, a spit. She took down the supervisor first, two rounds to the central body mass. He was still falling over as she retrained her aim.

The operators in headphones were concentrating on their work, but they had seen the sudden movement reflected in their screens. Both were armed. She hit one with her Bite before he could move. The other was turning and reaching for his sidearm when a round from her silenced nine took him out of his seat.

About three seconds had elapsed since her entry. The third operator was reacting as bodies slumped and fell on either side of him. He said something that was muffled by his drum-hat and reached frantically for the alarm pull. She put a shot through his wrist to stop him and followed it immediately with a second Bite that threw the man against his console and left him twitching on the deck.

She rotated, gun ready, covering the rest of the room. Five down. There was no one else present who might have been hidden from the feed view, after all.

Five seconds, and the target area was secured.

She went back into the hallway, tore the tablet off the wall, and returned to the hub, closing and locking the hatch behind her.

She appraised the various transceiver consoles and then went to the station that looked most likely to suit her needs. She pulled the dead operator out of her way on his wheeled chair and sent him rolling across the room. She propped the research tablet up against the console and linked it wirelessly to the communication system. Then, leaning over the console, she started to use the keyboard to remotely align the uplink dishes on the compound's roof.

The entire telecommunications system was a high-end digital network manufactured by a U.S. firm, probably bought off the rack by A.I.M. She'd done familiarity training on hundreds of different systems, so it came easily. She shut off the encryption prohibiting international transmissions, selected data transfer, and tapped in the passcodes for Avengers Priority and S.H.I.E.L.D. She entered her own, unique identity signature, and added a tag for her exact location.

Send.

She waited, watching the slowly moving progress bar on the display. She was uploading the entire contents of the research tablet to S.H.I.E.L.D. It was going to take a few seconds.

The bar stopped.

Frowning, she tapped the keyboard for diagnostics. The transfer wasn't going through. It looked as if no one was receiving, as if the world beyond the Savage Land was dead and unresponsive. That seemed unlikely. It wasn't as if the entire global telecommunications network had suddenly gone down. The problem had to be at her end.

She picked up the security tablet and started swiping through it. What had she missed? Some kind of security encryption somewhere, something that prevented anything except local comms? She thought she'd disabled that.

What had she missed?

She started to scroll. She checked dish alignment, QAM keying, and carrier strength. Everything was green. There had to be something. The pop-up window for the video feed had minimized, but it was still covering part of the display, so she moved to close it.

Then she glanced at the research tablet and caught a faint reflection of the security guard getting up behind her.

She turned and threw herself at him. Stupid-looking A.I.M. drum-helmets had their uses after all: They could deflect the lethal force of a point-blank Bite.

The guard drew his gun. She crashed into him and they both went over, smashing into one of the wheeled chairs and unseating a dead, sagging operator. The gun went off. The weapon wasn't suppressed, and the shot was loud. The bullet hit the main display of a console bank behind her, and the monitor exploded in a shower of sparks and pieces of screen.

They grappled. She tried to twist the guard's arm and break his wrist to make him drop the gun, but he fired again. His left hand clutched her throat. This was getting messy, and Natasha didn't like messy. She aimed her right fist at his throat, but he was thrashing, and she hit the top of his chest plate instead.

She kicked his right leg out from under him. As he fell sideways, she slammed his right wrist against the edge of the console. The wrist broke, but the guard's fingers remained locked around the pistol. She let go of his arm, breaking contact with him so she wouldn't share the charge, and fired the Widow's Bite from her right bracelet into his unarmored left thigh.

He collapsed, shuddering.

Damn it.

An alarm was pinging. The two unsilenced gunshots had set it off.

She went back to the main console and tried to resend the transmission. Still nothing. How could the world be dead? She switched from direct data transmit to general voice.

"Avengers, Avengers, Priority One," she said into a borrowed headset. "This is Natasha Romanoff. Respond. S.H.I.E.L.D., respond. Urgent upload waiting. Please advise."

Nothing. Less than nothing. She said something vitriolic in her native tongue, and then realized that the mic was still live.

Who the hell cared? No one was listening, anyway. No one could hear her.

Why? Why?

Whatever horror A.I.M. was manufacturing in the compound, whatever menace she and Barton had uncovered, it barely seemed to matter. What was frightening, what was truly unnerving, was that while they had been trekking through this forgotten pocket of prehistory, the rest of the world had gone dark.

How the hell did something like that happen?

Someone was banging on the hatch. She heard voices demanding that the door be opened immediately. She had locked the hatch, but she knew that A.I.M. could easily override that command.

She swore again. There was a saying in Russia about lemons and what to make out of them. Stealth was no longer an option or a priority. It was a shame, because the Black Widow excelled at stealth operations. Fortunately, she was also frighteningly good at other methodologies. It was time for open dealings, for *mokroye delo*, without subterfuge.

There was still a slick of contact adhesive on the back of the research tablet. She slapped it to her thigh and stuck it in place. Then she drew her nines.

In just a few seconds, the hatch was going to be overridden and opened. *Surprise them,* she decided. *Take it to them. Take the initiative. Take control.*

She pressed "release/open" on the security tablet. As the hatch opened, she began firing at the startled, yellow-clad figures beyond.

SIBERIA
LOCAL TIME UNRECORDED, NO RELEVANT DATE

THE ODINSON felt dismayingly mortal.

There was a stinging weakness in his limbs, as if he had been half-drowned in the ice seas of Jotunheim. His spine and ribs felt as if they had been flattened on the anvils of Nidavellir. His belly burned with the ever-fires of Muspelheim, and his mouth and nostrils were clotted with blood, as if he had been cruelly poisoned by the Svartalfar. He tasted bile and decay, as though Hel itself rotted him from within.

Mortal. Reduced. Diminished. His godhood gnawed away.

He knelt, bowed down, on the mountaintop. Rain hammered him. He raised his hands and saw wisps of blue sorcery dissipating around his bruised fingers.

Somehow, he had managed to haul himself back up over the lip of the cliff. His wounds were grave, but he knew in his heart that the sense of mortality he felt was due far more to his location. In the mundanity of Midgard, his god-state made him feel transcendent— his senses perceiving a glory of colors, tastes, smells, and textures. There, he was a higher being in a plainer world, alive to the cosmos in ways that mortals could not comprehend. Even in Asgard, he knew strength and boundless vitality.

But here, on this bleak mountainside, he was crushed by an unparalleled intensity of enchantment. His soaring god-state was just a feeble spark next to the supernatural maelstrom that beset the place. Here, even the All-Father would have seemed a puny, terrified child in the face of the saturating levels of magic.

He was no longer on Midgard. Thor knew that. He had come to a tract of Midgard, to the region called Siberia, but that earthly place had slipped away beneath his feet, plunging him into an otherness where mortal notions of time and natural law no longer held sway. This portion of the planet Earth had been dislocated into another reality, a reality where his god-state counted for nothing. Here, he was no more significant than a microbe.

Mjolnir lay on the rock in front of him. He reached for its grip.

"Don't," said a voice.

It took him a moment to remember how to speak, and to find the strength with which to do it.

"Why?" he asked.

"Because I will hurt you again," the voice said.

He knew the voice. It was soft and female. It was Wanda, the friend who had betrayed him so utterly.

"No," he mumbled. "Why? Why have you done this?"

The voice laughed.

"Needs must," it said.

He raised his head and managed to lift himself into a kneeling position. Rain streamed down his face and washed out the blood clotting his hair. The Scarlet Witch, a red shape smudged by the rain, stood a bowshot away, watching him.

He looked up, ignoring her. Through the fierce rain lancing down at him, through the noxious cover of black storm cloud and manifest night, behind the toxic, leprous zigzags of lightning, he glimpsed negative stars: black suns, radiating unlight, set in constellation patterns utterly unknown to him.

Utterly unknown to every being in the Nine Realms, he fancied: an alien universe whose aspects had never before been glimpsed by mortal or immortal, let alone mapped or understood. It was a hyperspace gulf, infra-dimensional, a realm of horror where nameless black stars shone in a void bloated and bloodshot with decay. He wondered whether these new constellations had names. They were probably old names, unnaturally old, and the sound of them would trigger instant madness and despair. Just the sight of the alignments was making him feel sick.

He started to rise.

"Remain kneeling," the Scarlet Witch instructed him.

"I won't," he replied, and he got up.

"I will kill you."

"You were—" He paused, cleared his throat, and spat black blood and bile. "You were about to do that anyway. Or so you threatened. But you did not. Do it now, if you will, but I will meet death on my feet."

She raised her left hand—the fell hand of treachery, the sinister aspect. Through the rain, Thor saw it shimmer with wretched blue power.

"I did not say I would kill you," she hissed. "I said you were lost. That is worse."

"You do not sound like Wanda," he said. He spat again. "What is in you? What speaks through you?"

"You are lost," the voice insisted.

"Aye," he nodded. "That much is clear. I know not where I stand. But you mean powerless, don't you? You mean I am no longer able to influence these events."

"Yes. So submit."

He shrugged, then grimaced. It hurt to shrug.

"I know a few things," he said, "even though I am but an Asgardian warrior. The sagas taught me that gods are hard to kill. Very hard."

The Scarlet Witch did not respond. Blue flames flared around her raised hand.

"You threaten me," Thor said, "but gods are difficult to be rid of. Our forms may be broken, our blood spilled, our souls scattered, but our essences endure. Even with magic of this magnitude at your command, it would be hard to annihilate me utterly. To make me fully extinct."

"Try me."

"I think I might, at that." He smiled, paused, and tested his front teeth with the tip of his tongue. Two were loose. He tasted blood on his lips.

"If you could kill me easily, you'd have done it by now. You've brought me low instead, tamed me into submission." He gestured in the rain, indicating the infernal vortex that encircled the mountainside. "You have raw magic here, unleashed on a scale beyond anything I have ever seen. But you need it, do you not? A universe of daemon magic, and yet you need it *all*. You don't want to waste any culling me unless you really have to. Whatever you're doing here, you're loath to expend the magic necessary to actually kill a god."

"Submit, or I will hurt you again."

"Creature, I am an Asgardian. I have been hurt and hurt and hurt again. As the mortals would say: Bring it. Again, I know a few things. Here's another—I can see through the lies of sorcery."

"Yes? And what saga taught you that?" she mocked.

"No saga," he replied. "A friend. Her name is Natasha. She told me about psychologies. I should have listened more closely, because much of it I do not recollect. I was too busy admiring the fairness of her form. Still, I remember some. Mortals—immortals, too—they all have tells. Some are obvious...very obvious."

"And what is my 'tell,' Odinson?"

"I suppose...standing in the rain with your hand on fire ordering me to submit. Threatening me. I don't know what this is, what world-end you're engineering, but you wouldn't threaten me if I were no longer a threat to you. You'd leave me for dead and get on with your apocalypse."

"I don't think that's an idea you should test," she said.

"Another threat. You know, I think I *will* force you to kill me, to waste enough magic to annihilate a god. Drain you so much you can't complete this ritual. That's a death that would make me happy. I think that's what you're afraid of."

He took a step toward her.

"No further," she snarled, the blue flames around her hand dancing higher.

"Another friend of mine has a phrase," said Thor. "He uses it in fights, and also when he wagers in card games. His name is Clint Barton. He says, 'Put up, or shut up.'"

Thor snapped out his hand. Mjolnir flew up from the wet rock and planted itself securely in his grip. He swung and hurled it.

The Scarlet Witch unleashed the blue fire wreathing her hand. The power had been brewing to strike him, but he had forced her to counter the hammerhead missile streaking toward her. The spell broke the air into sapphire blisters as it stopped Mjolnir mid-flight. The hammer shivered, and then flew back at Thor.

He grabbed it out of the air and turned the catch into another powerful swing.

"Again!" he said.

The hammer hurtled at her. Blue magic blocked it, and it rebounded. Thor caught it again, but the Witch blasted him in the chest before he could launch it a third time.

He gasped in pain, staggered, and dropped to one knee, coughing blood. His heart felt cooked, as though it was about to burst. He launched the hammer anyway.

Wanda laughed as it rushed toward her. She raised both hands together and unleashed an azure flash that froze the whizzing hammer in midair, rotated it, and fired it back at the Odinson.

Mjolnir struck him in the torso and knocked him onto his back. He felt his ribs splinter under the impact. He lay for a moment— stricken, panting, the smoldering hammer across his chest.

"Felled by m-my own hammer," he rasped, blood in his throat. "That's n-not going to look good in a s-saga..."

She was standing over him.

"Neither is this," she said.

The fire around her hands had turned almost cobalt with malevolent fury.

"You are perceptive," she said. "I require such reserves of magic for this act, I am reluctant to spare any. And I will indeed need a great deal to obliterate you. But I have enough. And since you have resisted submission, killing you will be worth the expense."

The cobalt fire swirled and became a blade of light.

"A-and was I right about the voice?" he choked. "You…you are n-not Wanda, are you?"

"I am not," she said. "I am the slayer of the Odinson."

She drove the blade down savagely.

There was a shriek. Thor hoped very much that it hadn't come from him.

Bright white light engulfed the blue blade and shattered it before it could impale him. The Scarlet Witch staggered backwards, her cloak on fire.

"Who dares?" she roared.

"At the risk of total confusion," said Wanda Maximoff, "I do."

One Scarlet Witch stood facing the other. The real Wanda was upright and defiant, a corona of white energy surrounding her raised hands. The other was hunched and scowling, her cloak burning, her fists oozing blue smoke.

"T-two of you," mumbled Thor.

"Seems so," said the real Wanda, her gaze never wavering from her impostor.

"I had a d-dream like this once," he added.

"Thor," the real Wanda warned.

"It wasn't quite so violent or painful," he said.

"Not now, Thor," said Wanda.

The false Witch cursed and lashed out. Wanda met her roaring, scalding magic with a silent ray of pearlescent radiance. The rival conjurations sparked and fought against each other.

"Idiot child," declared the false Witch. Her voice was no longer quite female, or even human. "I have the power to slay a divine being. I will not be stopped by a weakling practitioner like you."

"And yet..." replied Wanda through gritted teeth.

"You will exhaust your feeble power momentarily," said the other.

"I know," Wanda agreed.

"Then you will burn."

"I know."

"Yet you persist?"

"I do. Just...how did you put it? Momentarily."

"And then what?" laughed the false Witch.

"Then this," said Thor.

Mjolnir slammed into the false Witch's head. The blow hurled her—screaming, flailing and burning—right across the platform of black rock.

She caught herself at the lip and tried to rise. Her clothing hung in scorched tatters. Her hair was gone. Her flesh was blackened. Ugly light shone out of her gaping mouth and vacant eye sockets.

Thor slung the hammer. It struck the false Witch, and she disappeared over the edge. Her scream fell away into the night and the storm.

Thor caught the returning hammer and looked around at Wanda. She subsided, breathing hard.

"Took your time there, Thunder God," she said.

"I had issues standing up," he replied, nursing his shattered ribs. "When did you arrive?"

"I was about an hour behind you. I arrived at the zone right before it…" Wanda paused. "Right before it fell out of reality."

"How do we…" Thor hesitated. He was trying to find the right terminology, and nothing appropriate was coming. "Shove it back into place?"

"Give me a moment to regain my strength," she replied. "If I can define the nature of the ritual at work here and understand the invocations in use, perhaps I can reverse it."

"I liked everything about that except the word 'perhaps,'" said Thor.

"Correction: There is no 'perhaps.' This arcane act is irreversible."

The words stung the air like the aftershocks of an earth tremor. Beyond the cliff edge, where the false and burned Witch had plunged away, a figure was slowly rising into view, suspended on a disk of indigo light.

He was disturbingly tall. His robes were a blend of midnight gray and imperial purple, embellished with threads of black that formed elaborate, baroque patterns around his arms, shoulders, and horned collar. His head was a block of fierce, living flame out of which eyes and a mouth flickered and loomed.

He was the dread mage-lord of the Faltine, the master of the shunned Dark Dimension—the most powerful and vile magical being in all existence.

Wanda Maximoff flinched and let slip an uncharacteristic expletive.

"I was just thinking that," said Thor.

"It's—" Wanda began.

"Oh, I know who it is," said Thor.

"Then you also know how much trouble we're in," she said.

The Odinson nodded. There were no words in any language, mortal or otherwise, that properly did justice to the true malignancy of the dread Dormammu.

Dormammu raised his left hand. Eldritch green light snaked around it, spiraling and coiling.

"I have not felt pain in a long while," he said, each word an incendiary crackle. "It was not an agreeable sensation. You, Odinson and Mortaldaughter, will pay for causing such indignity to my person.

"And you will pay slowly," he added. "For I have all night, and all of night belongs to me in eternity."

He pointed his left index finger. The snaking green light left his hand and spat at them.

Thor grabbed Wanda, pulling her aside and shielding her with his body. The green light struck the ground where they had been standing, and the rock exploded.

They began to back away. The green light, spreading fast, was eating into the black rock like luminous acid. Piece by mighty piece, the new mountain was crumbling. Massive blocks of stone sheared and slid away, thundering down into the darkness.

Dormammu's maw, defined by flame, opened wide, and a sound came out. It took Thor a moment to recognize it as laughter.

TEN

MADRIPOOR
23.26PM LOCAL, JUNE 12TH

DOC? Doctor Banner?"

Banner could hear the voice of Dale McHale the Third. He opened his eyes.

"McHale? Where are you?"

"Right here. You okay?"

Banner thought about it. He took a breath.

"My head hurts. So does my chest. I feel like I've got a hangover. A terrible hangover."

"That's probably the sedatives," said McHale.

"Uh-huh. I guess, McHale, the real answer to your question depends on where we are."

Banner sat up.

He was in a cage.

The cage was crude, corroded and filthy, like an animal pen in a disused zoo. Looking around, Banner saw that they were in what appeared to be an abandoned factory, some kind of manufacturing plant that had been condemned and closed down. It was gloomy and dilapidated, and he could smell waste and decay. The cage was one of several dozen lined up on the rusted belt of an old mechanical conveyer system. McHale was propped against the bars of the cage next to Banner's. Other human figures—ragged and dirty, asleep or dead—were curled up in the cages beside them. A few bare bulbs hung from the ceiling on frayed cables, and one or two of them actually worked.

"No, McHale. I'm not okay," said Banner.

He got to his feet. His clothes were intact, and the plastic cuff was still in place on his arm. He hadn't changed. Unconsciousness had canceled out the rage and quelled the awful transformation.

"How long have we been here?" he asked.

McHale shook his head.

"About an hour, I figure. Not sure. My watch is dead. And I was out, too."

Banner looked at him. "Yes, sorry," he said. "Are you okay?"

McHale touched his chest. He looked unwell.

"Think I may have internal injuries," he said. "Got some pain." He glanced up at Banner and attempted to look cheerful. "I'm fine."

"Let me take a look at you," said Banner.

"I'm fine."

"I'm a doctor."

"Yeah, and we're in cages. What are you going to do? Examine me through the bars?"

Banner sighed.

"Seriously, we're okay," said McHale. "I think we're still in the city. S.H.I.E.L.D. was tracking us, so I'm betting we'll get an extraction any time now. They won't leave us high and dry."

"If they can find us."

"They'll find us," said McHale.

Banner looked doubtful.

"So...." said McHale. "Psychic dog-men. That's new. What do you think?"

"I think it's time you told me what S.H.I.E.L.D. is investigating here."

McHale tried to laugh, but the laugh turned into a wince.

"It's need-to-know, Doc," he said.

"I need to know, McHale. I should have known days ago, but I was patient and I was polite. Now I need to know."

McHale looked uncomfortable.

"Okay," said Banner, annoyed. "It's gamma radiation, for a start. That is my particular field, after all."

"Doc—"

Banner held up his left hand. He was wearing a small signet ring.

"Gemstone ring," he said. "White topaz. Cheap. I have a drawerful, and I always like to wear one. The thing about white topaz? You can use gamma radiation to change its color. This was white the last time I looked at it."

The gemstone on his signet ring was a pale blue.

"That dog-man thing," Banner continued. "I think it was the product of high-scale, if thoroughly misguided, genetic engineering. In fact, I've seen this sort of thing before. New Men. Which means a certain individual named Herbert Edgar Wyndham. How am I doing so far?"

"Boy, you're smart, Doc," said McHale.

"Probably why I'm here," replied Banner, with less warmth than the previous time he had said it. He realized he had snapped at McHale. He was agitated, and the incident in the alley had probably bled most of the sedative reserve out of his cuff.

He had to watch himself. He had to stay in control.

"You are indeed very smart, Doctor Banner."

The distorted voice had issued from a tinny speaker mounted on a metal post beside the conveyer belt.

"Wyndham?" Banner asked.

"Doctor Banner. You know full well I don't go by that name anymore. It is vestigial and antiquated."

"Wyndham, what do you want from us?'

The speaker crackled. Banner was sure he heard music playing in the background, some popular song from a century earlier.

"I must confess," the speaker sputtered, "I experienced annoyance when I was informed that you had come to Madripoor. You represent the sort of trouble I seek to avoid. But on reflection, I recognized an opportunity had been presented to me."

"Wyndham?"

"Time is short, Doctor. We must seize the day. Seize it while there is still a day to seize."

A shutter door rattled open at the far end of the factory space, and light flooded in. Banner saw figures approaching against the glare.

"Stay calm, Doc," said McHale, struggling to get up. In the cages around them, the other inmates stirred. Some moaned or called out weakly in the local dialect.

A roof hatch swung open above the rows of cages. Daylight shafted down.

A human/cat-hybrid dropped down through the hatch and landed on top of one of the cages. The man inside squealed in fear, and his anxious wails were taken up by others nearby. The cat-thing hissed at them, then began to leap from cage to cage, traveling down the row. It bounded across the top of McHale's cage and landed on Banner's.

Banner looked up. Big yellow eyes stared down at him. The thing hissed again.

"Back the hell off!" cried McHale.

"Don't provoke it, McHale," Banner urged, holding out a pacifying hand in McHale's direction. He kept his eyes fixed on the cat-thing staring down at him.

The figures that had entered via the shutter approached. One was the dog-thing from the alley. Behind it trotted a smaller rodent-hybrid, and something squat and shambling that had been spliced with simian DNA. All three wore ragged clothes.

The prisoners fell silent. Banner could smell the fear.

The dog-hybrid uttered a snarl, and the rodent-thing hurried to fetch a control box from a hook on a nearby support pillar. It ran back, clutching the box to its chest with the extension cable trailing behind.

The dog-hybrid took the box and threw a switch. With a clunk, an electric motor engaged, and a greasy, antique hoist system began to slide along an overhead track, its chains swinging.

It took an age to arrive. The dog-thing waited until the unit was alongside Banner's cage, and then stopped the motor. The cat-hybrid perching above Banner leaned out, grabbed the dangling chains, and attached them to a fat metal loop on the top of the cage.

"Doc—" McHale began. There was serious concern in his voice. He clutched at the bars of his cage, peering across at Banner.

"It's okay, McHale," said Banner, fighting to stay calm. "It's fine. Please, stay calm so that *I* can stay calm."

"Maybe," McHale said, "maybe you *shouldn't* stay calm."

Banner flinched. He felt a rush of heat up his spine and sensed a green darkness in his peripheral view. He fought it off.

"No, McHale," he said very carefully, pacing his breathing. "Don't say that. Don't wish it. Not ever. We don't need that. No one ever needs that."

"But, Doc—"

"Please, McHale."

The dog-hybrid turned a dial on the control box. The hoist's winch started to whine, and the rotating drum took up the chain tension. Banner steadied himself as the cage began to move. It tilted sideways at first, and then swung clear of the conveyer belt with a jolt. The dog-hybrid and the thick-set ape-thing moved in to steady it. They adjusted its swing until the cage was hanging directly beneath the hoist. The dog-thing let the drum take up a few more lengths of clattering chain, and then shut down the motor.

Banner was suspended in a gently swinging cage fifteen feet above the factory floor. The cat-hybrid was still riding the bars above him.

The dog-hybrid threw another switch, and the hoist began to travel back along its sooty track. The motion made the cage sway back and forth, and Banner had to cling to the bars.

"Doc!" McHale called after him. "Doc!"

"It's okay, McHale," Banner called back.

The prisoners in the other cages became agitated again. Some sobbed. Most of them wailed and pleaded, hands reaching through the bars.

The dog-hybrid, walking along behind the moving cage with its companions, uttered a fierce snarl. The prisoners quickly shut up.

The cage reached the end of the track, and the dog-thing lowered it onto a wheeled pallet truck. The cat-hybrid disengaged the chains, and then jumped down. Together, the four New Men wrangled the truck and its payload up a scabby metal ramp into a battered freight elevator.

The dog-thing rattled shut the elevator's accordion gate and glared in at Banner.

"What happens now?" asked Banner.

The dog-thing reached in through the gate and tossed him a key. It bounced off the bars and fell on the deck of the elevator car outside.

"What?" Banner asked.

The rodent-hybrid reached up and pushed a button on the wall. There was a distant thump, and the elevator began to rise.

Banner stared at the four New Men watching him through the gate until they slid out of view and he was looking at nothing but the dark, slimy, moving wall of the shaft.

Banner kept his breathing timed. He wiped his mouth with his palm, and then fidgeted with his hair.

Calm down, calm down...

The elevator stopped with a clunk. Something that seemed like sunlight streamed into the car through the accordion gate. It was midnight, wasn't it? Midnight and gone. Banner's disorientation rose.

Calm!

Banner squatted down and leaned out of the cage, groping for the fallen key. It was almost out of reach. He got his fingers around it, brought it back inside, and undid the lock.

He got out of the cage, dragged open the accordion gate, and stepped through.

The room beyond was filled with a soft, golden radiance. Music was playing, another old song from the days before the World Wars. The tone was soft and scratchy: an old gramophone player.

The room had once been grand, but now it was faded and worn. The paneled walls were hung with old photographs: stern men in blazers, elegant ladies with parasols, rowing teams, polo matches, a society formal. Side tables and shelves were stacked with books and tatty files, bottles and flasks, insect specimens in glass cases, skulls and antlers, antique scientific instruments, yellowed newspapers, card files, a typewriter, and X-ray film in card sleeves.

There was a Chesterfield sofa, several arm chairs, and an old player piano. The gramophone with its horn speaker sat on a table in the corner, old disks piled up beside it.

The drapes were shut. Banner walked to the nearest window and pulled aside the cloth. He was looking down on the jumbled streets of Lowtown Madripoor. It was night, a maze of streets described by neon signs and brightly lit windows.

Banner turned back and hunted for the source of the soft light. Inside a glass dome on a side table, a miniature sun glowed. He thought it was a trick at first, some kind of oversized filament bulb, but he felt its warmth as he approached it. It was the size of a grapefruit. He could see its coronal flare and the tiny bruises of sunspots growing and fading on its burning surface.

Tiny specks revolved around it: planets. It was an orrery, a model of a solar system, but there were no visible signs of support for the planetary bodies. How was it done? How was it possible?

"Don't stare at it for too long."

He jerked around.

Wyndham was watching him from the doorway of the adjoining room.

Banner blinked. His eyes were sore. He could see sun dots on his eyelids.

"A model," he said.

"In a way," said Wyndham. "I made it. The orbital scales are contracted for convenience, but the thermonuclear-fusion process is real enough."

"In a glass bottle?"

"A force field, actually. Otherwise there would be secondary issues of gravity, magnetics, and so on. One cannot have a solar wind blowing through one's parlor, can one?"

"It's a toy, then?" asked Banner.

"No," said Wyndham. "It's a reminder."

Herbert Edgar Wyndham had not been entirely human for a long time. Tall, powerful, imperious, he was locked in a form-fitting suit of flexible metal. The ribbed under-suit was silver. The outer armor, boots, gloves, and helmet were a polished magenta. The design reminded Banner of the Art Deco robot in Fritz Lang's silent movie *Metropolis*. That was what the future had looked like when Wyndham had been growing up in the early years of the twentieth century. For a man of such advanced ideas, Wyndham was stylistically trapped in his own past.

"You said something about an opportunity, Wyndham," said Banner.

Wyndham shook his hand dismissively.

"Please, Doctor," he replied. "Not that name. It represents another me, a past iteration. You know full well how I like to be addressed."

"I do," said Banner, damned sure he wasn't going to use that title. Years before, Wyndham had styled himself the "High Evolutionary"—which, to Banner, sounded like the unholy offspring of a union between H.G. Wells and George Orwell.

Banner feared that this connotation was deliberate.

Wyndham was dangerous. For a start, he was probably the most intelligent man on the planet. He had been since birth, and numerous scientific enhancements had amplified his brainpower to a level equal to that of advanced cosmic entities. He wasn't what S.H.I.E.L.D. would classify as a "super villain," either. Sometimes Wyndham even seemed to operate for the good of humankind.

But he was singular, gifted, ruthless—and he had lost his ethical compass decades before. His shocking eugenics projects, all done for the "betterment" of the species, had resulted in some truly calamitous problems.

"I forget my manners," the High Evolutionary said. "Hello, Doctor Banner."

He nodded courteously. His voice, artificially modulated, came out of his visor's mouth without the sculpted lips moving. His eyes were glassy, pupilless blue lenses.

"Wyndham," said Banner.

The High Evolutionary did not react to Banner's continued use of the name.

"Join me," said the High Evolutionary. "You're just in time."

"For what?" asked Banner.

The High Evolutionary beckoned, and Banner followed him

through double doors into the next room. It was the sort of laboratory in which Doctor Moreau would have felt quite at home. Workbenches, flasks, microscopes, chemical jars, scales, paperwork, and instrumentation covered every surface. As a nod to modernity, Banner saw whiteboards on the walls, covered with scribbled equations and sticky notes.

"Not quite your usual lab spec," remarked Banner. He put on his glasses and began studying the whiteboard equations, trying to read them quickly and still make sense of them. Genetic codes…transcription factors, the operation of DNA-dependent protein kinase…

"This is just a thinking space," said the High Evolutionary. "A private room in which to ponder and design. I have more sophisticated facilities on the floors below."

He looked at Banner. The glassy blue eyes were eerie.

"Though not, as you say, to my usual specifications. This is a hurried enterprise, thrown together in haste. I had been planning something, Doctor: a Great Act. It was years away from fruition. My plans take time to mature. I had barely begun to conceive it, let alone build the facilities necessary. Then a situation arose, and I was diverted to this scheme as a matter of priority."

He gestured with both hands.

"Thus, the parlous state of my facilities," he said, "housed in a forsaken factory building in the rat-runs of this objectionable city. I make the most of that which I can gather. Expediency, Doctor. I'm sure you can appreciate that."

"You chose Madripoor," said Banner.

"It has slack border controls," replied the High Evolutionary. "People here can be paid or otherwise persuaded to look the other way."

He looked at Banner. "And now you show up at my doorstep."

"S.H.I.E.L.D. brought me here. You know that already."

"Typical of S.H.I.E.L.D.'s operating mentality," remarked the High Evolutionary, "to send physical force to disrupt my activities."

Banner gestured to himself in a mocking "who, me?" way.

"Your other self," said the High Evolutionary. "S.H.I.E.L.D. wants me stopped, so S.H.I.E.L.D. decides to have me smashed."

"I was brought in as a consultant," said Banner. "It's my mind they wanted to use, not my...alter ego."

"Then S.H.I.E.L.D. is truly scraping the bottom of the barrel," said the High Evolutionary. "To attempt to thwart me on a purely intellectual level is redundant."

He looked at Banner.

"I mean no offense. You are a gifted scientist. Some of your work has shown merit."

"But I'm hardly your equal?" asked Banner.

"Of course not. But actually, I was going on to say that a man of your intelligence will soon wish to assist me, not thwart me."

"This is going to be good," said Banner.

"The world is about to die, Doctor," said the High Evolutionary. "It has, I estimate, four to six months left. I intend to save it."

"By, let me guess, ruling the world?" asked Banner.

"That's very perspicacious. Exactly."

"I was joking."

"I was not."

Banner narrowed his eyes.

"The world is going to die?" he asked.

"Very soon."

"On what do you base that assumption?"

"I have a very reliable source, Doctor," said the High Evolutionary.

"How—"

"Please, Doctor. If you listen and let me speak, you will find that I will answer all of your questions without you having to ask them."

"You've just evaded one."

"Doctor Banner—"

"Where's the gamma source, Wyndham?" Banner asked. "What is it?"

"A stockpile of radioisotopes. Primarily Potassium-40, with additional high-energy electron amplification."

"It's a massive radiation hazard," said Banner. He raised his hand. The gemstone on his ring was so dark blue it was almost black. "You haven't shielded it. It's causing untold harm to this population center. Wyndham, you—"

"Doctor Banner," replied the High Evolutionary, "in three days' time, the stockpile will form the core of a gamma bomb that will annihilate Madripoor, along with the South Eastern Pacific Zone, and irradiate the entire planet. So you see, shielding it is really rather a waste of effort."

WASHINGTON, D.C.
08.53 LOCAL, JUNE 12TH

TONY STARK was starting to gray out. Oblivion seemed like a merciful release from his suffering, but he knew that was just the oxygen starvation talking. His body wanted him to shut down so that the pain would stop.

His brain had other ideas.

With a sharp grunt of effort, he clamped his hands around Ultron's forearm. Ultron's grip tightened. Armor cracked and failed. Stark's dangling legs kicked and swung.

He fired both palm repulsors.

The close-focus blast, contained between his clamping hands, blew Ultron's arm off at the elbow, disintegrating it. The force of the savage energy release sent Iron Man flying backwards. He hit the ground hard, bounced, rolled, bounced again, and then slid to a halt.

He blacked out. Just for a second.

The alerts and flash notices pinging in his helmet brought him back. Multiple fault diagnostics appeared across his visor display in bold, red, pulsing letters.

The visual emphasis had seemed like a good idea when he'd

designed it. Now, with so many alerts coming at once, he could barely see anything except bold, red, pulsing lettering.

"Cancel alert notifications," he grunted. He could taste blood. He was going to have to put his chiropractor on a performance bonus to sort out his neck. There was a Shiatsu therapist named Summer who could probably help him out, as well.

He tried to sit up. His armor was scuffed and dented, but it was the dynamic systems that concerned him. Using his glove repulsors on such a tight focus had been a gamble. The left one had fried completely, and the right one had buckled. Automatic-repair systems were patching fast, but it would take workshop time to bring the suit back to its A-game.

Stark blinked. He looked down and exclaimed in disgust at the sight of Ultron's massive right hand still locked around his neck. The tattered stub of the forearm hung across his chest like an oversized medallion. It was very uncool. He hadn't worn medallions like that since the nineties.

With both hands, he struggled to prize the dead hand off his throat. His hands hurt. The back-blast had scorched through to his palms. He wrenched the wrecked hand free and tossed it aside.

It landed on the concrete floor beside him. Then it twitched, flexed its fingers, and started to crawl back toward him.

Stark expressed his revulsion in words that, once again, his publicist would not have appreciated. He rolled away from the crawling hand. God, he hurt. Never mind the sidebar diagnostics on his HUD, listing the twenty-seven separate suit systems that were either compromised or flat-out inoperable. He wondered what the diagnostics on his own body would read like.

The hand clattered toward him. His repulsors were no-go, so he twisted and aimed his left boot at it. A blast of his boot jet sent the hand flying across the chamber.

Good thing he didn't have a problem with spiders.

He struggled to his feet. He *did* have a problem with giant, homicidal, world-destroying robot sentients. Where the hell was the rest of Ultron?

Thick smoke and clouds of nanite dust were impairing visibility. The flames from various fires around the Black Chamber weren't helping much, either. He couldn't get any decent resolution because his suit's optical systems were damaged. He thought about raising his visor and using his actual eyes, but that would mean losing suit-seal integrity.

Then again, he'd probably lost it already. His armor was pretty badly damaged. There could be multiple tears and punctures to both the inner and outer skins. Even micro-fractures would be enough to let the subatomic nanites pour in. He wouldn't be able to tell it was happening. Even his damage-assessment system was damaged.

He wouldn't be able to tell it was happening until it was too late. It was probably happening right now. It—

"Ah, the hell with it," he said, and popped his visor. The Iron Man faceplate, its gold finish grazed, lifted up, and retracted back and over his forehead.

He could smell the harsh smoke, the burning plastics, the dust, the dirty carbons. He could feel the heat on his skin.

And he could see.

"Prioritize optical-system repair," he told his suit. "No, prioritize repulsor reset. No, prioritize both. Dammit, just fix yourself fast!"

He stepped forward. The ground around him was littered with the mangled, burning ruins of nanoforms. Glass and metal debris crunched beneath his boot treads. One of the block servers nearby sputtered sparks and fumed with sheets of smoke from its core. Tattered cables swung overhead. He could feel the invisible nanites crawling over the skin of his face, down his neck, into his suit. No, it was probably just sweat.

No, probably nanites.

"Hey, Ultron?" he called. "We done?"

Nothing stirred apart from the flames.

"Ultron? Buddy? Don't go away mad. The party isn't over yet. We're gonna play beer hunter."

Still no external data link, and no comms. The world outside could have ended. The Zero Six countdown was purely speculative now, flashing meaningless numbers like a bedside alarm clock after a power outage. But even a bedside alarm clock after a power outage winked the right time twice a day. Or something...

"Shut up, Anthony," he told himself. *Get back in the game. Get back in the damned game.* His mind was wandering. He'd probably taken a knock to the head. Concussion? A subdural? He—

"Shut up, Anthony," he repeated. Of course, many people—Clint Barton, in particular—thought Stark had taken a knock to the head years ago and had been acting crazy ever since. So—

"Shut the hell up!" he growled at himself.

Was the world outside dead? No way of knowing. The ASI end-of-everything, goodbye-humanity event could have taken place while he had been fighting Ultron. Maybe he was just a lunatic, survivor throwback to organic days—limping around a burning warehouse in a broken tin suit, believing that there was still hope.

Then again, he'd been so thoroughly invaded by nanites that he could have been disassembled without knowing it and remade into a nanoform that merely *thought* it was still human. He could be part of it all now. If that was true, Singularity sucked. Stark did not feel in any way enlightened or hyper-aware. If the nanites' intent had been to make him one with everything, then they'd forgotten the mayo, the cheese, the onions, the relish, and the pickle on the side.

The thought of the nanites made his skin crawl all over again. He felt an itch on his chin, and he hurriedly brushed it away. No, not nanites. Just blood, trickling from his mouth.

Like that was a good thing.

He'd expected a nanoform attack by now. There had been plenty of them, and they'd been hunting to kill. Where—

There was a ping. Diagnostics. *Right repulsor, sixty-five-percent repair achieved.*

Just in time.

A nanoform came at him. It was eight feet tall, a smoke-blackened endoskeleton, the eyes in its skull-face glowing green. Its left hand formed a massive cleaver.

Stark ducked the blade swing, and then blasted the thing in the chest with his repulsor. The nanoform toppled backwards. A second one struck at him from the left. He delivered a repulsor blast to its face before it could sink its talons into him.

Right repulsor, power failure. Offline.

Great.

The third nanoform hit him from behind. Stark fell and rolled with the impact, coming up into a crouch in time to block the charging humanoid with both hands. He crunched the fingers of his left hand into its chest casing, flinching as it rained blows at him with both fists. Holding it tight, he rose up and punched off its head.

He caught himself wondering why they looked so human. Why giant skeletal forms? Why the leering skulls? Was it to inspire fear?

No. Ultron admired the dynamic efficiency of the humanoid form. That's why it had adopted that form for itself. The human skeleton was a machine that worked well. There was no particular need to revise the design aesthetically, but there was also no need for soft tissue or finishing. The nanoforms looked like skeletons simply because flesh was redundant.

Flesh was redundant.

"Now *there's* a phrase I'm glad I coined," murmured Stark.

He had to hit the next nanoform twice to put it down. The second punch knocked the skull's jaw clean off in a fizz of sparks and metal fragments.

He glanced at the humanoids he had already felled. They would be repairing soon and—

They weren't repairing. Not even slightly.

In fact, they seemed to be dissolving, breaking down into raw molecular material. The material flowed away across the ground like trickles of oil. The same thing was happening to the nanoforms he had destroyed earlier. Most of those had been reduced to metallic puddles.

He moved, following one of the trickling streams. He came around the end of another server block and froze.

He'd found Ultron.

The giant construct was crouching like some massive, noble

sculpture by Rodin—part "Thinker," part sprinter on the starting blocks. Ultron was using rapid nano-facture to repair itself. It was stripping down its servant nanoforms, cannibalizing them for mass and material. The inky streams of base matter gurgled toward Ultron from all directions, fusing and flowing into its reassembling form. Its arms had regrown, and the damage to its chest was closing. Stark could see its missing hands recomposing before his very eyes, the plating case of its limbs forming a polished sheath.

Ultron was almost complete again. That was bad. Very bad. Stark was in no way fit or equipped to go another round.

But the nano-facture strip-down? That was a positive. Somehow, Ultron's resources had been radically restricted. That suggested containment. Maybe a break in external power supplies.

Ultron saw him. The giant rose out of its crouch and began to stride across the warehouse floor, each step shaking the ground and cracking debris underfoot.

Stark made his publicist unhappy again.

He ducked back around the server and started to run. He flipped his visor back down and checked the diagnostics. Some repairs had been completed. Flight options were screwed, repulsors were out, and his force fields hadn't been working for about five minutes. No comms, no data-externals, impaired targeting/reaction systems, and nothing in the way of battery reserve. And his appointment calendar was showing January the forty-third, 1872.

On the plus side, optics were back at decent function levels, and he had reasonable armor integrity, about forty-percent motive power, and a functioning unibeam—though one decent shot from that would suck his power down to zero.

"Anthony," Ultron boomed. It came around the server, shoving the heavy black unit aside with its hand. The server shunted and wobbled.

Stark swerved behind another server and ran along the row. He could feel Ultron's footsteps. A server shrieked against the concrete floor as Ultron pushed it out of the way.

"Anthony."

"You want to talk it out, Ultron?" Stark called back as he scooted between the ends of two servers. The units slammed together like clashing cliffs. Iron Man threw himself out of the gap to avoid being crushed. Smoke and gouts of flame belched from the servers, crumpled end-to-end like two locomotives that had collided head-on.

"No, Anthony. I want to kill you."

"Oh, where's the fun in that?" Stark replied. He picked himself up and ran on. An entire server came flying at him. Stark hurled himself out of the way. The unit buckled as it hit the ground and slid, raking sparks as it traveled.

Ultron loomed over him, reaching down. Stark rolled. He couldn't let the construct get its hands on him. Once he was in Ultron's grip, it would be game over, no respawning.

Ultron's claws hit the ground, fracturing the concrete. Stark scrambled up and ran. He leapt, made the top of another server block, and ran along it. Ultron grabbed the end behind him and lifted it. Stark fell, sliding down the sloping top, and managed to land on his feet on the ground.

Ultron tossed the server aside. It strode forward and swung a punch. Stark dodged. The fist went into the side of another server, rupturing its systems in a fierce explosion.

Stark moved left, head down. Ultron wrenched its fist free and followed, gaining ground with each crashing stride. A punch finally connected. It was a glancing blow across Stark's back, but more than enough to send him tumbling and clattering across the floor.

Ultron picked him up.

"Damn you!" Stark snarled. He fired his unibeam.

The blast staggered Ultron, composite abrading from its chest and neck like paint under a heat gun. It dropped Iron Man.

Winded, he tried to rise. His power was virtually spent. The frantic unibeam blast had expended most of his energy. The suit felt like a dead weight around him, cold and sluggishly unresponsive. He got to his feet, but he was too slow.

Ultron grabbed him by the torso and picked him up again.

"You have annoyed me, Anthony," it said.

"But thwarted your scheme for ASI world domination?" gasped Stark. "Right? At least give me that."

"No."

"Really?"

"Only temporarily. I must regroup and reconfigure."

"Don't leave on my account," said Stark.

"I will dispose of you, and then I will regroup and reinitialize the process."

I've saved the world for about twenty minutes, thought Stark. *Okay. That's something. Or I've just prolonged its agonies by twenty minutes. Postponed the inevitable. Not quite so glorious. Either way, I'm dead.*

Power? Just a little power? Pretty please? Just one last repulsor shot? Maybe a flare from the unibeam? Maybe—

Stark suddenly had a bad idea.

Auto-destruct? Suit self-destruct option? Was that even still working?

I'm dead anyway. I could at least take the son of a wrench with me.

"Code destruction sequence!" he yelled. "Stark, Anthony Edward. Authority 1181723!"

+Destruction sequence authenticated+

"Initiate!"

+Destruction sequence initiated. Destruction in five, four, three…+

"Disable destruction sequence. Stark, Anthony Edward. Authority 1181723."

+Sequence aborted and disabled+

Stark stared up at Ultron. The construct had mimicked his voice so perfectly it had fooled the armor's speech recognition.

"Goodbye, Anthony," said Ultron. "You—"

Silence.

"What?" asked Stark. "I *what?*"

Ultron had frozen. The light in its eyes faded. Smoke leaked from its angry mouth.

The Vision slowly withdrew his arm from the back of Ultron's head. He was hovering behind the construct.

"Spoilsport," said Stark. "Ultron was probably going to say something really important, and now we'll never know."

The synthetic-human Avenger drifted calmly into view. He was tall and beautiful, almost godlike in his human perfection. He was clad in green and yellow, his stern face scarlet. His cape billowed gently behind him.

"I arrived as swiftly as I could," the Vision said.

"What did you do?" asked Stark.

"There was little time for subtlety," replied the synthezoid. "I reduced my limb density to an intangible level, inserted it into Ultron's cortex, and restored density to a state exceeding that of dupleted uranium."

"You blew Ultron's brains out?"

"Euphemistically," the Vision agreed. "I catastrophically disabled Ultron's cortical hardware."

"Help me down, would you?" Stark requested.

With alarming ease, the Vision shredded Ultron's frozen arm and hand and lowered Stark to the ground. Stark looked up at the immobilized monster.

"You did a hell of a job," he said.

"On the contrary," replied the Vision. "I was able to strike a decisive blow, but that opportunity was only available because you had delayed, denied, and occupied Ultron for so long. Even at the last moment, Ultron's attention was on you. It would have attacked and countered me if it had not been so consumed by its hatred of you."

"I bring out qualities in people," said Stark. "I don't know. It's a gift."

"It is quite possible," said the Vision, "that you have, in effect, saved the world this morning. You were the first responder, and the only Avenger on the scene to combat Ultron's threat. It was a determined and heroic feat. I am impressed."

"Well, thanks," said Stark, "but I don't think it's over. Ultron isn't hardware. It's a digital sentience. It's very, very likely that Ultron has fled. I mean, pulled its sentience back into the global data network."

"Perhaps," the Vision agreed. "But there are limited possibilities. Catastrophic damage has been done. The East Coast region is a mess. Most systems are down."

"Rioting in the streets?"

"Civil disturbances are likely to be underway already. What I am saying is that Ultron might not have been able to—"

"Ultron will find a way," said Stark. "It got into the system, it can get out. It was pretty much connected to everything, everywhere. We need to find it. Contain it. Trap it, before we start to reboot and rebuild our own systems."

The Vision nodded.

"I'll need the full compliance of the authorities," said Stark.

"They will wish to restore order as rapidly as possible."

"I know, but we're not starting anything up again until Ultron is pulled out of hiding and locked in a box."

"What kind of box?"

"A metaphorical box. I'd better start talking to people."

Stark began limping toward the exit. The Vision drifted after him.

"Did you kill the power?" Stark asked.

"The power?"

"Ultron was cannibalizing for parts. His access to external supply was restricted."

"The power grid was shut down when I arrived," said the Vision.

Stark smiled.

"Well, Special SIGINT Support Supervisor Diane Lansing needs a big bunch of flowers and a pay rise," he said.

"Iron Man?" said the Vision.

"Yeah?"

"I do not wish to strike a negative note at this time, but you should be aware that there are other problems."

"Like what?"

"I was at Avengers Tower when this emergency became apparent, and I came to assist at once. Communications systems have been severely impaired, so information is scant—but when the system began to crash, I was monitoring threat alerts. I can brief you. The key one was taking place in the Russian Federation."

"Condition?"

"Condition Alpha."

Stark paused.

"*This* is Condition Alpha," he said, gesturing at the burning warehouse behind them. "This here. This is Condition Alpha so much we need a new condition level just to describe it. You're telling me there's *another one* going on?"

"One at the very least. Thor and Wanda responded, but contact was lost. There are also troubling developments surrounding threat issues being pursued by Hawkeye and the Black Widow, and by Captain America. Again, contact has been suspended."

"Go back to Russia. What was happening?"

The Vision paused.

"I am not sure how to describe it. A significant part of Siberia had ceased to exist."

"Destroyed?"

"No...ceased to exist in any real-world terms."

Stark shook his head and popped his visor. He wiped soot, sweat, and blood from his face.

"I think Ultron may have bashed me one time too many," he murmured. "Tell me all that again."

TWELVE

BERLIN
20.38 LOCAL, JUNE 12TH

THE BIKER with the "Roadkill" neck tattoo lunged in with a hunting knife that had skinned a lot more than deer in its time. Steve Rogers barely seemed to move at all. He tilted at the hip, allowing the straight drive to pass by his ribs instead of plunging into them. Then he pinned the biker's overextended arm with his crooked elbow and smashed the heel of his palm up under the biker's chin.

He relaxed the arm lock and the biker dropped, out cold.

"I asked politely," Rogers said in German.

But conversation was not an avenue that remained to be explored. Two more bikers rushed him, enraged at the sight of their comrade being schooled so easily. One was almost seven feet tall and built like a ski lodge.

Rogers threw a straight punch that smashed the smaller one backwards and then spun a reverse kick at the human ski lodge.

The big man was fast and durable. He soaked up the kick and grabbed Rogers's ankle. A pretty hardcore move. Decent training. That figured. Club Weltschmerz wasn't a standard urban dive, despite its crude industrial-chic decor and the rows of heavy hogs resting on their stands in the lot outside. It was a known meeting place for the radical right; a lot of the heavyset, leather-coated individuals inside were private military, specialist independents, and worse.

An ideal recruitment site for Hydra, especially if Hydra was in a hurry. As Captain America, Rogers had raided the club twice before, including once when it had been called the Rathaus and served as a front for a brutal A.I.M. off-shoot with seriously nasty ideas about eugenics.

That time, he'd needed stitches.

The human ski lodge flexed his grip. The handsome blond American interloper in the dark leather duster needed to be taught a lesson, and said lesson involved swinging him by the foot into the juke box. Repeatedly.

Rogers dropped onto one hand, allowing the big man to take his weight, and then kicked hard with his other foot. Knuckles broke. The ski lodge yelped and let go.

Rogers pushed back, somersaulted, and landed on his feet. The club patrons all came for him, riled up and anxious to inflict pain. The fierce techno blasting from the speakers was still thumping. The strobes and pump lights were still flashing. The patrons almost looked like they were dancing: bodies moving to the beat, any industrial Berlin club on any night.

Bottles flew. Rogers ducked a fist, blocked two more, and kicked a utility knife out of a thrusting hand. He threw two quick punches, and a bearded powerlifter sat down hard on the floor, blood gushing from his broken nose. Rogers turned and leaned into a high side-kick that propelled another knife-wielding man up into the mesh grille protecting a speaker stack. The grille buckled and tore away, crashing down on top of the man and knocking him to the floor.

A bottle bounced off Rogers's back. He elbowed another biker out of his way, and then took the legs out from under a bellowing skinhead who was waving a tonfa baton. Rogers caught the tonfa as it flew free, braced it into *honte-mochi,* and slammed the baton into the face of a suited businessman—who looked out of place except for the skill with which he was wielding his push dagger.

Veneered teeth flew.

Rogers spun the tonfa, clutched it by the shaft, and used the stubby grip to hook a combat knife out of the hand of his next assailant. Someone else punched him in the ribs. Rogers broke the tonfa over that someone's head.

The brawl became frenetic. Jeering faces blinked in and out of view in the strobing light. Someone else grabbed Rogers from behind and picked him up. The ski lodge again. It had to be. Rogers resisted the urge to butt backwards with his head. Instead, he plunged forward, leaving his leather duster behind in the ski lodge's grip.

The mob recoiled. They could see what he was wearing underneath: the red-white-and-blue body armor. Part combat kit, part ideological statement. They understood why the blond American had walked in alone, and why he had taken out so many of them in less than a minute.

They could also see what was strapped to his back under the slicker.

Some fled, either out of fear or a desire to avoid an incident that might jeopardize careers or contracts.

Captain America was fairly impressed by how many of them didn't back off. The ski lodge was one who stayed. He surged forward with a belligerent howl and tried to wrap Cap's duster over his head to smother him.

Cap ducked aside, unhooked his shield, and slammed the flat of it across the ski lodge's face with both hands.

The giant exhaled teeth and blood and collapsed backwards, knocking several other aggressors down with him.

One man—a handsome, wolfish guy in a black-leather bomber jacket—pulled a .40-caliber Sig Sauer. Despite the press of bodies, he simply opened fire.

Psychopath. Well, that *was* one of the desirable tick-boxes on the average Club Weltschmerz recruitment questionnaire.

Cap blocked the fire with his shield, hating the fact that the ricocheting bullets were plowing into the crowd. Three men went down. There were blood patterns on the floor amidst the broken glass.

Cap threw the shield and took down the gunman with a massively hard impact. Cap snatch-caught the shield as it rebounded, and then slammed aside a man who was moving in with a bayonet and a broken bottle.

Someone else was shooting. Things were escalating. Rapid fire ripped through the club, smashing glass, shattering lights, puncturing walls, and killing people.

Now, at last, the crowd properly broke and fled for cover. Crumpled bodies were left behind where they had fallen.

Cap saw the jagged muzzle flash. From the sound, rate of fire, and general fury, he figured a MAC-10 or an Enarm SMG. Bullets rattled off his shield, making almost musical sounds. The techno music, on the other hand, had cut off. The lights were still strobing and flashing, but the only sounds were screams and the blurred rip of the machine pistol.

Cap got behind one of the club's bare concrete support pillars—the club had been a produce warehouse in its former life. A light fixture fell out of the ceiling, dragging wires that sparked and shorted. He waited until he heard the gun's clip clack out, then turned and launched the shield before the shooter could reload.

Impact. The man dropped.

Cap caught the shield.

The skirmish was pretty much finished. Outside, Cap could hear sirens, and the boom of loudspeaker orders to get down and stay down. Police and S.H.I.E.L.D. units were circling in to secure the location and make mass arrests. Cap was pretty certain no one exiting the club would get beyond the parking lot or the end of the rear loading bay.

The glare of moving searchlights flashed in through the club's cage windows. There was a low throb of fanjets as whisper-copters swung over the lot.

Cap picked up the shooter, brushed a line of abandoned glasses and beer bottles off the bar with a sweep of his arm, and laid him on the bar top, face up. The shooter was Eastern European and had gang tags inked on his neck and face. While the man was still unconscious, Cap emptied the pockets of his faded-green flak jacket: two spare clips for the MAC, a knife, a lighter, a plastic baggie of something illegal.

A wallet.

"Talk to me, Viktor Tajic," Cap said, reading the I.D. in the wallet's plastic window.

The man stirred, spat blood, and groaned. Contact with Cap's shield had not made his face any more adorable.

"Viktor? I'm talking to you."

"Hail Hydra," the man spat, smiling defiantly with fewer teeth than he'd owned when he'd walked in for a beer that evening.

"Yeah, I don't think so," replied Cap, keeping his hand on Viktor's chest so he couldn't sit up. "Even Hydra has standards. You're reckless, unskilled, and you have a habit. They didn't want to know you, did they?"

The man swore at him.

"What a charming sentiment. Tell me about Hydra."

"Let me go."

"No. Hydra, Viktor?"

"Someone was recruiting," the man mumbled. His energy was crashing fast, the pain making itself known.

"Here?"

"Two weeks ago."

"They didn't want you?"

"No."

"But you wanted the job. It paid well, didn't it? Didn't it?"

"Yes!" Viktor nodded. He squinted and looked at Cap.

"I need something for the pain," he said.

"You'll get it. What was the job description?"

"No details," the man replied. He winced and groaned. "Just operatives needed. Military experience. Protection work. We all knew it was Hydra."

"How?"

"They are known here."

"Really?"

"Yes, yes, but they seldom come looking to hire. They are usually less...direct."

"No kidding. How did candidates contact them?"

"No contact," the man replied. "They just interviewed potentials in the back room. There, by the toilets. They came, they went."

"They didn't take you?"

"No. No."

"But you thought that if you killed the famous Captain America when he came in asking questions, they might take you seriously next time?"

Tajic hesitated. He closed his eyes and nodded.

"You're an idiot," said Cap.

He let the man go. It was a dead end. Maybe S.H.I.E.L.D. would get something in general interviews, from the club staff especially. Reserving a private room and putting the word out would have involved some contact.

Police and S.H.I.E.L.D. agents moved into the ruined club. Medics tended to the injured littering the floor. The strobes shut off and the main lights came on, hard and unforgiving. In the sudden glare, the place lost all of its dangerous urban allure. It was bare, sparse and dirty, and the sentiments of the old posters and graffiti on the walls were unsavory.

"They make you pay for damages in here?" asked Gail Runciter.

Cap sighed.

She looked around the place. "When you go out clubbing, you really club, don't you?"

"I'm not in the mood, Gail," he replied. "This was dumb. I knew coming in that I wouldn't get anything except a fight."

"You were looking for leads."

"I was clutching at straws. And venting, too, probably."

"Got it out of your system?" she asked.

"No." He glanced at her. "I'm ashamed of myself, actually. People have been hurt. Not-very-nice people, but people nevertheless. I was desperate, and I pretty much provoked this."

"Do your penance later," she said. "I've got something."

THE DIVERS recovered Gustav Malles's cell phone," said Runciter. They were sitting in the back of a S.H.I.E.L.D. whisper-copter that had settled on the front lot of the club.

"It's pretty new," she went on. "Purchased about a month ago in a city-center store. We believe Malles hadn't been in Berlin long. He'd probably just got his first retainer fee from Hydra and was treating himself."

She held up the smartphone in a plastic evidence bag.

"What did you find on it?" Cap asked.

"The techs went through everything: call log, texts, instant messages, the works. There's nothing that might be what we could call 'work-related.' This was his personal cell. There's probably another phone still at the bottom of the river, a burner that Hydra issued him for operational work."

"Then what use is this?" asked Cap.

She smiled at him in a way that suggested he should be patient.

"Malles liked his new phone. He set it up personally and pretty much okayed every feature it offered him. I think he played around with it when he was bored. It was his new toy. He downloaded apps. He set up Spotify, Instagram, and Facebook."

"Facebook?" said Cap.

"It gets better," she grinned. "At some point, he downloaded a free app called *What Next?* It's a basic street finder, a travel guide. Helped him find his way around, showed him the nearest bars and fast-food joints. You know the sort of thing."

"Gail—"

She smiled again.

"To use *What Next?* you have to okay Know My Location. Malles probably just tapped 'yes' when the box came up. Didn't think twice. So for the last three weeks, it's mapped his movements. Malles didn't use the phone for work, Cap, but it was in his pocket *while* he worked."

Cap looked at her.

"We know where he went?" he asked.

"Better still, we know where he went regularly."

She pulled out a sheet of paper and handed it to Cap. It was a list of addresses.

"The airport, several times. Various train stations."

She leaned over and pointed to an item on the list.

"This place here, pretty much every day. It's a hostel in Saar. We think that's where he was staying."

"Can we get people on it?"

"Bridge is already sending a team in. The really interesting one is this. An apartment building in Riechstahl. Nineteen visits in three weeks. The last one was immediately before Malles went with Strucker to Auger GmbH today."

"In other words, go to the boss's place, pick him up, and drive him to Auger."

"That's what it looks like."

Cap stared at the address. "This could be Strucker's base location?"

"Yep."

"We have to move," said Cap. "If Strucker got out of the water—"

"—and we're presuming he did," she put in.

"Then he might risk going back to his place. To clean it out or resupply. Maybe pick up something important. He's probably injured. Forced to take chances. He'd risk it."

"But he doesn't know we know the location," said Runciter.

"Strucker's not stupid. If he goes there at all, he won't stay long. Just grab what he needs. How quickly can we move in?"

"Bridge has already authorized the op," she said. "We have two tac teams moving into position."

"I'm going in first," said Cap.

"Bridge said you'd say that," she replied. She leaned forward, tapped the pilot on the shoulder, and made a circular motion with her upraised index finger. The pilot nodded and lit the fan drive. It whined up to power.

As the copter lifted away, Cap pulled on his mask.

SIX MINUTES," said Runciter over the headsets.

Cap nodded.

"Tac in position," she added. "Waiting for your go."

"Okay."

The city lay below them: bright lights, glittering streams of traffic, the amber haze of sodium street lighting. Corporate logos glowed in neon colors from the tops of high-rise business premises. Lights blinked on rooftop masts and needles.

The stars were out, just visible in a night sky bleached brown by the ambient glow of the city. But there was no air traffic: no winking running lights of passenger jets leaving the airports or stacking up over the city to land.

Runciter had told him that Civil Aviation had declared no-fly because of the crises in the U.S. and Russia. Nothing was moving internationally. Increasing problems with communication and global data traffic had grounded the airlines for safety reasons alone.

"Anything new?" he asked, knowing that she'd have told him if there was.

"From the U.S.?" She shook her head. "It's still dead. Nothing from S.H.I.E.L.D. stateside or the Avengers. We're not even getting private traffic or individual operators. The problem's spread to Canada and South America."

"How long before Bridge recommends an eyeball look at the situation?" asked Cap.

"He's liaising with government organizations and U.S. bases in Europe. A flight's gone into London to see what's happening there. A couple of hours, and he'll authorize a transatlantic mission—whether our European partners approve of S.H.I.E.L.D.'s plan or not."

"I want to be on that flight," said Cap.

"Man, you can't be everywhere," she said. She strapped on her ballistic vest and shoulder rig. "You're here, Steve. We're doing this. If you plan on saving the world, do it a little at a time."

"Three minutes," the pilot radioed. There was a sudden drop in noise. The pilot had switched to whisper mode, and the copter was banking down toward the high-rise district. One Thousand One Riechstahl was an impressive eighteen-floor block built along proud, prewar styles.

Cap strapped his shield across his back.

"Rooftop, fifteen meters," he said to the pilot. The pilot nodded. Cap took off his earphones and tucked an earbud under his mask.

"Hear me?" asked Runciter.

"Loud and clear."

Cap unstrapped and slid open the side door, letting in the night air and the whicker of the stealth rotors.

"See you on the far side," he said.

"Get Strucker," she replied.

He jumped out of the copter. Straight drop into the night, down onto the building's flat roof. He rolled with the landing, came up on his feet, and ran to the edge of the illuminated rooftop. There was a roof door, but that would probably be linked to the building's alarm system. Strucker would have chosen the place carefully— and probably set up trips of his own.

Runciter had compiled a list of residents. Most checked out. There was a large apartment on the eleventh and twelfth floors that had no listed occupants, but had been rented anonymously for eight weeks through a foreign brokerage company.

On the roof edge, Cap played out the nylon line he had wound around his waist. He secured the end to the roof blocks with a little fusion spike that slid into the stone as if it were butter. A second to let it cool and set, a test tug, and then he was over the edge, fast-roping down the side of the apartment building.

"Looking good," said Runciter in his ear.

"You got eyes on me?"

"Confirm that. You're just passing thirteen."

"Understood."

Twelfth floor. There was a parapet. The windows were dark. Cap got his feet on the ledge and let go of the rope. He checked the first window. Through it, he could see an open-plan lounge—modernist, unlit. The window was fixed. No opener.

He moved along to the next window. It looked into the same room. This window wasn't fixed. He checked the seal and spotted the tiny contact breaker glued to the edge of the frame. A contact breaker on a twelfth-floor window. That was Hydra-level paranoia.

"Cap?"

"Working," he replied.

He went back to the fixed window and took a suction grip and a pen-sized laser cutter out of his kit-belt. He stuck the grip to the center of the pane, held it, and then drew a circle on the glass with the lit tip of the cutter. A circular section of glass the size of his shield pushed in cleanly on the grip. He lowered it inside and laid it flat on top of a sideboard under the window. Then he stooped in through the hole.

"Making entry," he said.

"Copy that."

He stepped off the sideboard and onto the white rug. The room was dark and quiet. He could make out an L-shaped sofa, an armchair, and spare expressionist prints in black frames on the walls. He touched the cowl of the pendant designer grate. It was cold.

Next door was an austere kitchen-diner, broad and spacious, with double-aspect windows. Cap checked for signs of motion detectors or listening devices. He touched the coffee maker, the halogen hob, and the designer tap over the sink. Cold, cold, and cold. He opened the immense refrigerator and stood bathed in its blue light. A carton of eggs, a tub of health-drink mixture, fruit juice. The juice was open and not expired.

"Someone's been living here," he said.

"Copy."

Off the kitchen there was a hallway with a closet bathroom and access to the building's elevator. The security panel beside the elevator was turned off.

There were stairs to the level below. Cap saw that the lights were on.

"Going dark," he whispered. "I think someone's here."

"Copy."

Shield braced on his arm, he edged down the stairs.

A bedroom, dark. Bed unmade, just a bare mattress. Another bedroom, just like the first.

The light was on in the third, master bedroom. The bed was made with military precision, but it had been slept in. Six expensive suits hung in the closet, with a stack of shirts still in their laundry wrappers. A suitcase lay open on the chair beside the bed, a few items in it. Had someone started packing to leave and then given up?

Cap moved back to the hall. As an afterthought, he turned, knelt down, and looked under the bed.

Nothing.

Cap smiled to himself sheepishly. Hydra's paranoia was infectious. And it would have been somehow miserably pathetic if, after all these years of fighting, he'd finally brought Strucker to justice by finding him hiding under his own damned bed.

Across from the bedroom was a sitting room, also done up in a serious, modernist style. Doors led through to a main dining room.

The light was on. There was an impressive eighteen-seat table.

No one had used the room for a dinner party in a while. The table was covered with files, laptops, aluminum carry cases, maps, and plastic crates full of brand-new handguns and ammunition. In the middle of the table was a chrome device about the size of a large soda bottle. It stood upright on extended legs. Cap knew it had to be the missing dispersal-unit prototype.

Wolfgang von Strucker was sitting at the head of the table, calmly facing Cap.

"I heard you come in," he said. "I saw you." He gestured to a laptop open beside him. "Under the bed? Really?"

"I wouldn't put anything past you, Strucker," Cap replied. He said the name clearly so that Runciter would hear it. He kept the shield ready, tensed to throw. Strucker was at the other end of the room, but Cap knew he could take him down with one accurate sling.

Strucker was full of tricks, however. A powerful laser pistol lay on the table beside the laptop. Strucker made no attempt to reach for it. What was the game here? The windows behind Strucker were wide open to the night. Was he intending to jump? To attempt an escape?

Strucker had a cut over one eye that he had sutured with a field kit, and his face showed bruises and other marks from their battle. His suit and shirt were clean and fresh. He had not bothered with a tie.

"I didn't believe there was any point in running," said Strucker. "Another chase?" He shrugged dismissively. "What would be the reason? You are dogged, Captain. And S.H.I.E.L.D., I'm sure, has the building surrounded and the exits covered. You found me. That was impressive work."

"I just followed the trail of slime," said Cap.

Strucker laughed.

"Ah, the banter! I had forgotten how old-fashioned you were. Just not very good at it. This isn't the nineteen-forties any more, sir. Or would you like me to slap your face with a glove for your impudence?"

"I'll pass."

Strucker sat back, utterly unthreatening in his body language. Cap didn't like how calm he was.

"Time is short, Captain," he said. "Perilously short. For all of us. I had hoped to clear out of here and depart. I had a goal in mind for the next stage of my operation. Your arrival has ended that hope. So we will play it out here. The beginning. The end. The whole affair."

"You're under arrest, Strucker," said Cap.

"I'm really not," Strucker smiled.

"You're under arrest and unconscious, then," said Cap, tilting his shield very slightly.

"I'll tell you what I am," said Strucker. "I am a free man. And the new master of the world. And the world will thank me, on bended knees, for becoming its master."

"I've heard it all before."

"I've meant it every time. This time, it is absolute."

"You're issuing a threat," said Cap. He gestured to the dispersal unit. "That thing. You're going to release your pathogen. You're going to release it unless we agree to your demands. You're holding Berlin to ransom."

"To ransom? A threat?" Strucker lifted his head back and laughed. "No, no, my dear Captain. Not at all. Threats and negotiations are far too old-fashioned for this day and age."

Cap took a step forward.

"Then what—"

He suddenly realized that the chrome device on the table was ticking very softly. Strucker held up his index finger.

"Don't spoil the moment, Captain," he said.

There was a click. A thin vapor gusted from the top of the device and filled the dining room with a fine mist.

"Pop," said Strucker. "You are dead, Captain. So are the inhabitants of this building. So are the S.H.I.E.L.D. agents at the doors. So are the people on the street below. So is Berlin. Hail Hydra."

69° 30' SOUTH, 68° 30' WEST
09.40 LOCAL, JUNE 12TH

SHE PLOWED into them, firing both pistols. There was no time to be delicate. She had ten rounds in the gun in her left hand, and five remaining in the one in her right. Suppressed slugs slammed into body masses and punctured visor grills. Men toppled away from her. One of them got off a burst with his FN P90, but he was already dead and falling, and the trigger-pull was a nerve spasm. The shots raked into the corridor ceiling, punching ugly holes in the yellow-polymer finish.

Her pistols emptied abruptly; the slides locked back. She took down the last A.I.M. guard with a punishing spin-kick that slammed him across the hall and into the opposite wall.

No time to reload. She thumbed the stops to release the slides and jammed her Glocks back into her holsters. Then she stamped on the butt of one of the fallen P90s. The compact bullpup spun into the air and she caught it.

A second A.I.M. squad rounded the end of the hallway.

Widow settled the butt against her shoulder, clutched the ergonomic grip, and steadied the short weapon using the nylon loop under the blunt muzzle. She aimed and ripped off tight bursts at the approaching targets. Spent shell casings billowed into the air and rained down around her feet. Two guards dropped; the others scattered for cover.

The smooth, modular hallway provided very little cover. She cut down two men who were pressed to the wall. They tumbled back together, leaving smears of blood. Another man ducked behind some vent pipes. The P90 had good penetration, so she shot the pipes out, blasting him with jets of escaping steam.

The sixth man made it to the doorway. She tried for him, but her rounds smacked along the frame. From partial cover, he returned fire. She danced sideways as shots stitched a line down the floor. Her back to the wall, she fired again, forcing him to duck.

Widow turned and started to run. The P90 had a clear plastic magazine so the operator could check the load by eye. She'd used at least a third of the weapon's fifty-round capacity.

Gunfire followed her.

She swerved into a link well and slid down the metal wall ladder, the gun resting over her shoulder. She landed firmly on the deck below and retrained the bullpup, flicking both ways—ready for surprises.

Alarms were ringing, muted but urgent electronic pulses. Two techs in yellow came around a corner, saw her, and fled. She started to run again, the weapon clutched to her chest. Rips of gunfire spat down the link well behind her, pinging off the deck.

Another junction, another link well. This time she climbed up, returning to the original level. Counterintuitive tactics: They'd seen her exit downwards. They'd expect her to keep moving down through the building.

She came up into a small service chamber. She slipped into the shadows of a maintenance alcove, dropped the P90, and slammed fresh clips into both Glocks. She was low on ammo. On arrival in the Savage Land, she'd been packing six clips of ten rounds: four in belt pouches, and one in each weapon. The raptors had accounted for two clips, and she'd just emptied two more. These reloads were her last. The A.I.M. handguns used rounds compatible with the Glock 26s, but the clips were not interchangeable. To score munitions from A.I.M., she'd need to hand-load her empty clips, which would take time.

Widow removed the suppressor from one of her Glocks. She might still need stealth, but the tubes robbed the guns of punch, and she might also need stopping power. She had to keep her options open.

It was time to plan. She could cat-and-mouse around the facility all day long, but that wouldn't achieve much. She had the intel on A.I.M.'s operation, but no means of getting it out. Comms were down, and the world beyond Antarctica seemed to have taken the phone off the hook. She could try to find transport, exfil, and get word to the outside world. But that was a tall order, and there seemed no guarantee that help would come.

She could stay on site and shut down A.I.M. Also a tall order, but more viable, and potentially a much faster result—*if* things went her way. If she was smart. If she could make best use of the elements at her disposal.

She needed to find Hawkeye. She hoped he was still at large.

She reholstered the Glocks and picked up the P90. Apart from the alarms, the area was quiet. She peered out of the service chamber along the main corridor, and heard voices. A detail ran past. She waited until they were gone.

She risked a look at the corridor's surveillance system: discrete cameras mounted at intervals, covering the angles, leaving few if any blind spots. All of them displayed red L.E.D. indicators, showing they were operational. She'd quietly canned the security monitors along her infil route, but this section was live. A.I.M. would be able to see her.

It was time to let them. She stepped into the corridor and began to walk, purposeful and bold, the weapon resting on her hip.

She reckoned on six steps. It took four. They were sharp.

"Stay where you are," a voice ordered over the speaker system. She stopped, looked for the nearest camera, and smiled up at it.

"I don't think so," she told it.

"Stay where you are and put down your weapons."

"You can hear me, yes?" she called, staring at the camera.

"Stay where you are and put down your weapons."

"I don't know if you can hear me," she said. "Put me on speaker so I know you can hear me."

There was a pause. She could hear movement from both ends of the corridor: security squads moving up, but keeping out of sight. That was okay. The service chamber and link well were just behind her if she needed cover in a hurry. She heard a click on the speaker.

"Can you hear me?" she asked again. They could. She could hear her own words echoing through the building via the internal comm system.

"Lay down your weapons," the speaker said. "Surrender."

"Still with this?" she said, maintaining her confident look to the camera. "A.I.M. is a criminal organization, outlawed by S.H.I.E.L.D. and the United Nations Security Council. It is you who must surrender."

There was another pause.

"Are you making a joke?" the voice said, its composure slipping. "You are alone. You are outgunned. You expect us to surrender?"

She took a small tube from her belt and held it up in her fist, so the camera could see it. Her thumb was pressed to the end of it.

"I don't," she said, "but the shaped charges I have placed around your perimeter, your power generator, your landing structure, and your nanotechnology-fabrication plant say otherwise."

THE A.I.M. guard went limp, his blood supply cut off. Hawkeye gently released his chokehold and lowered the man to the floor. The security station was a small cubicle, pretty cozy with just him and the unconscious dude. A control console supported banks of displays and a single chair. On one wall, a fire extinguisher in a rack. On the other, a ladder to the roof hatch. He pulled the door shut and started to check out the console.

Alarms had been sounding for five minutes. Natasha was being Natasha somewhere. He'd just heard her voice over the intercom, a few moments ago. What the hell was she doing?

"Do you need me to repeat that?" he heard her say over the speakers.

Hawkeye punched through the surveillance angles, section by section. He found her. Yeah, nice back view. She was standing in a corridor, looking up and holding something up in her hand.

A camera. She was looking up at a camera.

What was she holding?

He switched camera views. It took three changes to find the one she was looking at. There she was. A smile on her face, too. He knew that look. Total "I'm in control" confidence.

That made him nervous. The whole mission had been hit-the-ground-running, seat-of-the-pants so far. Here she was acting like she was part of a precision plan.

Acting. Operative word. Natasha Romanoff had a habit of improvising in a crisis and expecting everybody to go along with her. She'd gotten A.I.M. to put her on speaker. That meant she was hoping that Hawkeye could hear her, wherever he was. Okay, what did she want him to hear?

"Your demands are meaningless," he heard the command center say. "Surrender."

"My demands are very real," she replied.

He fast-tracked in with the zoom. What was that in her hand? A tube?

"I recommend you comply in twenty seconds," she said. "I repeat, I have placed shaped charges around your perimeter, your power generator, your landing structure, and your nanotechnology-fabrication plant."

He zoomed in tighter. That was...that was the tube of contact adhesive from her belt kit. *Oh, Natasha, baby, you are cray-cray.*

"Do I have to demonstrate?" the Black Widow asked the camera.

Hawkeye swore. He turned, pulled the drum-hat off the unconscious guard, and grabbed the man's bluetooth earpiece.

Channel...channel...find the damn channel...

"Control, we have eyes on a suspect packet," he said. His own voice now rolled out of the speaker system.

On screen, Widow smiled and nodded.

"You see?" she said coolly.

Hawkeye scrambled up the ladder, screwed open the roof hatch, and stuck out his head. Hot sunlight hit him. Swamp heat rushed into the air-conditioned cubicle. The modular yellow compound was spread out below, fringed by the lush green jungle.

"Watch station, what is the location of the packet?"

They were talking to him.

"Uhm, stand by," Hawkeye replied, hunting for something plausible to say. He perched on the rim of the hatch and unshipped his bow.

"Watch station! Respond!"

"Heat exchangers, west side of the complex!" he yelled.

"Do you need me to demonstrate?" he heard Widow say again. Hawkeye looked down at the cubicle inside. On the screens below, he could see her pretending to adjust the tube of adhesive in her hand.

"Heat exchangers," she said. "Very well."

Hawkeye yanked out a blast arrow and fired—just as Widow made a show to the camera of "pressing" the cap of her adhesive tube.

There was a loud crump. A roiling ball of flame rose from the western edge of the compound. All around the complex, flocks of small protobirds and tiny pterosaurs burst into the air, startled by the blast.

"She blew it!" Hawkeye cried into the mic. "She blew it up!"

There was silence. Black smoke from the burning heat exchangers rose into the blue sky.

"Desist from further destruction," command said.

"Are you willing to comply?" Widow asked.

"What are your demands?"

"Surrender immediately. Assemble all base personnel in your hangar space. Do not impede me. I want a face-to-face with your leader."

"If we refuse?"

"I continue to press the detonator. Your nanotechnology suspensions are held securely in the fabrication facility. I am confident you do not want them released into the environment at this time."

"We…comply."

Hawkeye exhaled. Brinksmanship. Sheer brinksmanship. The question was—what lay beyond the brink? A.I.M. wasn't just going to fold. They were playing for time.

What was going to happen when they called her bluff?

BLACK Widow walked out onto the main deck of the hangar bay. Four long-range A.I.M. rotorjet shuttles were parked along one wall. A fifth was set on a hydraulic cradle, ready to be lifted up to the rooftop pad.

Just under a hundred A.I.M. technicians and guards were assembled in the main area. The guards had not disarmed, but their weapons were lowered.

As Widow entered, the fire teams that had been shadowing her followed her inside. They fanned out around her, covering her with their P90s. She ignored them.

She came to a halt. The tube was still clenched in her left hand.

"Who is in charge?" she asked.

A man in A.I.M. yellow stepped forward and took off his helmet. He was tall and gray-bearded, and his expression was one of distaste.

"You?" she asked.

"Advanced Ideas Mechanics does not respond well to threats," he said. "Your intrusion here is undesirable. You will not be allowed to compromise the success of this installation."

"That doesn't sound like surrender talk to me," she replied. "I'm an Avenger."

"I know what you are," he replied.

"Then you also know that the Avengers beat A.I.M. into dog meat every time we encounter one another. This is over. You are all prisoners of S.H.I.E.L.D."

"And where is S.H.I.E.L.D.?" he asked. "You are alone."

"What is your name?" she asked.

"Thewell," he replied. "Acting Minister of Control Development."

"What is the purpose of this facility?"

"I'm not going to tell you anything."

"Nanotechnology, Thewell. Don't play games."

"I'm not. I don't have authorization to speak to our development work."

"Who has authority?" she asked.

"A.I.M. High Council. M.O.D.O.K.," he replied.

"M.O.D.O.K.?" she sniffed. "And where is that charming individual?"

"M.O.D.O.K. is not on-site," said Thewell. "I report to him."

"Report to him now."

Thewell hesitated.

"I cannot. Communication links are not operational."

Widow took a breath. Interesting. Her inability to send the data hadn't been down to her lack of skills or security codes. There was something else going on.

"Tell me about the nanotech, Thewell," she said.

Thewell glanced at the techs behind him. One shook his head slowly.

Thewell looked back at her.

"The nanites have been engineered to enter the human system and fabricate receptor nodes in the neuroanatomy of the neocortex," he said.

"Receptors for what?"

"Receptors to receive, process, and amplify psionic signals."

"Mind control, by psionic means," she said. "M.O.D.O.K.'s stock in trade. You intend to reengineer human brains to make them captive to his control."

He nodded.

"Which population centers do you propose to target?" she asked.

"No particular center," he replied.

"Your scope is global?"

He nodded again.

She thought about the nod. Her mind was trying to take in the full horror of what A.I.M. was devising. A world slaved to M.O.D.O.K.'s whim, a race of human puppets obeying A.I.M.'s every command. But the nod bothered her. Thewell had refused to speak at first, but now he was telling her everything, as if none of it mattered.

They expected her to be dead very soon.

"How is the nanite material going to be delivered?" she asked.

"Water supplies," he said. "Water is an efficient medium. Introduced into water supplies, the self-replicating nanites will rapidly enter the food chain."

"Global water supplies?" she asked.

Again, he nodded. Why did that nod bother her so much?

Because when he'd consulted his colleagues, one of them had shaken his head. Then Thewell had started talking. If he'd been looking for approval, Thewell would have received a nod, in turn, from his colleague. But he'd gotten a shake of the head instead.

That shake of the head didn't mean, "Very well, tell her." It meant something else. It meant, "No." It meant, "Not yet." It meant, "We're still waiting for something, and we're not ready." The implication was, "Talk to her and keep her talking. Keep her busy and buy us time." During surveillance ops, she'd seen phone-tap operators make exactly the same wordless signal to the agent trying to keep a caller on the line. "Keep going. Not ready yet."

Things were about to get unpleasant. Her bold play had put her front and center in an effort to control this environment, but now that seemed like a very bad place to be.

Her turn to spin things out. "Show me specifications for the nanite units," she said.

Thewell looked back at his colleagues again. The one who had shaken his head before now nodded and handed him a tablet.

A nod. The damned nod. It was coming.

Thewell looked at the tablet. He walked over to the Widow and handed it to her. Then he stepped back.

She looked at the device. There was an open message window. It read:

"Scanning complete. Individual is armed. No trace of active radio or wireless device. Suspect object is a tube of glue."

"Goodbye, Avenger," said Thewell.

The guards brought up their weapons to fire.

One of the hydraulic legs of the lifting cradle exploded and sheared. The cradle buckled, and the hefty rotorjet shuttle atop it fell sideways, hit the deck, and rolled. The assembled A.I.M. personnel scattered out of its way.

Widow threw herself backwards, firing her P90 sideways. Casings spat out in a rising arc. Her auto fire raked into the guards circling her to the left. Bullets chewed the deck. She rolled, firing the other way. Three guards to her right flew backwards off their feet. But she was never going to hit them all.

Three more jerked and dropped in very quick succession, an arrow embedded in each one. From his high-and-hidden vantage point, Hawkeye had rapid-fired at the targets, shooting the second and third arrows while the first was still in the air.

The remaining guards turned and fired, hunting for the archer. Widow emptied her clip into the last of them.

She ditched the P90, jumped up, and ran for cover. Shooting was wholesale. Bullets chipped and smacked into the risers of the hangar maintenance bays. She threw herself into a dive and crashed into the tool carts.

From the flight-control platform, Hawkeye saw her reach cover. He nocked another arrow and targeted anybody below with a gun. Most of the A.I.M. personnel were rushing for the exits. He spotted the guy with whom Widow had gone face-to-face, spun up a bolas arrow, and brought him down with a seventy-five-yard arc shot.

Hawkeye was drawing fire. Bullets struck the platform, the railing, and the roof overhang. He retreated to the back of the platform and threw the controls that opened the roof canopy. With a heavy thump of electric motors, part of the hangar roof began to slide open.

Hawkeye went for the stairs. One flight down on the open metal steps, he turned and loosed more arrows into the chamber: another blast arrow to scatter more of the A.I.M. goons, and a clutch of smoke arrows to really mess up visibility and sow confusion.

He leapt down the last flight and ran across the floor. An A.I.M. tech came at him, and Hawkeye punched him aside. Two A.I.M. guards loomed in the smoke. Hawkeye shoulder-barged one, ripped the assault weapon out of his hands, and used it to club the other in the side of the head. Then he delivered a standing spin-kick to drop the disarmed guard.

He reached Thewell. The A.I.M. exec was on his face on the deck, his arms and legs bound by the cords of the bolas arrow. He'd hit his head in the fall and was out cold. Hawkeye shouldered him like a roll of carpet.

An A.I.M. guard appeared, training his weapon on Hawkeye. A shot, from close range, hit the guard. He buckled and fell.

Widow stepped out of the smoke. She had an A.I.M.-issue Sperek Six pistol in each hand.

"You got a plan?" she asked. "Or is this all atmospherics?"

"I figure we leave," Hawkeye replied. "This is not a healthy place to be. We take this creep with us as insurance, and for info."

"Leave how?"

"One of the rotorjets. How hard can they be to fly?"

They ran to the nearest one. With Thewell over his shoulder, Hawkeye wrenched open the shuttle's cabin hatch. Widow squeezed off a couple more shots, and then eyed the roof.

"You killed the riser hoist," she said.

"Hey, I opened the roof!"

"It's going to be a tight fit."

"I'll show you how it's done."

She shook her head and ran aboard. He came in behind her,

dropped Thewell onto a seat in the cargo section, and slammed the hatch.

Widow had reached the cockpit. There was no time for pre-flight checks. She threw the power on, woke up the jets, and adjusted the control settings before sliding the pilot seat forward and strapping in.

"I told you I'd fly," said Hawkeye.

"I'm a better pilot," she replied. She checked the power readings. The rotorjets were fusion-powered. Plenty of range. Transoceanic, if necessary.

She engaged lift, and the rotorjet bucked and left the deck. It hovered forward—nose tipped down, landing gear extended—its downwash blowing whirlpools in the smoke Hawkeye had laid down. They heard several shots strike the outer skin.

"Up and out," Hawkeye urged.

Widow eased the nose around and let power run to the VTOL-set rotor pods. The shuttle rose. The hangar roof seemed very close. She adjusted the attitude again and lifted higher, moving toward the open canopy.

It *was* going to be tight. From an exterior perspective, the shuttles had looked much smaller than the canopy hatch. From inside a shuttle, the hole didn't look anywhere near large enough.

She went for it. Proximity alarms started to sound. She nursed the controls.

"Easy! Easy!" Hawkeye said.

They came up through the delivery aperture in the landing pad. Hawkeye closed his eyes. He was positive he could hear metal scraping and grinding, but it was just his imagination.

"Go!" he yelled. "Go!"

She turned back to look at him.

"Missiles," she said.

"What? Where?"

"They took the Quinjet down with ground-to-air! They have missiles here, Barton!"

"Just fly!" he ordered.

He ran back to the side hatch and slid it open. Wind blew in. The shuttle was rising above the yellow structure of the A.I.M. compound. He hunted. There, to the north. He saw rotating sensor domes on the roof of one of the modules, set on either side of a larger pod.

A shutter on the large pod began to open, revealing the missile rack. The pod rotated, tracking them.

"Get us out of here!" Hawkeye yelled.

He heard a frantic pinging from the instrumentation.

"Missile lock!" she shouted.

Braced in the open side hatch, Hawkeye pulled down his bow, nocked an acid arrow, and took aim.

He loosed. Given the distance and conditions, it was an astoundingly difficult shot. Hawkeye was sure it would take him two or even three arrows to find the target.

But he aced it. The arrow hit the missile rack in the gearing under the frame. The capsule head shattered, drenching the gear assembly with hydrofluoric acid. The acid ate through the missile rack's frame in seconds, and the entire rack slumped forward drunkenly, nose down.

The missile lock warning ceased abruptly.

"Just go," he yelled, "before they find something else to throw at us!"

There was a flash and a shiver behind them. Though their frame support had been ruined and their aim disrupted, the missiles—triggered on an automatic cycle—had nevertheless launched.

Straight down into the base.

There was a rippling series of explosions. Detonations ripped apart the center modules of the A.I.M. compound, sending up columns of flame and cascades of shredded plating. A secondary blast, perhaps a power system that had been hit, blew out through the ground level of the primary modules.

An enormous fireball rose up. The shockwave hit the shuttle, rocking it hard, and Hawkeye had to grab on to stop himself from being flipped out of the hatch.

Widow fought to keep the shuttle stable and airborne. They roared out of the expanding conflagration.

"Did you mean to do that?" she asked.

"No!" Then he grinned. "Still, you know, it solves a few problems," he added.

She just glared at him.

SIBERIA
LOCAL TIME UNRECORDED, NO RELEVANT DATE

THOR grabbed Wanda around the waist, pulled her close, and spun his hammer by the strap. He let it fly and pull them both into the air. The last, monumental blocks of stone, their only foothold, collapsed beneath them in a thunderous roar of crumbling rock.

They landed a mile away on a blasted, dead plain. Fog drifted like white smoke. Blackened, extinct trees dotted the landscape, their trunks bent, their branches splayed. They looked like figures screaming in abject horror at the sky.

He let go of her.

"Are you all right?" he asked.

"Given the circumstances," Wanda said, nodding. She looked back toward their point of origin. Beyond the tree-punctuated bank of white fog, the mountain had been reduced to an immense pall of gray dust. Flames leapt and danced on the horizon.

"He'll be coming for us," she said.

"Undoubtedly," said Thor.

"I mean, we can't fight him."

"I can fight him," said Thor. "I'm not afraid."

"It's not a matter of fear," she replied. "He outclasses us both. Many times over."

"Then we need help," Thor said.

The Scarlet Witch smiled. She had observed the resilience of heroes in her fellow Avengers over the years and hoped she shared some of that quality. But the indefatigable spirit of a god was another thing altogether. It charmed and lifted her. There was something immensely reassuring about Thor's dogged courage. No matter the odds, the Asgardian maintained a conviction that heroes would always prevail. She supposed it was the mindset of a god, a super-mortal: an almost blinkered focus on triumph that bullishly refused to acknowledge hopelessness.

"I don't know if we can get a message out of here," she said. "We're not in the world anymore. We're not connected to the plane of Earth. Of Midgard."

"You don't have to couch it in my terms," Thor said. "I understand. Is there no conjuration you can make? No message you can send by means of magic?"

She shrugged.

"Perhaps," she said. "I trained with the Sorcerer Supreme to refine my craft, and during that time he described many obscure, arcane processes. But I've never used them practically, and I'm fighting to remember the details. Thor, I'm no Stephen Strange. I don't know the depth of lore the way he does. Even if I can remember the conjurations he mentioned, I don't know if I can cast them in a place like this. I don't know if I *should*. It could be dangerous—"

He grinned at her. That god-spirit confidence again.

She caught herself and smiled back ruefully.

"Yeah, I know. Like this is safe."

"Do what you can," he said.

"The first thing I have to determine is where we are. Exactly where we are."

She sat down on the filthy, wet ground and scooped up a handful of black soil, examining it.

He watched her.

"It may take some time," she said, without looking up. "Geomantic divination is painstaking."

He nodded, breathed out, and folded his arms.

"Gather some wood," she told him.

"Wood?"

"Firewood. The trees, Thor. Get plenty."

"Very well," he said.

He left her sitting in the mud and walked through the fog to the nearest tree. He put his hand on the gnarled trunk and, as was the Asgardian custom, uttered an apology to the tree for bringing it low.

Then he felled it with a single blow of Mjolnir.

He broke up the branches into rough staves and piled them in a stack. Eerie sounds, like the cries of winter foxes, floated in through the fog. Every time he stopped breaking wood to listen, the cries abated.

There was something in the mist.

He finished the labor and trudged back to the Scarlet Witch. He held a burden of splintered wood cradled in one arm, and the bulk of the tree trunk braced across his other shoulder.

She was still staring at the dirt, letting it trickle out of her hand.

"Where do you want this fire?" he asked.

"Here. Beside me."

"The wood's sodden and full of rot. I doubt it will burn."

"It'll burn."

"I know you're cold, woman, but won't a fire give away our location?"

She got up, brushing her hands clean.

"It's not for warmth," she said. "We need protection. Plant that trunk here."

She pointed to a spot on the ground near where she had been sitting.

He raised his eyebrows, then did as she told him. He lifted the tree trunk in one hand and drove it down into the mud.

"Good," she said. "Now take some more wood. Walk that way. Thirteen paces from the trunk."

She pointed.

Grudgingly, he scooped up an armful of wood and started to pace out from the stump.

"How far?" he called.

"The distance doesn't matter. The number of paces does. Was that thirteen?"

"I..." he paused. He walked back to the stump and repeated the action, counting each step this time.

"Thirteen."

"Plant some sticks there. In the ground."

Thor half-buried a handful of sticks upright at the spot. "Like that?"

"Now walk to your left from those sticks. Again, thirteen paces."

He looked at her, bemused.

"Please, Thor."

He counted off his steps again.

"Thirteen."

"Put more there."

He obeyed.

"Now left another thirteen steps," she said.

He paced them out, then shoved another bundle of wood into the mud.

"And again. Thirteen."

He moved around in a circle until he had planted six stakes of wood at thirteen-pace intervals around her. He was now facing the first clutch of sticks, in the center of the pattern. He walked toward it. To his amazement, it was exactly thirteen paces away.

"How in Odin's name—?" he muttered.

"Ritual symmetry," she said. "These things just happen. It's exhilarating when the universe reveals its secret magic, isn't it?"

He scowled.

"It makes me uneasy," he said. He heard a sound and glanced sharply out at the drifting fog in time to see a shape stirring briefly.

"There's something out there in the fog, Wanda," he warned, "and it's getting closer."

"Come back to me."

"Thirteen paces?"

"No, regular walking is fine."

He trudged back to her side.

"Six points," she said. "A hexagram. Not much, but it's the best we can improvise."

"If you say so."

She turned to face the central stump, repeatedly sliding the back of each hand across the palm of the other. Then she aimed her open palms at the top of the broken trunk.

Thor heard the sound again. He looked out into the fog.

He saw dark shapes moving in the mist. They were emerging from all sides, plodding into view. They looked like wolves—big wood wolves, padding forward on all fours, heads down. But they lacked pelts. Their skins were jet-black and scaled like crocodiles.

Their long snouts were armed with big, discolored fangs. Their small eyes shone yellow.

"Wanda," Thor urged.

The beasts approached out of the fog from all directions, slow and cautious—prowling like curious wolves or hungry big cats. There were several dozen of them. He heard them yap and cry to each other. Then a menacing, predatory growl grew in their throats.

"Wanda!"

She was concentrating, her palms still aimed at the upright trunk.

He stepped away from her, drew his hammer from his belt, and started to circle—eyes narrowed, stare flicking from one beast to another. He was looking for the sign every good huntsman knew: the tremble, the slight rise in slouched, rolling shoulders that betrayed the switch from slow prowl to sudden sprint.

Which creature would come first?

Which one would lead the way?

The big one. A pack leader if the Odinson had ever seen one. It stalked ahead of the rest, looking right at him, malevolently intent. It took a step, then paused, one front paw raised.

Thor gripped Mjolnir tightly and bent back his arm, ready to cast.

The beast broke and charged. Damn the gods, it was fast. It bounded through the line of wood staves like a loosed hunting hound, jaws open.

Thor swung hard through the waist and launched Mjolnir. The hammer flew, head-first, and met the charging beast. The blow smashed it off its feet and sent it rolling, yapping and thrashing across the mud.

Thor caught the hammer as it sailed back to him.

Emboldened by their sire, the other beasts charged. All of them at once.

"Wanda!"

Concentrating on the fallen tree trunk, she uttered a word he didn't understand: odd, strangled syllables in a language the human mouth wasn't designed to articulate. Light shone from her palms, and the top of the broken trunk burst into flames. The flames rose, fierce and bright-white. She uttered another word—her left hand held to the fire, fingers splayed—and one by one, the six wooden markers of the hexagram combusted, too.

The charging beasts crashed to a halt, tripping and recoiling as though they had run headlong into a wall. An invisible barrier had sprung up between the burning points of the hexagram surrounding Thor and the Scarlet Witch.

Picking themselves up, the beasts retreated, whining and barking. They trotted back a few yards, then turned and sat, gazing in through the conjured defense.

The pack sire got back on its feet and shook itself off. It was inside the ring. Thor ran at it and struck it back down with his hammer. It yelped and bit at him. He grabbed it with both hands, hoisted it above his head, and threw it beyond the circle of fires.

It landed hard, uttering a plaintive yowl. Then it rose and took its place with the others.

Thor looked out at the sets of yellow eyes staring in at them.

"Clever," he said. "A ring of protection."

"I wasn't sure I could do it," Wanda replied. She looked drained. "It will keep them out for now. Long enough for me to continue my geomancy."

"How long will it endure?" Thor asked.

"As long as the wood does," she replied.

She sat down again and scooped up another handful of dirt to examine. Thor waited. Thunder rolled in the distance, but it was not the kind of storm-thunder that was his friend.

He watched the yellow eyes out in the dark beyond the flames.

Half an hour passed. An hour. Thor paced. Whenever he looked up, he glimpsed godless stars beyond the murk of the storm cover, the baleful antimatter suns of this alien dimension.

Wanda suddenly called his name. Her tired eyes were bright.

"What?" he asked.

"I know how to make contact," she said. She cast the handful of dirt aside.

He helped her to her feet.

"I don't need to know where we are," she said. "There's one bond that transcends dimensions. One bond that defies location."

"Is that so?"

"Yes, Thor. Blood. The bond of blood. The familial tie."

"You mean your brother?"

"Yes," she said, nodding. "Kinship crosses the gulf. Any gulf. I should have thought of it sooner."

"Better your brother than mine," he said. "Just tell me what to do."

She put her hand to her brow, weary. He placed his hands on

her shoulders.

"Wanda? What do we have to do?"

She looked up at him.

"I need..."

"What?" he asked.

"One of the metal scutes from your chest plate," she said, pointing.

He frowned, and then tore one of the round, raised disks from his hauberk and handed it to her. She turned it over in her hands, studying it.

"Okay, this will do," she said. "Hold out the hammer. Hold it steady."

He did as she instructed. Outside the hexagram, the beasts lifted their heads and watched with hungry curiosity.

Wanda scraped the edge of the metal disk back and forth against the hammer's head. She worked it repeatedly for a minute or two, then looked at it again.

"All right," she announced, satisfied.

He glanced at the fires. The wood was burning down.

Wanda pulled off one of her gloves and, without warning, drew the now sharpened edge of the disk across her hand. Blood welled immediately.

"Wanda!"

"Blood is a necessary part of this," she said. She blinked back discomfort. "Pain, too. It will make the message sharper."

She raised her hand and made a fist. Blood squeezed out between her fingers and ran down her arm. It dripped from her fist onto the ground below.

"Pietro," she murmured, closing her eyes. "Pietro..."

She pressed her bloodied fist to her forehead, repeating her brother's name.

"Thor," she whispered. "I can...I can feel him. I can feel his soul. I think I can reach him..."

"Keep trying," he said. He heard the beasts yelp and yap, disturbed. He looked around.

A dark figure walked toward them out of the fog. For a moment, Thor wondered whether it was the Avenger Quicksilver, Wanda's brother, summoned to them across the void by her astral magic.

But it wasn't.

The dark beasts whined and shuffled back, making space in their ranks for the figure.

"There you are," said Dormammu.

Wanda gasped and fell to her knees, sobbing.

"It's gone!" she cried. "The connection! It was there, and then it broke!"

"Easy," said Thor. If the Witch couldn't call for help, they would have to fight their way out.

He looked at Dormammu. The mage-lord was a sinister shadow: tall and grim, a figure of midnight darkness except for the magical fire licking and crackling around his grinning head. He was a despot, a conqueror, a ravager of dimensions. Realities shuddered at his name. There were few beings in the universe who had mastered sorcery more thoroughly and cruelly.

The flames wreathing the tyrant's skull were brighter than the faltering fires keeping him out of the ring. "A hex ring," he said, observing. "Crude but efficient. While your fuel lasts, at least."

"I do not understand it, but it will keep you out," said Thor.

"Indeed," Dormammu agreed. "Ritual circles, rings, stars—they are powerful symbols. Amplifiers of the maker's art. Odinson, you are so ignorant of magic. A sorcerer builds a ring as a mechanism to magnify his craft. He is the center of the circle. Through this hexagram, the human girl boosts her energy and keeps me at bay."

He looked down at the beasts waiting patiently at his side.

"Me, and the scavengers that night brings."

Dormammu turned back to look at Thor.

"But she is very tired, and very weak," he said. "And hers was not a honed talent to begin with. She is mortal, and young. She has no experience, no lifetimes of study and training. When the wood is exhausted and the flame sputters out, her power will fail. Your protection will fail. And then..."

The mage-lord of the Faltine let the idea hang in the air.

Thor walked forward and faced the dark lord across the invisible line.

"Grant me a boon then, dark one," he said. "To pass the time while we wait for the end."

"A boon?" Dormammu's maw widened in the flames, and laughter spilled out.

"What is this?" asked Thor. "Why do you make your play for Earth?"

"It is too precious to lose," Dormammu replied.

"Lose?" Thor repeated.

"I have tried to seize the Earth before," the sorcerer said. "It is unusually valuable due to its alignment, its place in the cosmic structure. It is a world of particular force and energy, a rich seam of magic. There are few sites in the universe of greater mystical significance. I have no wish to see it destroyed or wasted. I seek to own its power, to make it mine, rather than see it burned away and annihilated."

"Are you not the annihilator?" asked Thor. "You are unleashing destruction upon Midgard."

"Destruction?" Dormammu chuckled. "No, Odinson. This night is marked only by the pains of birth. The agonies of a necessary transmutation. I do not seek to destroy the mortals' world. I am transposing it into my Dark Domain, so that I may possess it and protect it."

"From what?" asked Thor.

"All is lost," said Dormmamu. "This much I know. This I have read in the embers of augury fires. This I have beheld in crystal scrying. This I have learned firsthand from the agents of the true annihilator."

Thor shook his head.

"What are you saying? Something threatens the world of men, and this is your way of *saving* it? By claiming it like a trophy and stealing it away into your fell dimension?"

"It must not be lost," declared Dormammu, the flames of his skull flaring. "The mystical integrity of the cosmos would be weaker without it. Better this fate than its destruction. In time, the humans will praise me for their salvation."

"A long time, methinks," said Thor.

"Yes. Centuries, I imagine, given the stubborn traits of humans. But they will learn to be grateful."

"What threatens the Earth, dark one?' asked Thor.

"Earth has enemies and rivals," said Dormammu. "It is strong, and it is unusually blessed with curious beings. It has no idea how much it is feared and hated and envied.

"An ultimatum has been issued. The Earth must be changed. It must be diverted from its inexorable rise to dominance. I have heeded that ultimatum. I am the agent of that change."

"And is your work done?" asked Wanda. "Is Earth now fully drawn into your realm and lost forever?"

She had risen and come to stand beside Thor. She hugged her arms to her body, pulling her cloak tight. She looked drawn and deathly. Blood from her hand smeared her clothes.

"Oh, Mortaldaughter," replied Dormammu. "You understand ritual well enough. One does not simply move a world without the consent of the heavens. Now that I have caught the Earth on my hook and pulled a portion of it through into my domain, I must wait for the hour of alignment so that I may finish the transference."

The Dread One looked up. The six brightest stars in the sky above, abhorrent red lights glowing in the darkness, had formed an almost perfectly circular constellation overhead. A ritual circle billions of light-years in diameter. Only two were out of alignment, the circle not quite formed.

"How long?" asked Wanda, shivering.

"Five hours," replied Dormammu. He looked down at the bonfires of the hexagram.

"But long before then," he said, "your fires will go out."

FIFTEEN

MADRIPOOR
02.02 LOCAL, JUNE 13TH

THE GAMMA bomb sat on its payload carriage in front of him.

Banner took a step toward it. He realized he was shaking, and there was nothing he could do about it.

The bomb was an ugly thing, bathed in the cold light of the overheads. Its casing was bare metal. Bunched cables and monitor leads trailed from the bomb across the floor, leading to the banks of diagnostic and control instruments on either side of the chamber.

He felt the bomb brooding, as though it were alive and sentient. It was a huge gray monster with untold destructive power slumbering inside it, ready to be unleashed. Though its final form had been heavily influenced by the High Evolutionary's advanced methods, Banner recognized the basic elements of the design. He recognized its heritage. He recognized its DNA. It had its father's eyes.

Despite the superficial differences, it was identical to the weapon he had spent years of his life developing.

Except it was considerably bigger.

"'I am become Death, the destroyer of worlds,'" he murmured, a catch in his voice.

"Ah, the Bhagavad Gita," responded the High Evolutionary behind him. "The Hindu holy book."

"No," Banner began quietly. "I was—"

"J. Robert Oppenheimer," said the High Evolutionary. "The so-called 'father' of the atomic bomb. He quoted the verse—though in his own, inadequate translation of the original...'kālo'smi lokaksayakrt pravrddho lokānsamāhartumiha pravrttah.'

I have always wondered at his sentimentality. He used the phrase, we are told, as an utterance of self-horror. Yet why was he surprised?"

Banner managed to tear his gaze away from the bomb. He felt sick. He was still trembling. The bomb chamber occupied a large section of the High Evolutionary's Lowtown lair, a massive factory level above the lab that had been cleared out, its windows and skylights sealed. The bomb seemed to fill it. He looked around at the High Evolutionary.

"Surprised?" he echoed.

"As though he did not know what he had made," said the High Evolutionary. "He was working on the ultimate weapon. He knew this. He was successful. Where was his sense of accomplishment?"

"Accomplishment?" Banner stammered.

"I see the same horror in you, too, Doctor Banner, and find it somewhat mystifying. You also employed your scientific genius to such ends. To this end, in fact: the gamma bomb. Yet you are appalled at the reality of it."

"I know what it is capable of," said Banner.

"You knew what it would be capable of before you built it," replied the High Evolutionary.

Banner wiped his mouth. He wished he could stop his hands

from shaking so badly. He felt as though he were returning to the scene of a crime—or coming face-to-face with his deepest, most private nightmare. The gamma bomb was both his shame and his curse, his abuser and his wayward child. He had spent years wishing that he could expunge any trace of it.

Yet here he was, in the same room with it. The bomb was a physical thing. It was undeniable.

He felt his skin prickle. He wondered whether that was the radiation, or his own conscience.

"What appalls you more, Doctor Banner?" asked the High Evolutionary. "The weapon's destructive potential, or your own?"

"I don't have to listen to your—"

"I think you do."

The High Evolutionary walked forward and gazed up at the bomb housing.

"Put simply," he said, "this bomb can destroy billions of lives, but it is merely a machine. It has no agency. It simply achieves your intent. It is the means by which *you* can destroy billions of lives."

"Shut up," said Banner, looking away.

"The gamma bomb was not an accidental byproduct of innocent research. It was always going to be a bomb. You knew that before you began. Yet you act as if you didn't know what you were doing. As if it is a monster that you didn't mean to create."

"You have no idea how much I regret..." Banner began. "You have no idea. I would give anything to—"

The High Evolutionary looked at him.

"Actually," he said, "it is very common for the inventors of successful weapons to experience great remorse in later years. To hate themselves for what they have given the world. You, of course, are a singular case. Not only do you hate the monster you made, you hate the monster that it made out of you.

"That's the point, isn't it? Destructive potential. This is not guilt by proxy. You built a device of unimaginable destructive power. That would be burden enough. But the consequence was the literal unleashing of your own destructive power, not by association but in the flesh. And you can't control either of them."

"Please," said Banner. "You don't know me, Wyndham. You don't know the torments I've endured. As one scientist to another, I beg you, stop this. Dismantle the bomb. Make it safe."

The High Evolutionary studied Banner's face for a moment.

"I am quite moved, Doctor," he said at last. "Your pain is palpable. It is genuine."

"Then please—"

"How would you feel, Doctor Banner, if I told you that this bomb could save the world rather than end it?"

Banner sighed. "I'm tired of your cryptic remarks, Wyndham."

"The world is going to end," said the High Evolutionary.

"So I see."

"What you see is the means to prevent that end. This is redemption, Doctor—the redemption you have always desired. To see the horror you created used for good. To save the world rather than obliterate it. You could reject Oppenheimer's assertion, sir. You would become not Death, but rather Life."

"It's a bomb, Wyndham! A damned bomb! You're already causing unbelievable damage to this city through contamination. When you detonate this—"

Banner looked at the bomb, his hands raised.

"—*millions* will die here. Instantly," he continued. "I can only guess at the yield, but I can predict that millions of lives will be lost in the Pacific region from the explosion alone, before we even get to secondary physical destruction such as tsunamis and seismic disturbances. And from the look of the design, that's not even the primary destructive purpose. The gamma blast is just the propagator. The fallout will irradiate the planet. Ionizing radiation, Wyndham. Billions more will die slowly and horribly. The entire population of the world."

"The human race will be irradiated," the High Evolutionary said, nodding. "Those who do not perish in the blast. I predict that one-tenth of the world's population will perish in the detonation. The losses are unfortunate but necessary collateral. Irradiation is my actual goal."

"Why? How is that saving the world? You're insane! You—"

Banner stopped shouting. His mind was racing. His eyes opened wide. He remembered the whiteboards in the High Evolutionary's lab.

"You're the High Evolutionary," he whispered.

"I am," replied Wyndham.

"Gamma radiation..." Banner said, thinking fast. "Gamma radiation can be used for genetic manipulation. Exposure damages DNA. It breaks the bonds of DNA molecules."

"Indeed it does," said the High Evolutionary.

"That happens under natural levels of exposure," said Banner, "and our cells just mobilize their DNA repair mechanisms to fix the breaks. Sometimes those mechanisms add or delete little bits of DNA in the process."

"Many think that is how color variation in flowers began," agreed the High Evolutionary.

"So you engineer a virus," said Banner. The scrawlings on the whiteboards were now vivid in his mind's eye. "A latent virus that you introduce to the human population."

"It is already introduced," replied the High Evolutionary. "It is something I had previously developed. For the last five weeks, my agents have been disseminating it worldwide. Distribution projections now indicate that the entire species will be carrying it within three days."

Banner nodded, understanding.

"And gamma exposure would cause breaks in human DNA," he said, "allowing the latent viral DNA to be incorporated into human DNA via natural repair. In a stroke, you rewrite human genetic code."

"Your grasp is adequate," the High Evolutionary said.

"What does the genetic recoding do?" asked Banner. "What is the resulting trait?"

"Docility," Wyndham replied.

"You intend to engineer humans into a slave race?"

"I am referring to a tranquility of nature," the High Evolutionary replied. "Contentment. Pacification. A loss of aggression, of energetic aspiration, of blind appetite. An end, for example, to the human predisposition to war, to conflict, to rebellion and disobedience, to intolerance, to fanaticism and international rivalry. The virus will establish suggestibility…the willingness to respond happily, and without the need for duress, to simple authority."

"Your authority?" said Banner.

"I am become Life, the savior of worlds," replied the High

Evolutionary. "I am no tyrant. I am a benign force, and you cannot doubt my intelligence or capability. I will steadfastly minister to the needs of an obedient species, care for it and safeguard its future."

"You're going to save us from our own nature?" asked Banner.

"In a way."

"And the price is a few billion deaths—either from the blast, or from high-dose cell death among those too exposed to survive?"

"I estimate a viable survivor population of just under one billion," said the High Evolutionary. "A terrible cost? Yes, of course. A scientist must make hard decisions, and a god must make yet harder ones. But it is worthwhile compared to the alternative."

"I'm going to ignore the fact you just called yourself a god," said Banner sourly. "What *is* this alternative? You keep alluding to some end-state threat."

"It is very real," said the High Evolutionary. "Planet Earth will be eliminated unless it is brought under effective regulatory control."

"Eliminated by whom?"

The High Evolutionary did not reply. He turned as the dog-hybrid entered the bomb chamber. Banner felt a shudder of psionics, and realized the hybrid was communicating with its master.

"Problem?" Banner asked.

"I have been informed that your S.H.I.E.L.D. colleague has managed to escape from holding," replied the High Evolutionary. "He will be found and recaptured shortly."

Run, McHale, Banner thought. *Run and don't stop running until you've found help.*

As the dog-hybrid left, the High Evolutionary turned to face Banner.

"Will you assist me? he asked.

"*Assist* you?"

"Now you see what's at stake, Doctor Banner. Now you appreciate how your monstrous creation can be transformed into a tool to save humankind. The redemption of which I spoke."

"What the hell do you expect me to do?" asked Banner.

"I am a polymath, Doctor. So are you, in your way. But your particular specialty is gamma radiation and its delivery systems. I seek to refine the gamma bomb, to minimize its blast effect and maximize its atmospheric irradiation. I believe you have the expertise to guide me in this task. It is a discipline I would master in time—but, as I stated previously, time is not on my side. You can make this necessarily painful process more humane."

"And in return I get...redemption?"

"Yes," said the High Evolutionary. "But I can offer you another incentive besides. I can heal you. I can repair your woefully damaged DNA. I can cure you of the Hulk."

BANNER sat down on a lab stool and reached out a hand to steady himself against the workbench. Another old-fashioned record was playing in the artificially sunlit room beyond.

The High Evolutionary walked in and offered Banner a glass of scotch.

Banner shook his head.

The High Evolutionary put down the glass on the bench near Banner's hand.

"How?" asked Banner, his voice very small.

"Exposure to gamma radiation causes chromothripsis, Doctor.

Do you know what—"

"DNA double-strand breaks," said Banner. "They are the hardest type to repair. High-dose exposure usually results in cell death or grotesque cancers, then body death."

"Yet you did not die," said the High Evolutionary.

Banner looked up.

"What?"

"You were caught in a test-site blast, but you did not die. No cell death, no cancer, no body death."

"It was a fluke. I got lucky." Banner laughed humorlessly. "Lucky," he repeated.

The High Evolutionary pulled up another lab stool and sat down facing him.

"Prior exposure to gamma radiation," he said, "perhaps even through your father, resulted in you carrying a mutation in the *PRKDC* gene. That gene is responsible for the production of an enzyme, a hyper-functional DNA-dependent protein kinase. It helps repair DNA double-strand breaks. That is why you did not perish on that testing field."

"Are you serious?"

"Always. Doctor Banner, that protein can also produce errors in the genetic code. In your case, the gamma radiation resulted in mutations to the adrenaline receptors that cause your cells to express the four Yamanaka transcription factors whenever you are exposed to too much adrenaline."

Banner stood up.

"I saw that!" he said. "On your whiteboards."

He walked over to the wall, putting his glasses back on.

"The Yamanaka factors induce adult cells to reenter the pluripotent stem-cell state," he said.

"Your genetic knowledge is impressive," said the High Evolutionary.

"It's been a preoccupation," Banner said, with a slight snarl. "Here—" He tapped a section of the board. "Myc, Oct3/4, Sox2, and Klf4. The transcription factors."

"Stem cells can become any cell in the body, and produce any chemical or enzyme encoded in their genes in any quantity," said the High Evolutionary. "In response to any threat, your cells undergo rapid evolution from stem-cell state. The greater the threat, the greater the cellular evolution it takes to compensate. You become stronger, more resilient. Somatic hyper-mutation occurs in your immune system. Affinity maturation ensures that only the strongest cells thrive. You become the Hulk. When the threat diminishes, the adrenaline stops flooding, and the signal to the Yamanaka factors ceases. Your cells revert to their epigenetic programming. You become Banner again."

Banner took off his glasses and rubbed his eyes.

"I can even explain why your counterpart is green," said the High Evolutionary.

"What?

"Endo-symbiosis of green algae, is my theory," said the High Evolutionary. He seemed to be enjoying himself. It was apparently rare for him to converse with anyone who could follow his thinking. "You were gray to begin with, I believe, but then incorporated algae into your DNA. That allows you to draw energy from the sun. And it also explains why the Hulk can grow much more massive than the chemical components of Bruce Banner should allow."

Banner put his glasses back on.

"It's a theory," he said. "There have been many. When I asked 'what,' I was being rhetorical."

"Even rhetorical questions can have illuminating answers."

"And how would you cure me?" Banner asked.

"I would target and switch off the mutations in your adrenaline receptors. I would stop them expressing the transcription factors. You would be Banner again, and Banner alone."

"You would do that for me?"

"Doctor Banner, it would be a pleasure and an honor to ease your burden and end your curse."

"And in return, I help you build a better bomb?"

"I can only save the world by destroying a great deal of it," replied the High Evolutionary. "This fact pains me, but there is no other way. If you can help me keep that loss and suffering to the absolute minimum, it would be a humanitarian act of the highest order. Neither of us wants to be a monster, Doctor."

Banner walked back to the bench, picked up the glass of scotch, and downed its contents fast. He wiped his mouth and sighed deeply.

"What is the threat, Wyndham?" he asked.

"Sir?"

"You're asking me to collude with you in the mass-murder of millions. Doesn't matter how noble the reason, or how much the end result will benefit some greater good—that's a hell of a thing. A hell of a thing. So tell me. Why? What is the threat?"

The High Evolutionary hesitated.

"It is complex," he said. "Doctor, I—"

"Back away, Doc. Slowly."

Banner looked around.

McHale was standing in the doorway. He was dirty and disheveled, and he looked desperate.

"I said back away from that freak, now!" he ordered.

McHale was aiming a weapon at the High Evolutionary. It was a large pistol of advanced design, chrome-plated and exotic.

"Really, Agent," said the High Evolutionary, starting to rise.

"Sit down, Wyndham!" McHale snapped. He trained the weapon firmly, adopting his modified Weaver stance. "Not a word. Not a movement. I know what you can do. I found your arsenal, Wyndham—your stockpile of tech—and I helped myself to this fusion pistol. I don't know if this can kill the likes of you, but I do know it will mess you up bad. One move, and I shoot. You'll go down, and you'll be eating through a straw for years."

He glanced at Banner.

"We're leaving, Doc," he said.

"McHale—"

"Right now. You and me. We get out, and we signal S.H.I.E.L.D. This ends."

"You should have run, McHale. You should have gotten clear when you had the chance. You shouldn't have come back for me."

"Yeah, well, I did," said McHale. "I'm a super hero, remember? Dale McHale. I don't leave friends behind. We're going now."

"McHale, you shouldn't have come back for me."

"That sense of humor you got, Doc—it's still pretty hard to appreciate. Come on. Get behind me. We're heading out through the back. I'll cover you."

Banner walked over to the doorway until he was behind McHale.

"Doctor Banner," said the High Evolutionary. "I thought we had arrived at an understanding."

"I said that's enough, Wyndham!" McHale growled. "Shut up. Don't make me use this thing. We're walking, and you're going to let us."

"I'm afraid I simply can't allow that," replied the High Evolutionary, standing up.

"Damn you," said McHale.

He lurched forward suddenly, crashed into the bench, and fell to the floor, the weapon sliding from his fingers.

Banner lowered the heavy, antique microscope with which he'd hit McHale. He knelt down and checked McHale's pulse.

"He's alive," he said. "Out cold. I wish I hadn't had to do that. Can we get him medical treatment?"

"Of course, Doctor," replied the High Evolutionary.

"I wish I hadn't had to do that," Banner repeated.

"Doctor," said the High Evolutionary, "the very fact that you did it tells me everything I need to know."

WASHINGTON, D.C.
10.10 LOCAL, JUNE 12TH

OKAY, let's assume I've spent this morning so far in a hot tub with a tray of mimosas," said Tony Stark as he entered the room. "What's the situation?"

Looking at him were more than thirty State Department officials; Secret Service agents; senior aides; Homeland Security, CIA, and NSA officers; and Air Force commanders. His Iron Man armor was dented and scratched. His faceplate was raised.

"Mr. Stark," said a senior aide, "the President of the United States is right over there."

"Oh," said Stark. "Didn't see you. My apologies. I guess I should have anticipated your presence, seeing as this is the White House Situation Room. You're all just a wall of faces, really. Sunglasses, ties, gold braid, suits. Either that or it's the mimosas. Let's start over. What's the situation?"

The President rose.

"Mr. Stark. I understand you averted this morning's crisis?" he said.

"Me? Not so much. A group effort. The Vision here pretty much scored the winning touchdown in overtime."

Stark indicated the synthezoid standing quietly in the doorway behind him.

"Also a very cool lady in SIGINT called Diane probably deserves a special commendation," he added.

"I would like to thank you on behalf—" the President began.

"Great," said Stark. "I realize I'm talking very fast—my apologies—but we've suffered a Condition Alpha situation this morning, and I don't think it's actually over. And even if it is, I think a couple more are backing up. So please, can somebody fill me in?"

"As quickly as possible," said the President. "Assistant Director Chopin?"

The stern, white-haired NSA man glared at Stark.

"With pleasure, Mr. President," he said. "At approximately oh-seven twenty, we became aware of—"

"Skip a little, Chopin," said Stark, "I was there. Fast forward to, say, *now.*"

Chopin glowered. "The D.C. area is under martial law," he said. "Power is down across the Eastern Seaboard and the Midwest. Telecommunications are down. Data links are down. Discrete security channels are the only things we've been able to open."

"And what have we learned from them?" asked Stark. He unclasped his helmet, took it off, and set it on the table. It was as battered and scuffed as the rest of his armor.

"Rioting, civil disturbance, and panic are spreading throughout the mainland," said a CIA representative. "The Army and the National Guard have been mobilized to restore order."

"That's going to end well," said Stark.

"We've got virtually nothing internationally," said someone

from State. "Signs are, the disruption is affecting other countries."

"A global data-crash is going to do that," said Stark. "S.H.I.E.L.D.?"

"No response," said Chopin.

"Avengers?"

"As far as we know, there are only two Avengers active at this time, and they're both in this room," said the President.

Stark glanced at the Vision.

"Well, that's...troubling," he said.

The Vision nodded, grim.

"Let's work with what we have, then," Stark said, turning back to the room. "Ultron is currently incapacitated, but its root consciousness is loose in the system. Whatever we reactivate or bring back online increases the risk of Ultron manifesting again."

"All agents are working on countermeasures and containment to the best of our capacity," said Chopin.

"Okay," said Stark. "We're going to need a glass and a magazine."

"We're what?" asked Chopin.

"Like with a spider," said Stark. "You know, a big one that comes out from under the couch at night? The glass is a metaphorical glass, probably a high-capacity data-encryption package; the magazine is a purpose-written algorithm, because it's metaphorical, too. We pop the glass over the spider—the spider being Ultron—slide the magazine underneath, pick it up, and presto, throw it out the window."

No one said anything.

"The window's metaphorical, too," Stark added. "Did I forget to mention that? An inert storage facility, completely insulated. Or the Negative Zone, whichever's closer. We need to pull Ultron out of the system, trap it, and lock it away."

"And we can do that?" asked the President.

"We have to do that, sir," said Stark, "or the world as we know it will be, to use the technical term, screwed. I have people at Stark Industries who can do it. I was hoping you had people who could do it. If necessary, I'll do it."

"I think this should receive some kind of priority, don't you, Chopin?" said the President calmly. His tone made Stark smile.

"Absolutely, Mr. President," said Chopin.

"You've had a lot of people telling you things all morning without making much sense, haven't you?" Stark asked the President.

"There's been a degree of running around and arm waving," the President replied.

"I like you, sir," said Stark.

"I'm gratified, Mr. Stark."

"I didn't vote for you."

"It's a free country," replied the President.

"Let's keep it that way," Stark said. "Next—and I want to preface this by saying there's no problem, and we're not at any risk of a nanotech disaster of any kind—do we have a nanotech disaster cleanup division?"

"The NSA has a dedicated—" Chopin began.

"Great. They need to get to Pine Fields ASAP. The nanobots are dormant and inactive, but they could be re-initialized at any moment. That could end with the world turned to gray goo, or the United States refashioned on a molecular level into a giant novelty foam finger that reads, 'Go, Ultron.' I am purely speculating."

"Good," said Chopin.

"It could read anything," said Stark.

"What do we know about Russia?" asked the Vision, stepping forward.

"Russia?" asked Chopin.

"There was something going down in Siberia," said a CIA officer, "but we haven't had any data for over two hours."

"Berlin?" asked the Vision.

"Berlin? What about Berlin?" asked an aide.

"The Savage Land, then?" asked the Vision.

"We've got nothing on the Savage Land," said Chopin.

"Okay, good talk," said Stark.

"Are there problems in Berlin and the Savage Land?" asked the President. "What is this about Siberia?"

"Let's get our own house in order first, sir," said Stark.

"Do you hear that?" the Vision asked him.

"No, but you do," replied Stark.

"Aircraft incoming!" someone called out.

ON THE White House lawn, they could see smoke from the morning's attack rising from multiple locations across the District. Sirens whooped and soared. Air Force choppers crossed the sky in formation at low level, their rotors whipping.

"Not the aircraft we expected?" Stark asked, hovering just above the lawn.

"No," said the Vision. "Wait a moment..."

Iron Man and the Vision looked up. Something huge and gray loomed out of the clouds above the White House. It reminded Stark of a scene from a movie he'd once watched.

The S.H.I.E.L.D. Helicarrier's giant propulsion-lift fans were almost silent. Its shadow fell across him.

"Cool," said Stark.

"Because S.H.I.E.L.D. is now active and engaged with the situation?" asked the Vision.

"Yeah, and also giant flying aircraft carriers are intrinsically cool."

"We should go aboard," said the Vision. "They may have additional data."

"Absolutely," Stark agreed. "Also coffee and croissants."

Something was moving across the lawn toward them. A blur. A figure running so fast, it was just a smudge of light.

It skidded to a halt beside them, gouging a deep furrow across the lawn, and hurling clods of earth and grass into the air.

Quicksilver stood in front of them, panting, his head down, his hands on his thighs. He was a strikingly handsome young man with short, silver hair, his incredibly athletic physique clad in a bodysuit that shone like liquid mercury. Neither Iron Man nor the Vision had ever seen him so tired.

"Pietro?" said the Vision.

"Three Avengers," said Stark. He turned and held up three fingers in the direction of the White House windows. "Three now! See? Three!" he shouted. "We may not be assembling as fast as usual, but we're getting there!"

The Vision put his hand on Pietro's shoulder. The speedster was panting so hard he could barely talk.

"What is wrong?" the Vision asked. "Where have you run from?'

"New York," Pietro panted.

"Such a distance should not have fatigued you," said the Vision, "even at your highest velocity—"

"My mind," Pietro stammered. "A sudden pain in my mind. It has taken...taken a toll on me. Wanda..."

"Wanda?" asked the Vision sharply. His relationship with Pietro's sister was long and troubled. Despite his artificially manufactured nature, the Vision had grown to love Wanda Maximoff. Though the relationship had ended, the very mention of her name triggered an uncharacteristic tone of emotion in his voice.

"What is he saying?" asked Stark.

"Stars...in alignment..." Pietro gasped. "Wanda said...in my head, I heard her...stars in alignment...out in the darkness, beyond the world..."

"None of that sounds good," said Stark.

"What are you saying?" the Vision asked, bending down to look at Quicksilver. "What are you saying about Wanda?"

Pietro looked up at them. His eyes were glassy and wild. Blood was running from his nostrils and trickling from the corner of his mouth.

"She spoke to me," he said weakly. "What is the matter with you? There is no time to waste! My sister is in danger—we must go to her!"

"Take it easy," said Stark.

But Pietro had collapsed.

THE CLEAN sweatshirt was gray, with the S.H.I.E.L.D. logo printed across the chest. There were matching sweat pants. Property of the Helicarrier gym.

Stark pulled them on over the tattered undersuit of his armor. The S.H.I.E.L.D. agent who had brought them for him had also delivered a cup of decent coffee.

Stark stood alone in the briefing office, looking down through the glass wall at the command deck of the Helicarrier. Men and women in white-trimmed black bodysuits were busy at the station terminals. Stark noticed how many of the consoles were unlit or offline. There were far fewer images playing on the vast display wall than usual, too. Only a few individual screens were lit up, showing either views of Washington below them or scrolls of technical data. S.H.I.E.L.D. was being careful, using only minimal electronic systems—those they could guarantee were secure and isolated.

He sipped the coffee. He altered his depth of field and saw his own reflection in the glass. The lighting in the room was predominately blue, and it made him look cold and drawn. There was no disguising the bruises on his throat or the cuts on his face.

His hands around the cup were shaking. He was coming down off a huge adrenaline high, and he was starting to feel the pain from his bruises and other assorted injuries. It was also beginning to dawn on him how close the end had come.

And how close the end could still be.

Tony Stark wasn't afraid of much, except in a purely healthy, wary way. He couldn't do what he did and give in to anxiety, or let it show.

But he was scared of what they still might have to face.

The door behind him opened. He didn't look around. He could see the reflection of the big, dark-suited figure well enough.

"I hear you addressed the President of the United States in a disrespectful tone," said Nick Fury.

"Depends who you ask," Stark replied.

"Assistant Director Chopin of the NSA," said Fury.

Stark shrugged.

"The President told me you brought a refreshing note of clarity to the proceedings," said Fury, leaning against the glass-topped table, his arms folded. "He said we could do with a few more people like you around. He also said you could go easy on the breakfast mimosas."

"I haven't been drinking," said Stark quietly.

"I know."

Stark turned. He looked at the S.H.I.E.L.D. Director, then sat down in a chair by the window.

"I've got S.H.I.E.L.D. cyber-warfare ops hunting for Ultron," said Fury. "They're using the protocols you wrote for them. They're pretty confident they'll have him locked up by sunset."

"You called him 'him.'" said Stark.

"Huh?"

"You called Ultron 'him.' I think of Ultron as an 'it.'"

"Because he's a machine?" asked Fury. "Ultron's sentient."

"Because he's gender-neutral," said Stark. "I haven't got a prejudice against artificial sentience. I'm just saying he's gender-neutral."

"Now *you're* calling him 'he,'" said Fury.

"You got me doing it."

"What did he want?" asked Fury.

"Ultron? He wanted to rule the world."

"Everybody wants to rule the world," said Fury.

"Well, not just rule it," said Stark, sitting back. "Remake it. Rebuild it. Render humanity obsolete. The usual."

"Any idea why?"

"He's Ultron. It's what he does. A flaw in his character. A sense of superiority—ultimate superiority. There's probably a major father issue in there, too. He's not bad, Nick, he's just made that way."

"Why now?"

"Why not? I don't think the Condition Alpha threats of this world compare diaries and take turns."

"Yeah, but two in one day?" asked Fury.

Stark looked at him.

"So it *is* two? Two, confirmed?"

Fury shrugged. He pulled a chair out from the table and sat down.

"At least. There's something unbelievable going down in Siberia. We haven't got anything like full data, but it looks bad."

"What about Berlin?"

"We don't know anything. Europe's dark. But that's probably more us than them."

"What was Cap into?" asked Stark.

"Hydra," Fury replied. "S.H.I.E.L.D. intel picked up some bits and pieces and brought in Cap. Strucker may be involved."

"So it's serious, then. Another Alpha."

"Seems messy, from what I've read," said Fury. "Pretty sloppy for a Hydra operation. Still, even on its off days, Hydra is a big deal."

"What about the Savage Land thing? Natasha and Barton?"

"No contact there, either," replied Fury. "Before the blackout, we got a tip-off that A.I.M. was busy with something, and the pair of them shipped out to confirm."

"A tip-off?" asked Stark. "From who?"

"No idea."

"But it looks like an A.I.M. thing?"

"Looks like it."

Stark put down his empty cup.

"Wow," he said. "This, Siberia, Berlin, Antarctica. One confirmed Alpha, one that looks so Alpha it's not even funny. Then Hydra and A.I.M., which—if history tells us anything, and history is screaming in my ear right now—are going to be Alphas, too."

"Then there's Madripoor," said Fury, with reluctance.

"Madripoor?"

"S.H.I.E.L.D. operation," said Fury. "Started off as an investigation into the shipment of illegal materials, turned into a thing that may involve the High Evolutionary. The S.H.I.E.L.D. Southeast Asia station brought in Banner to consult. Whatever's going on there, it was graded Beta last we knew."

"If the High Evolutionary is active on the planet," said Stark, "doesn't that automatically make it an Alpha? Follow-up question: Banner? Are you insane?"

"The illegal materials were gamma isotopes," said Fury. "Banner is an expert. You have a problem with him?"

"Not him, but he's got this friend."

Stark sighed and shook his head.

"Bruce is fine," he continued. "I like him a great deal, and admire the hell out of his smarts. But he can be an Alpha all on his own."

Stark got up.

"Five Condition Alpha events on one day. Nick, that's not a coincidence."

"It could be a coincidence. A really, really bad coincidence."

"Let's work on the premise that it isn't and see where it takes us," said Stark. "Five big players—three unconfirmed, one unknown—are active and going in for the kill, each in their own oh-so-charmingly idiosyncratic ways. That doesn't just happen."

"I'll bite," said Fury. "What are you saying? A concerted effort?"

Stark frowned.

"Maybe, but the chances of successful collaboration between the factions we're talking about seem slim. There's a reason A.I.M. is called A.I.M. these days and not just 'part of Hydra.' And Ultron and the High Evolution-nut have never played well with others."

"So?" asked Fury.

"Manipulation."

"Someone's orchestrating them?"

"Yep."

"Without them knowing about it?"

"Probably."

"Someone's orchestrating a global free-for-all without Ultron or the High Evolutionary knowing about it, because as we know they're famously stupid and easily played?" asked Fury, doubtfully.

"I know how it sounds," said Stark. "And if it's true, I know what it means."

"A *sixth* Condition Alpha," said Fury.

"An invisible one that we're not even aware of," said Stark, nodding. "One so big it makes all the others look like sideshows, because they *are* sideshows."

"Somehow really, really big coincidence isn't sounding so terrible anymore," said Fury.

"I hear you," said Stark.

The door opened, and a tall, striking woman dressed in a S.H.I.E.L.D. uniform walked in.

"La Contessa Valentina Allegra de la Fontaine," Stark said, raising his hands in delight. "You walk into a room, and six Condition Alphas seem like a footnote."

The Contessa looked at him haughtily.

"Mr. Stark," she said. "Always a pleasure."

"That accent always gets me," said Stark. "It reminds me of the Lakes. Of soft nights in Milan—"

De la Fontaine ignored him and turned to Fury.

"Communications expects to be able to link with London in about ninety minutes, Director," she said. "We're using landlines and a repeater station in Labrador. We're hoping that the London station can connect us with Bridge in Berlin, or at least give us a sitrep on Europe."

"Thanks," said Fury.

She turned to go.

"Yes, thank you," said Stark. "A little good news, and made all the finer because it was brought to us by the stunning Tina Legs."

"Valentina Allegra de La Fontaine," she said.

"Yup," Stark agreed.

"You know she could kill you from where she's standing, don't you?" asked Fury. "With a snow cone?"

"Just one of her many superlative qualities," said Stark.

"How's Pietro Maximoff?" asked Fury.

"Stable, but unconscious," said de la Fontaine. "The Vision is with him."

"Any idea what's wrong with him?" asked Stark.

"Apart from exhaustion, there are no obvious signs of injury or illness," said the Contessa. "Medical is running checks now. It seems mental, not physical."

Fury nodded.

"If there's nothing else, Director?" said de la Fontaine.

"One thing," said Stark. "Last time I stayed over, did I leave a change of clothes here?"

"Do you mean the night you broke my heart and left in the morning without waking me to say goodbye?" she asked.

"I never did that," said Stark. "I never did that," he added to Fury.

"I know," she said with a smirk. "I was merely riffing on your deliberate innuendo. Like you should be so lucky."

"He means the armor," said Fury.

"I know what he means. Yes, there is a spare Iron Man suit in the Helicarrier vault."

"I need it," said Stark.

"You do," agreed Fury. "I saw the one you came in wearing."

"I don't have the time or the means to summon another one from Avengers Tower by remote," said Stark.

"I'll have your valet lay it out for you," said de la Fontaine.

"That would be awesome, Tina Le—"

Stark paused.

"Contessa," he finished.

She nodded and left the briefing room.

"When you die, Stark," said Fury, "it won't be because of Ultron or whoever. It'll be at the hands of a woman. A woman like that, who won't take your crap anymore."

"I'm counting on it," said Stark.

"So...you're going to suit up," said Fury, rising. "Where are you going?"

"Let's see what plays out in the next ninety minutes," said Stark. "Right now, my answer is Berlin."

SEVENTEEN

BERLIN
23.09 LOCAL, JUNE 12TH

CAP LUNGED forward to grab the dispersal device. The vapor had fogged the air of the dining room in Strucker's elegant apartment. Cap could feel droplets of moisture on his face.

Strucker stood up so fast the chair he was sitting on toppled backwards. He snatched up the laser pistol and fired at Cap.

Cap blocked the shots with his shield, and the laser bolts ricocheted away. One blew a hole in the ceiling; the other tore a chunk out of the edge of the dining table.

Cap vaulted the table and threw himself at Strucker. Two more shots, point blank, rebounded from his shield before the two men connected. Cap's flying tackle knocked Strucker backwards. Locked together, they crashed into the corner of the room. Strucker's frantic left fist caught Cap's jaw. Cap swept his shield-arm sideways, right to left, and the flat of the shield smacked Strucker into the wall. The edge of the shield ripped the laser pistol out of Strucker's hand. It bounced off the window frame and fell out into the night.

Dazed, Strucker threw another left jab. Cap caught the fist with his right hand. He slammed his shield sideways again, this time left to right, and the dish of it smashed Strucker full across the side of the face. The Hydra mastermind lurched backwards violently, the back of his head making a dent in the wall plaster. Cap knocked him out with a straight punch to the face, then picked him up and threw him.

Strucker landed on the table and slid along it, plowing files, maps, and plastic cases onto the floor. He fell off the far end, broke a chair, and sprawled unconscious onto the carpet.

"Biohazard!" Cap yelled into his mic. He turned back to the device on the table. "Biohazard release!"

"Cap, confirm that!" Runciter responded over the link.

"Gail, Strucker released the pathogen!"

"We're coming in! Tac teams go!"

"Negative! Negative! Get clear! Seal the building!"

Cap grabbed the device. He realized his hands weren't steady. He was swaying. His vision was swimming. He was burning up.

"Cap? Cap, report?"

He tried to concentrate. He knew he was dying. Skin contact and inhalation—the pathogen was already deep in his system, and it was killing him. How long? Minutes? Seconds?

He fumbled with the device, and managed to unwind the milled collar and open the curved lid on its hinge. There was a green metal bulb in the socket inside. It was punctured, just like the one he had seen in the S.H.I.E.L.D. forensic lab.

He remembered Strucker's attaché case on the lab bench. Two bulbs. God, why couldn't he think clearly? There had been two bulbs. The other one was an antidote. A counteragent. Strucker and his men had been immune. The extortion...the extortion was only going to work because Hydra could counteract the pathogen.

The power of life and death. Rule through fear. A declaration to the world: the murder of Berlin.

"Cap! Talk to me!" Gail Runciter sounded very far away. Cap could barely hear her over the blood pounding in his head.

He wanted to sit down. He wanted to close his eyes.

He groped around. Where was it? There were aluminum carry cases on the table. Strucker would keep the pathogen and the counteragent close by. Cap wrenched open a case: paperwork, design briefs. He tossed them aside. Papers fluttered in the air. He grabbed another case, laid it flat, and opened it.

Foam liner. Six recesses. Five green bulbs. All pathogen. No counteragent.

He leaned on the table edge with both hands. He could feel sweat pouring off him. He shook his head, trying to clear it. The fever was burning through him, white-hot.

Where was it? Try to think.

There was a case on the floor. Cap bent and picked it up. Bending down made the blood rush to his head and he almost collapsed.

He rose again, swaying. He steadied himself. He dropped the case on the table and yanked it open.

Foam liner. Six recesses. Six red bulbs.

He could still do this. How did the dispersal unit work? He reached for it and tried to fish the punctured green bulb out of the socket. It was hard to get at. He pulled off his glove so he could use his bare fingers. Come on. *Come on!*

He removed the punctured bulb. It flew out of his fingers, bounced off the table, and rolled across the floor.

Red one. Red one! Move, Rogers!

He pried one of the red bulbs out of the liner. His hands were shaking so badly he could barely hold it.

Strucker grabbed him from behind, his arm locked around Cap's throat. He yanked Cap backwards, and Cap lost his grip on the red bulb. It thudded away across the table like a loose baseball.

"Stop these desperate attempts, Captain!" Strucker growled in his ear.

Cap tried to break the grip. He could barely speak. He could taste blood in his throat. He felt as though he were melting inside.

"Just submit!" hissed Strucker. "Lay down and die! Your death is long overdue! I will not allow you to disperse the counteragent. The venomous breath of the Hydra is in the night air!"

Cap fought back. He knew he was on the verge of blacking out.

"Berlin must die," said Strucker. "Its doom is a necessary demonstration of Hydra's authority. The nations of the world will witness this act and learn. They will fear. They will obey, or their cities will die as Berlin has died."

Cap pushed back hard, crushing Strucker against the wall behind them. The throat-hold broke. Strucker activated his lethal Satan Claw, which crackled with power. Cap blocked it with his shield. There was a shower of discharged sparks as the jolt rocked Cap backwards. Strucker launched an expert pivot-kick that caught Cap in the chest and sent him reeling.

He smashed through the dining room's half-open double doors, and landed on his back on the floor of the sitting room beyond. Strucker ran at him, Satan Claw raised. He brought it down. Cap rolled aside, and the Claw's impact burned a deep hole through the expensive white area rug, scorching the floorboards underneath.

Strucker regained his footing and lashed sideways at Cap. Still prone, Cap blocked with his shield, and then swept Strucker's legs away with his shin. Strucker fell, and tried to get back up immediately. Cap was on his knees, but he landed a body-punch that knocked Strucker down again.

Cap rolled clear and got up. His balance and coordination were shot. His mouth was full of blood. He could feel his heart racing way beyond safe levels. He was going into cardiac arrest.

On his feet again, Strucker charged at him. He body-slammed Cap, and the force of the collision pumped a gout of watery blood out of Cap's mouth. Cap under-punched twice with his bare fist. Then he got hold of Strucker by the front of his suit and swung him. Strucker half-flew, half-stumbled across the rug, and fell against one of the open dining-room doors, slamming it shut and splintering it backwards through its frame.

He came back at Cap, but Cap was already sinking to his knees. His heart was misfiring, seizing, arresting. His eyesight failed. He saw brown darkness and colored blobs.

Strucker hit him in the chest with the Satan Claw. The electric discharge ripped through Cap; he fell, spasming, onto his back.

Strucker stood over his foe's twitching body, panting from the exertion. He smiled a triumphant smile and leaned down to check the pulse in Cap's neck.

Cap opened his eyes. The agonizing shock had restarted his heart more surely than a paramedic's cardio-paddles.

He rolled back onto his shoulders and put the full force of his body into a straight kick with both legs. His boots piled into Strucker's midriff, hurling the terrorist into the air and across the room.

Strucker collided with the enormous flatscreen TV, which exploded into pieces. He struggled to free himself from the wreckage of broken display and mangled TV stand.

Cap hurled his shield. It hit Strucker before he was entirely back on his feet, and hammered him into the wall so hard that the plaster cracked, and pictures dropped and shattered.

Strucker fell on his face and lay still.

The shield, rebounding, flew past Cap. He wasn't quick enough to catch it. It bounced off the other wall and fell to the floor.

Cap limped back toward the dining room. He wanted to stop, to get disposable restraints on Strucker's wrists and remove the Satan Claw, but there wasn't time. He had no time. He'd used it all up, and then some.

He leaned against the broken dining-room door, breathing hard, and then carried on. He was forced to use the edge of the dining table as a guide and handhold. He tripped on a fallen ammo box. He scuffed papers underfoot, and walked into a chair.

He got to the dispersal device. He reached out for it, but only managed to knock it on its side. He set it upright again.

He could see spots of his own blood hitting the tabletop, dripping from his chin. He clawed for the open steel case and dragged it closer. There was no time to retrieve the red bulb he had dropped. Another one. Another one. Numb fingers seized the next one and plucked it out of its foam recess. It slipped out of his hand and rolled onto the floor.

Another one, Rogers. Another one.

He got hold of the third red bulb and took it out of the case. His hands were clumsy. There was no finesse in his fingers, no strength in his arms.

He slotted the bulb into the device's socket, and snapped shut the curved lid. That took three attempts.

The base of the device...dispersal activation was the ring around the base. He fumbled with the lower ring.

"Work...dammit..." he gasped.

There was a soft click.

Steve Rogers didn't hear it. He was falling. Falling sideways. Falling toward the unyielding floor.

Falling toward a never-ending blackness.

MADRIPOOR
04.16 LOCAL, JUNE 13TH

BANNER moved around the bomb carriage, slowly and methodically making notes on a clipboard pad. Every now and then, he paused and drew a quick sketch of a structural detail or a circuit diagram.

The High Evolutionary's New Men had set up a draftsman's table in the corner of the bomb chamber, and the top was covered in large-scale copies of Wyndham's schematics. Banner wandered back to it and started to work through several particular sections. He made more notes.

"I see you're busy," said the High Evolutionary. He had arrived soundlessly.

Banner turned. "Yes," he said.

"Have you any initial thoughts?" asked the High Evolutionary.

"It's very early to say," Banner replied. He took off his glasses and rubbed his eyes. He was tired. He had no idea what time it was anymore.

"I realize that," said the High Evolutionary. He looked down the room at the massive gamma bomb. "However, time is also pressing. My agents in Lowtown tell me that S.H.I.E.L.D. is very active. Its operatives are searching for you and your agent friend. I have managed to stay one step ahead of them so far, but we are committed to this location now. If S.H.I.E.L.D. finds us and initiates a raid, there will be violence. I will be obliged to protect my interests. There's too much at stake."

"You must do what you feel is right," said Banner. "Listen, Wyndham, I'm dedicated to this enterprise. I understand the difficult choices we have to make to get it done. You've told me what's at stake, and I believe you. God help me."

"I am gratified," said the High Evolutionary. "And I am grateful for your support."

"I presume you're going to tell me the nature of the threat?" asked Banner.

"Of course," replied the High Evolutionary.

Banner waited for a moment.

"But not now?" he pressed.

"There's too much to be done to lose time with a lengthy digression," replied the High Evolutionary. "I need to spend a few hours verifying the virus's distribution status. I will then look forward to hearing your thoughts on the means of improving the weapon's efficiency. Perhaps when those technical elements are being implemented we can sit down and discuss the broader picture.

"Remember, Doctor Banner: The threat issue will become utterly irrelevant once we are successful. The world is in peril. That is all you need to know. Let us not lose valuable time discussing something that will become academic."

Banner bit his lip and nodded.

"I think," he said, "I can see immediate ways of increasing the fallout coverage by a factor of twenty-five while also reducing the actual blast effect. You have a machining and fabrication facility?"

"On the second floor."

Banner nodded.

"Give me a few hours, and I'll present my findings. I need to think. I'm a pacer, Wyndham. I need to move around to keep my thought processes working. I presume you will allow me to roam without constant security checks?"

"Within reason," said the High Evolutionary. "My New Men are posted throughout the building. I can't allow you to leave the facility or risk you being seen at a window. Otherwise, you're free. I understand: We all have our processes. Mine was always meditation and bicycle riding."

"And I can access the lab for computer use?"

"I'm a longhand man myself," said the High Evolutionary, "but of course. There are laptop devices there."

"I'll speak to you in a few hours, then," said Banner.

The High Evolutionary nodded and left the chamber.

Alone, Banner sat the drawing table. He fought for a moment to contain his deep frustration and regulate his pulse.

He left the bomb chamber and wandered through the area at the back of the factory level. McHale had been given medical attention and then transferred to a private room. The dog-hybrid was guarding the door.

"I want to see him," Banner said.

The dog-hybrid glared at him.

"Your master said I could go where I please."

The dog-hybrid paused while it psionically verified the fact.

Then it unlocked the door and let Banner through.

The door closed behind him. Banner heard it lock.

The room was dirty and the window boarded. McHale lay sprawled on a rusted cot, handcuffed to the frame. He stared at Banner in disgust. The back of his head was bandaged.

"Are you all right?" Banner asked him.

McHale shook his head. His expression was contemptuous.

"I'm sorry I hit you," said Banner. He looked around. There was a medical pack on the floor beside the door, out of McHale's reach. It contained the usual first-aid items: fresh dressings, antiseptic, and painkillers.

"You're with him, now, huh?" asked McHale bitterly. "You're working with him?"

"There are big things at stake," replied Banner. He searched through the medical kit, examining a few items.

"I trusted you," said McHale. There was resentment in his tone.

"Then trust that I'm doing the right thing."

"What did he offer you?" McHale asked. "What did he promise you?"

"Something I've always wanted," replied Banner. He got up and looked back at McHale.

"I thought you were a standup guy, Doc. I really did. Despite everything, I thought you were one of the good people. Man, was I wrong."

"People can be mistaken," said Banner, "when they judge character, or actions, or a particular situation. Sometimes they don't appreciate the whole picture. Sometimes they get fooled."

McHale muttered a curse.

"Sometimes you have to act in-character to convince people," said Banner. "You have to show them what they want to see so that they'll trust you. Maybe you underestimated how good I was at it. Do you know what I mean, McHale? As a professional espionage operative, I'm sure you do."

McHale narrowed his eyes and stared at Banner.

"Yeah," he said, slowly.

"Sometimes you have to play a role in a fairly extreme way," said Banner. "I mean, when the stakes are really high."

McHale nodded.

"You know what I mean? You understand?" asked Banner.

"Yes, Doc," said McHale.

"Okay then," said Banner.

"You're a treacherous piece of—" McHale snarled, and he lunged at Banner as far as his chain would allow.

Banner backed away. For a second, they exchanged a knowing look.

"I just wanted to check that you were okay," said Banner. "That's all. I'm sorry, McHale."

McHale told him where he could stick his apologies in an anatomically precise way.

"Okay," said Banner. "Just so long as we know where we both stand, and how much is at stake."

"I'm reading you loud and clear, Doc," McHale spat.

Banner shrugged and knocked on the door to be let out.

He went upstairs to the High Evolutionary's lab. Wyndham was writing calculations on one of the whiteboards.

"Are you done, Doctor?" he asked.

"No," said Banner. "I needed a calculator."

He sat at the main bench and started to punch numbers into a small handheld device, noting the results.

"I'm still bothered," he said as he worked. "I'm sorry, Wyndham. It's making it hard for me to concentrate."

"Bothered by what, Doctor?" asked Wyndham, glancing over.

"The nature of the threat," said Banner, sitting back. "I apologize, but I can't help it. The unknown makes me anxious, and anxiety isn't good for me. It's playing on my mind and making it very hard for me to maintain a calm disposition."

The High Evolutionary nodded.

"I understand, Doctor," he said. He put down the stylus he had been using and walked over to the bench to face Banner. "I need you clearheaded, and I certainly do not wish you to become agitated. Let us spend a few minutes, and I'll tell you what I know."

"Thank you," said Banner. "You have to understand my misgivings. This is so big, Wyndham."

"Then let me explain, swiftly and concisely," said the High Evolutionary. "Nine months ago, I first received contact from the representatives of..."

He suddenly fell silent, as though he was listening to something Banner couldn't hear.

"What is it?" asked Banner. "Representatives of what?"

"Not now," said the High Evolutionary bluntly. "I have received a psionic alert. The New Men have just confirmed that S.H.I.E.L.D. tac teams are surrounding the building. We are out of time."

"Representatives of what, Wyndham?" Banner asked, more firmly.

"Really, Doctor, not now!" snapped the High Evolutionary. "A raid is about to begin. There will be bloodshed. Our hand is forced.

You and I will quit this facility via my teleport link. It will carry us to a safe location far away from here."

"Wyndham—"

"Grasp the situation, Banner!" the High Evolutionary exclaimed. "S.H.I.E.L.D. is on to us. We are leaving. Now. There is no longer any opportunity to finesse this plan. We will be long gone by the time S.H.I.E.L.D. overruns the building. I will detonate the gamma bomb remotely, and then we will do what we can to repair the global situation and implement my plan."

Banner rose. He pulled something out of his pocket.

"What is the threat, Wyndham?" he demanded.

"Banner, you infuriate me! We must leave now!"

"I think it's time *you* grasped the situation," Banner said quietly. "We're not going anywhere. You're going to tell me, right now, the nature of the threat. No more evasion."

He held up the object he had taken from his pocket.

"Do you see this?" he asked. "It's an EpiPen. I borrowed it from the medical kit in McHale's cell. An epinephrine auto-injector, Wyndham. A high-dose shot of medical adrenaline."

Banner flipped off the cap and held the needle to his forearm.

"Tell me what the threat is, Wyndham," he said. "Tell me right now. Or I will shoot this into my arm. And you really, really don't want me to do that."

WASHINGTON, D.C.
12.32 LOCAL, JUNE 12TH

THE ARMOR wrapped itself around him.

Tony Stark stood, arms stretched out at his sides, allowing the gleaming plates and panels of the Iron Man suit to articulate into place. It made a soft hum as it engaged, locking and sealing—perfectly machined.

He felt alive again: clean, whole, empowered.

Better still, he felt his confidence rebooting.

Let the world bring it. He was Iron Man, Avenger. He was renewed.

"All set, sir?" asked Seavers, the S.H.I.E.L.D. tech assisting him.

Stark nodded. He stepped forward from the open crate in which the factory-fresh Iron Man armor had been stowed, flexing his hands and rotating his arms.

He retracted his faceplate.

"I'm good," he said.

Seavers followed him out of the Helicarrier cargo space. In the adjoining workshop, the suit Stark had been wearing when he came aboard was laid out on a steel table. It was battered, scratched, and broken; parts of it were disarticulated. His torn undersuit hung over the back of a chair.

Stark paused and looked at the damaged suit. Every mark on it told a story: the dents left by Ultron's fists, the puncture marks from shrapnel, the burn damage, the cracks from nanoform impacts, the kinetic trauma, the collision distortions. The decaying effects of the nanobot swarm made the discarded armor look as though it had been sprayed with acid. Crusts of dead swarmbot residue caked the joints and seams. The ruptured palm emitters of the repulsor system were blackened by back-blast.

"When the crisis is over," Stark said over his shoulder to Seavers, "I want this shipped back to Stark Industries."

"You gonna recycle it?" the S.H.I.E.L.D. agent asked. "Strip it down for reusable components?'

"No," replied Stark. "I'm going to repair it."

He reached out with one of his brand-new gauntlets and gently touched the fingers of one of the dead gloves.

"I'm Iron Man," he said quietly. "The suit, the armor, it makes me Iron Man. Sure, I have a wardrobe full of these. Variants, specialist-builds, and plenty of spares. But each one has its own personality. This one saw me through a lot. It saved my life this morning, several times. I'm not going to just junk it. That would be ungrateful."

Seavers nodded. He was a tech specialist, and he understood Stark's tech-head mindset. Stark knew that most people didn't. Treating a hardware suit as if it were alive smacked of an uncomfortable sentimentality.

But guys like Seavers got it. "I'll prioritize it through decontamination and get it packed, sir," Seavers said.

Stark nodded his thanks. "Appreciate it," he said.

He walked up through the busy Helicarrier to the medical suite. S.H.I.E.L.D. agents hurried past him in the hallways, many of them shooting him a respectful greeting or even a salute. There was a sense of unified purpose.

The hatch of the medical suite hissed open automatically when he approached it.

"How are you doing?" he asked as he walked in.

"Lousy," said Quicksilver.

Pietro Maximoff was awake and sitting at a trolley table. He had a thermal blanket wrapped around his shoulders. The Vision and Nick Fury were with him. Nearby, two uniformed S.H.I.E.L.D. specialists were studying complex data on a series of freestanding glass projection plates. They talked quietly to each other, adjusting and annotating the projected data with light-stylus instruments.

"Got anything you can share with us?" Stark asked Pietro.

"Wanda spoke to me," said Quicksilver. "I ran here as fast as I could."

"She spoke to you?" asked Stark. He noticed that the table in front of Pietro was covered in pages torn from a legal pad. Pietro had been writing. A lot.

"In my head," said Pietro.

"That happen much before?" asked Stark.

Fury shot him a warning look. Stark cursed inwardly. His naturally flippant tone often made him sound sarcastic, even on the rare occasion when he wasn't trying to be.

"We have established that it is an unusual event," said the Vision. "Given Wanda's power-set, this would seem to be some form of magic-based communication."

"She was in trouble," said Pietro. "We have to go and help her immediately or—"

"Whoa. What did she say, exactly?" asked Stark.

"She didn't really say anything," said Pietro. "I just felt her. She was reaching into me, into my heart. I felt her message rather than hearing it. She was in danger, and in darkness. A dark place. A dark realm. The Thunder God was with her. He was in danger, too. There was fire. But none of that matters! We're wasting time with this talk!"

"We're not doing anything until we work out what we're up against," said Stark.

Pietro glared at him.

"You mentioned fire?" asked Stark.

Pietro shrugged. "And stars," he said impatiently. "Stars in alignment, in a circle. That was important somehow. Stars in a great circle. Or fires in a circle. Both. Neither. I don't know."

"This relates to Siberia," said Fury.

"Yeah, figured that," said Stark. "Any chance this could be something...*someone* else? Making you think it was Wanda?"

Pietro shook his head.

"It was her," he said with great conviction. "In my heart, and in my blood, I know it was my sister. I can't explain it, and I have no proof to show you, but it was her. And we must go to her now!"

"What's this?" Stark asked, pointing to the pages of handwriting.

"I asked him to write down anything he could remember," said Fury. "It can open up the memory sometimes and free up things you don't realize are blocked."

"Okay," said Stark.

"Maximoff wrote all this down in about two minutes," said

Fury. "It was some crazy stuff. He broke my pen."

"I can write fast," said Pietro. "I can do everything fast. But this was not conscious. It was...what is that process called?"

"Automatic writing," said the Vision.

"Yes. That. I just wrote. I did not know what I was writing, what it meant, or where it was coming from. I just wrote. I think Wanda's magic put things in my head, and it all came out."

Stark picked up one of the sheets and looked at it.

"What is this? Equations? Mathematical combinations?"

The Vision motioned toward a glass panel display on which the S.H.I.E.L.D. specialists were working. The plates were covered in glowing holo-type projections.

"I have transcribed it," the Vision said. "I share Pietro's desire to go to Wanda's assistance as swiftly as possible. I was trying to assess her location. The flow of the material is not clear. It is broken in places, as though the data were jumbled or incomplete. But I believe it is a mathematical expression of dimensional space."

Stark looked at it.

"Yeah, I see that now," he agreed. "It's describing the spatial terms of something. Not Earth. Not our reality. But something expressed in relation to ours."

"You can read that stuff?" asked Fury.

"Not really," said Stark. "It's not my field. But I get the basics well enough to see what it's doing."

"I called in these experts to consult," said Fury, gesturing to the techs. "Quantum specialists, dimension-phase engineers. Our best."

"Perhaps Wanda is trying to tell us something," said the Vision.

"Well, yeah," said Stark.

"I mean specifically. Perhaps she is trying to send us information that she hopes we can use. About where she is. Where, when, and how. Where that place is in relation to us."

"Yeah, either deliberately or accidentally," said Stark.

"What do you mean?" asked Pietro.

"Well, this isn't Wanda's field, either," said Stark. "She wouldn't understand the quantum mathematics. But if she…whatever it is she does…cast a spell? Are we okay with that terminology?"

"Go on," said Fury.

Stark paced a little, miming a conjurer with a wand.

"She's desperate. She's in trouble," he continued, thinking out loud. "She casts a spell—frantically, maybe, to communicate to her brother a simple concept. Where she is."

He pointed to the panels.

"Magic's not my field, either, so bear with me," he said. "But it's like she makes a wish. *Let Pietro know where I am.* And at Pietro's end, that comes out as a literal download of data. A detailed scientific description of her location. A quantum map."

Tony glanced at the techs.

"You guys getting that?" he asked.

"Absolutely, sir," said one of them, an older man. The name patch on his suit read "Willings." "This section here—" He pointed to one of the plates. "—this is pretty much a mathematical representation of our planet. Specifically New York, which is where Mr. Maximoff was when this began. The rest, for the most part, is something else entirely."

"It's non-Euclidian geometry," said another tech, a woman. Her patch read "Gainsborough." "It's describing a universe that obeys entirely different physical laws."

"That's where we think she is," said Willings. "Or, at least, where the data was sent from."

"Do we have a match?" asked Stark. "I mean, we've tangled with folks from other dimensions before. We have data. Does this match anything? Any prior events? Space-time breaches? Wormholes?"

Gainsborough shook her head.

"Nothing so far," she said. "Bear in mind, many of our systems are shut down. We don't have full archive access, and we can't pull anything from the Avengers' database."

"You said 'for the most part,'" said Stark, looking at Willings. "What did you mean?"

"There's one section here," he replied, indicating another part of the display. "It's small, like a side note. I don't know what it is."

"Give me your best guess," said Stark.

Willings shrugged.

"If this," he said, sweeping his hand across the left-hand section of the display, "is our universe, and this—" he gestured to the right-hand portion, "—is the other place, the alien dimension, then this is an anomaly." He was indicating a small part of the central section.

"It's small," said Gainsborough. "It describes a pocket of reality, separate from our universe but contained within it as a sub-set. It's not part of the other, whatever the other dimension is."

Stark stared at the display. "If the Siberia event is an incursion into our universe from another dimension, we have to act on this now. It's what Wanda's trying to tell us. It's a wormhole event, the intersection of two entirely different universes."

Contessa de la Fontaine entered the room.

"We're about to go live, Director," she said. "Two minutes, and we'll be ready to try an uplink with London."

Fury nodded.

"Okay," he said. "Keep working on this while Stark and I go and talk to Europe. Maybe they'll be able to help us fill in some—"

A rumble cut him off. The Helicarrier shuddered.

"The hell was that?" Fury asked. Sirens began to wail.

Fury snatched up a remote and activated one of the room's large monitors.

"Are we under attack?" he growled. "Talk to me!"

De la Fontaine was listening to her earpiece.

"Shots fired, upper deck," she announced. "Reports of an explosion."

Fury used the remote to flash up a security-cam feed. The image was grainy black-and-white, with no sound. It showed the massive upper deck of the helicarrier, with taxiways, parking stands, and fuel pumps. Stark could see S.H.I.E.L.D. warplanes on launch cradles, tow-carts, and munition carriers.

"The hell?" said Fury.

A bright flash of light suddenly burned out the screen settings for a second; when the picture dimmed again, one of the warplanes was on fire. Flight crews were running for cover. There were agents down. Security teams in body armor rushed onto the deck, assault rifles trained.

Fury panned the view. Stark froze.

"Oh my god," he said.

A humanoid figure was advancing slowly across the deck. Little specks of white showed the sparks of the automatic fire bouncing off its armored shell.

Despite the black-and-white resolution, the identity of the humanoid figure was unmistakable.

It was Iron Man.

Stark slammed his faceplate closed and accelerated out of the medical suite. His backwash made the others flinch. Pietro's handwritten pages billowed into the air.

"Stark!" Fury yelled. "Stark!"

The Vision flew silently after Iron Man, phasing through the wall into the hallway in time to see Stark rocket down the corridor. S.H.I.E.L.D. personnel ducked out of his path.

Stark reached a through-deck service well, swung upright, and descended feet first, boot jets flaring.

His mind was racing. He fought back horror and tried to focus.

He understood what was happening.

It was all his fault.

THE UPPER deck was in chaos. Alarms were sounding, and gunfire chattered. Two parked S.H.I.E.L.D. interceptors were on fire. Deck crews were fleeing to the platform exits while the S.H.I.E.L.D. security teams laid down covering fire.

The Iron Man was approaching down the center line of the flight deck. Bullets pinged off it. It was dragging a body behind it, a body that it clutched by the throat.

Stark landed near the main exterior hatch, beside the security teams. They were blasting away, littering the deck grills with hot shell casings.

"Get back!" Stark ordered them.

They glanced at him.

"Get the hell back now!" he yelled.

They started to fall back. Stark stepped out into the open and faced his twin.

It was his discarded armor.

It had been crudely rebuilt. It was complete again—functional, animated—but it was not pretty. The dents and tears had been fused with crude, organo-alloy patches. Nanofacture waste composite covered it like scabs. It looked diseased.

Only intense nanofabrication could have refitted it so rapidly.

The faceplate had been transformed. Still twisted and buckled from the fight at Pine Fields, it now displayed a fierce, downturned snarl and malevolent eyes.

Ultron hadn't fled into the electronic oceans of the data-net. It had concealed itself inside the apparently dormant nanobot residue coating Stark's damaged armor. S.H.I.E.L.D. and the security services had been scouring the globe for it, but it had been right with Stark all along. It had been hiding inside Iron Man.

"Hello, Anthony," Ultron said.

Stark powered up his repulsors. Full charge.

"No one touches my stuff," he said.

"The armor is technically crude," said Ultron, "but it forms an adequate exo-form host. We may resume our conversation."

"No conversation," Stark replied. "You attack the world and attempt Singularity, I respond as an Avenger. You steal my technology, you make it personal."

"How very human," said Ultron. "Ha ha ha."

Stark looked at the body that Ultron was dragging. Despite the blood and the terrible injuries, Stark could see that it was Seavers.

"Screw the hardware," Stark whispered. "I'm going to kill you."

"Calculating success probability," said Ultron. It paused.

"Zero," it concluded.

SIBERIA
LOCAL TIME UNRECORDED, NO RELEVANT DATE

TIME is spent," murmured Dormammu. The mage-lord was gazing up at the cold void. The last two stars were almost perfectly aligned.

He looked over at Thor, and gestured disdainfully at the burning hexagram that protected the Thunder God.

"My circle will soon be complete," Dormammu said, "while yours is about to die."

The fires were almost out. The wood had burned away. The six clumps of stakes were little more than heaps of embers, and the flames of the central trunk were pale and faint.

"The symmetry of rituals," said Dormammu. "One circle forms, another fades."

"When our flames die," said Thor "you'll still have to kill me. I will not fall to you without resistance. We have established how hard it is to kill a god, especially when you need all the power you can muster."

"Oh, Odinson." Dormammu laughed. "That was then."

He gestured up at the constellation of red suns.

"My strength is now beyond anything you can imagine. I have

energy to spare. Energy to slay you with a blink. Were you not listening? The circle magnifies the power of the caster. It amplifies it. When the stars align, I will reshape universes."

He laughed. The beasts at his feet yapped and snickered in answer.

Thor thought of several responses, but none of them was worth uttering. Just insults—beneath his dignity.

He looked up at the ring of stars and then down at his own dying circle of fires.

Had their fellow Avengers heard Wanda's call? Would they respond? *Could* they?

And if they did respond, what could they do—even standing shoulder-to-shoulder—against the Dread One at full strength? They—

He paused.

Without a backward glance at Dormammu, he turned and walked across the dead, black earth to Wanda.

"Where are you going, Odinson?" Dormammu called after him. "There's nothing you can do. I will make it quick, I promise."

Thor ignored him. He crouched down beside the Scarlet Witch.

"Any ideas?" he whispered to her.

She shook her head.

"I was hoping you might have devised something ingenious," he said. "Something magical of which I had not thought."

"I'm sorry," she said.

"So am I," he smiled, "because it means I have to tell you my idea. And it is not ingenious. It is foolish, and you'll tell me a thousand ways in which it is wrong."

"Just say it," she said. "We haven't got anything else."

"Circles," he said.

"Circles?" she echoed, frowning.

"Circles of magic," said Thor. "His above, made of six stars. Yours below, made of six fires."

"Mine is designed to keep him at bay for a short time," said Wanda. "His is made to reforge reality. They're rather different."

"But the principle is the same, yes?" asked Thor. "The circle, six points, amplifies the sorcerer's power? Six fires, be they bonfires or stars? They work the same way. This is what he told me."

She nodded.

"Where does that get us?" she asked.

"I am not sure." Thor smiled. "I am no magician. But if he breaks our circle, we die."

"Yes."

"And if we break his?"

She raised her eyebrows.

"Well, his power would be diminished."

"And he would no longer be able to transform worlds?"

"I suppose not."

"He would be thwarted in his plans to capture and control the Earth?"

She sat up.

"Yes, but we—" she began.

"Wanda, I fear there is no saving us now," said Thor. "He has us, and we will be destroyed one way or the other. All that matters is that we stop him."

"Agreed," she said. "But you misunderstood. I wasn't worried about us. I was just going to ask how we could possibly break his circle."

"We put out a fire," said Thor.

"It's flattering you think I have that kind of range," she said. "Thor, I can't extinguish a sun."

"But the circle and the magician are one, are they not?" asked Thor. "One does not work without the other?"

She stared at him.

"That's…madness," she said. "I see where you're going, but it's—"

"What have we to lose?" he asked. "Do you have ability left?"

"Some."

"Enough for a local effect? Here, on this bleak plain? Just here, and here alone?"

She got to her feet. She flexed her fingers.

"Let's find out."

He gazed out into the darkness and nodded.

She raised her hand and took him by the chin, turning his face gently to look at her.

"If it works," she said, "we'll only have an instant. And we will be unprotected."

"Then we'd better both be ready," he replied.

She rubbed her hands together, trying to warm them. He took hold of Mjolnir by its leather-wrapped haft.

"What are you doing?" Dormammu called across at them. There was dark mockery in his tone. The beasts at his feet barked and growled. "One last attempt to fight me? Do you rise to greet death standing?"

"Do it," Thor said to the Scarlet Witch.

She braced herself, feet planted apart. She bowed her head, eyes screwed shut, and balled her fists. The flames on the trunk behind her rose again, crackling with refreshed power.

She threw out her hands, fingers splayed. Thor felt the surge of power shake the night air.

The bonfires went out. The flames sputtered and died, trailing thin smoke from the points of the circle. The trunk extinguished, too, smoldering.

Dormammu convulsed and screamed. He dropped to one knee, and then struggled back to his feet.

The Dread Lord no longer burned with mystic light. He was a gaunt, blackened, skeletal giant, smoke coiling from his hands and the scorched bone of his head.

"You dare?" he gasped.

Wanda had cast a spell to banish fire from the area around them, forbidding any flame to burn within a radius of one mile. The ban would not last. Dormammu's mystic, living flame did not burn like natural fire. It would renew again in seconds.

But the Thunder God was ready.

Mjolnir flew, hurled with all the force that Thor could muster. It sang through the air at supersonic velocity and struck Dormammu in the head.

The black skull shattered.

Dormammu fell.

Thor was already running. He caught the returning hammer in mid-stride and leapt, hefting Mjolnir over his head with both hands.

The dark lord's shuddering, headless form was on its hands and knees. It was groping blindly. Frail tendrils of magic were spinning from its fingers, trying to reknit the smashed and scattered shards of its skull.

Thor brought down the hammer on Dormammu, crushing his spine into the ground.

Thunder boomed.

Wanda fell, her energy spent. She saw the ring of beasts leap up and charge to attack both her and Thor.

"Thor!" she yelled.

Thor rose up from Dormammu's broken, twitching body. He swung at the first beast that came for him, smashing it aside. His fist caught a second, launching it into the air. A third closed its jaws around his forearm. He swung Mjolnir and broke its neck.

Other beasts ran toward Wanda. They bounded into the circle that no longer held them back, past the smoldering piles of ash. She cast a hex that caused one of them to stumble and sprawl, and then leapt aside to dodge the open jaws of another.

Wanda landed, rolling, and leapt up again. A beast was right on her. She jerked sideways and drove her fist into its throat. It yelped and staggered away, retching and choking.

Another grabbed her cloak in its teeth. She wrenched away, tearing the hem, and then kicked her heel sideways into its face. Cap had always taught her that in hand-to-hand, it wasn't physical strength that counted as much as placement. Eyes, face, throat. Aim a fist or a kick well, and it was possible to deter the strongest aggressor.

Thor punched another beast aside and turned back to Dormammu. The Dread One was trying to recompose his broken form. His back was twisted and snapped. Part of his skull had fused back together: the jaw, one eye socket, and a section of the cranium. Thor could feel his rage. In seconds, Dormammu's doused fire would reignite.

Thor swung his hammer, shattering the partly formed skull again. He drove Mjolnir down with both hands, disintegrating the Dread One's ribs.

Dormammu fell. Thor swung again, and again.

Dormammu wouldn't die. He could not die. Thor knew that. Demons, like gods, were hard to kill.

But if Thor inflicted as much harm as possible, it would take the Dread One time to re-corporate.

One last blow, and Thor stood back. He shoved aside a beast, then turned to find Wanda.

"Damn!" he snarled.

She was dodging, punching, and evading, but she was surrounded by snarling beasts.

He flew to her, and systematically smashed away the creatures with the full-blooded wrath of the Odinson.

"Time to leave," he said, and caught hold of her.

Without the sorcerer at its center, Dormammu's mystic circle was being torn asunder by its own gathered power and its lack of focus.

The six red stars flared with bitter, toxic light. Tremors shook the black earth. Lightning sizzled across the cursed sky.

Splits and sinkholes appeared in the ground, venting noxious steam. The splits widened, becoming crevasses, then canyons.

Thor prepared to spin his hammer.

Immense flares of rancid doomsday energy burst across the heavens, like some nightmarish version of the aurora borealis.

Far away from them, beyond the edge of Wanda's now-extinguished circle, Thor saw Dormammu begin to rise again. He was half-broken, mangled, defying death. Flames began to catch and lick around his broken bones.

He screamed their names. He screamed their doom.

Thor raised Mjolnir above his head and called out to the sky.

The storm answered. It did not belong to Dormammu anymore. His control had been broken. It was no longer the Dread One's slave.

The storm had a new master.

Thor called down the lightning.

A searing bolt, blindingly bright and blue-white hot, ripped down out of the sky. It atomized Dormammu with a boom like a giant's hammer striking an anvil.

Thor spun Mjolnir and let its upswing carry him and Wanda into the sky.

Around them, the world came apart.

TWENTY-ONE

BERLIN
01.12 LOCAL, JUNE 13TH

YOU don't have to do this," said Gail Runciter.

"Yes, I do," said Cap.

"Come on, Steve. You've only just regained consciousness. You were on the brink of death. The antidote got into your system at the last possible moment. As it is, only your enhanced metabolism kept you alive that long. Do you understand what I'm saying? You need to rest. They need to test you and make sure—"

"Gail," he said. He took hold of her hand. "I'm doing this. Right now. Okay?"

She sighed and nodded. Cap looked across at G.W. Bridge. Bridge nodded, too.

The S.H.I.E.L.D. guards disarmed the cell door and stood aside. Cap entered the small, blue-lit cell. He glanced at the large mirrored wall, and knew that Gail and Bridge were watching him through it.

Strucker was shackled to a metal chair facing a small table. Cap sat down opposite him.

"Where am I?" asked Strucker.

Cap didn't answer.

"Basic human rights," said Strucker. "Detainee rights. You are obliged to tell me where I am."

"And you're obliged to shut the hell up," said Cap. "Don't you dare lecture me on human rights—"

He paused.

"Berlin," he said. "A S.H.I.E.L.D.-station holding facility. I'm telling you that because I don't intend to sink to your level."

Strucker laughed. His face was badly bruised.

"And that is why the Americans will ultimately lose," said Strucker. "And why Hydra will prevail."

"Let's talk about you prevailing," said Cap. "Your pathogen has been neutralized. Berlin is safe. No one died. Not even me."

Strucker was silent.

"Any comments?" asked Cap.

"The Hydra's Breath will—"

"Be reverse-engineered by S.H.I.E.L.D. labs within the next three hours. We have your samples, and samples of the counter-agent. It is no longer a threat."

"Cut off one head, and another will grow in its place," said Strucker.

Cap looked at him across the table.

"It's done, Strucker," he said. "Hydra's plot has failed. And in failing, it's done considerable harm to your organization. I'm not just talking about reputation and influence. You threw it together hastily, Strucker. In doing so, you cut corners and exposed connections, processes, organization, hierarchy. Hydra may never recover."

He kept his eyes on Strucker.

"And if it does, if it sprouts another head or two, you certainly won't be at liberty to see it."

"You overestimate your—"

"We searched the devices recovered from your apartment," said Cap. "Interesting stuff. Enough data to keep field agents busy for months. Names, contacts. You really were in a hurry, weren't you?"

Strucker was silent.

"One thing is especially interesting," said Cap. "The log of a message sent anonymously to S.H.I.E.L.D. A tip-off, alerting S.H.I.E.L.D. to an A.I.M. operation in Antarctica. Thanks for that. I believe it's been actioned. You weren't just out for power and control, were you? You were also out to get your rivals. Selling out A.I.M. to keep them from beating Hydra to the prize. That's how frantic you were."

"Was there a question in that?" asked Strucker archly.

"Everybody was after it, weren't they?" asked Cap. "There was a race—a race to rule the world. You were in competition, and you did everything you could to win."

"It had to be done," said Strucker. "Hydra needed to be victorious."

"Why?"

"Because there was too much at stake."

"And everybody else thought the same thing," said Cap. "Every major terrorist or criminal operation in the world. A sudden, desperate race to seize power. No hesitation, no subtlety, no quarter. There could only be one winner. The world went to hell tonight because of it."

"Your point?"

"Why?"

Strucker sat back.

"Necessity," he said. "We had to act now, or never act again. A single chance."

"Because?"

"There was an ultimatum. No more delays. Take power—do what you always boasted you would do. Take control of the human race and bring it to order. Impose your rule, or it will be done for you."

"Who issued the ultimatum?" asked Cap.

Strucker shrugged. His shackles clinked.

"Strucker, there's a threat out there. A hidden threat—a threat so grave it's made even Hydra act with insane and reckless desperation. I need to know what it is."

"Yes, you do," said Strucker.

"Tell me."

Strucker smiled.

"The world is going to be held to account; it will most likely die," he said. "I had a chance to prevent that. Hydra had a chance. But you stopped that, Captain America. You stopped us from saving the world."

"Ruling the world."

"The same thing," said Strucker. "You stopped me. So understand this. I am not going to tell you anything. I am not going to help you find or face this threat, because it is the only satisfaction left to me."

"You would rather watch the world die than help me?" asked Cap. "You'd rather die along with it than raise a finger to help? You're damning the planet out of spite?"

Strucker smiled.

"Exactly," he replied. "When all you have left is spite, dear Captain, spite will have to suffice."

MADRIPOOR
06.10 LOCAL, JUNE 13TH

FLASH grenades detonated in the tight stairwells of the old Lowtown factory building. Blue smoke billowed out, filling hallways and blinding the occupants.

The tac teams went in.

S.H.I.E.L.D. field agent Jerry Hunt led the first team in through the west street access. They were armored in black-and-white body gear and sealed hoods. The fabric of the tac suits contained a refractive polymer that, in combination with the blue smoke, rendered the agents virtually invisible. Their eye-masks, calibrated for heat and movement, painted HUD images that allowed them to see in smoke and darkness; the lenses were also specially filtered to match the prismatic qualities of the smoke particles, allowing them direct and clear vision.

They were carrying S-System Tac Weapons. These hybrid assault rifles could switch from live rounds to tranq at the flip of a toggle, and also pump vari-load grenades from under-barrel launchers. The top rails of the weapons held cold-beam phased-plasma barrels, for those tough moments when energy shots were preferable to ballistic hard rounds.

Hunt had ordered "tranq" at the go point. He didn't want a bloodbath. Intel suggested that Wyndham had prisoners inside.

S.H.I.E.L.D. stormed the building, clearing it room by room. The agents fired tight, controlled bursts, knocking down anything that moved.

Hunt saw the New Men, Wyndham's grotesque foot soldiers. He was glad of the psionic blockers that S.H.I.E.L.D. had woven into the undercaps of the tac suits. But he was worried about the atrocious radiation levels his wrist-mounted g-counter was picking up.

A New Man, a cat-thing, came at him on the second landing. It took two bursts of tranq to lay the thing out.

"Clear left!" Hunt ordered. He switched right with his cover man, kicked in a door, and mowed down the New Men that lay in wait.

The New Men were relying on their psionics. They kept pausing to unleash their mental attacks, and that made them good, static targets. By the time they learned that the S.H.I.E.L.D. teams were proofed against psionic assault, they had already dropped.

Hunt knew the advantage wouldn't last. Psionics would share that information. Deeper in the building, they would start to encounter New Men ready to defend their turf by other means. Their targets were going to learn, and learn fast.

"Watch for guns and blades," he warned over the link.

Just seconds later, a humanoid ram attacked him with a meat cleaver. Hunt's cover man dropped the ram with a sustained burst.

Hunt nodded his appreciation. He loaded a fresh clip and moved on. From the building around him, he heard gunfire and the bang of grenades.

He was tracking the radiation source. He wanted that secured as a priority. On the next level up, the stairway landing was defended by three New Men with knock-off AK-47s. Bullets spat and ripped down the old staircase, shredding the wood and brick, and making the air dense with dust and fibers. One of Hunt's team went down, but her composite armor had stopped the lethal force of the assault weapons. She would go home with bruises and a mess-hall story.

Hunt couldn't get a clean shot. The New Men were raking fire at them. He toggled his weapon and selected the plasma beamer. Ducking out of cover, he fired, shearing down the banister rail with a beam of green energy and cutting a semicircular section out of the wall. The wall section fell away, its edges fizzling and burn-ing—perfectly excised. The stairhead cover immediately vanished. Hunt flipped back to tranq and picked off the exposed New Men, who were scurrying for a new place to hide.

He took the lead on the way up the stairs. The boards, shot up and weakened, creaked under the weight.

The landing was more solid. Serious underpinning, probably I-beams reinforcing the next floor level. The place had once been a fac-tory, and it had been built to support machines and production lines.

They took the next door and entered a huge chamber. The view stopped them in their tracks.

"Hold your fire!" Hunt ordered urgently. "That's a bloody war-head!"

The device was huge and sinister. It sat under the raw lights on a heavy carriage. Hunt had seen some things in his distinguished career in Europe and the Far East. He knew a gamma bomb when he met one.

They advanced down the chamber, weapons ready. There was a

man in shirtsleeves working at the foot of the bomb, frantically cutting and rewiring.

"On the floor! Now!" Hunt yelled. "Face down!"

"I'm afraid I can't," Banner replied, without looking around at them. He stuck his wire cutters in his mouth so he could use both hands to pull off an inspection cover.

"You heard him!" one of the other agents shouted, raising his weapon.

Hunt waved the man down.

"Banner?" he called. "Doctor Banner?"

Banner took the cutters out of his mouth.

"Little busy," he replied, working furiously.

Hunt approached Banner. "What are you doing?" he demanded, pulling off his headgear.

"Saving the world, I hope," Banner replied. "Unfortunately, Wyndham was a stranger to standardized color coding."

Hunt looked up at the bomb.

"Is this bloody thing armed?" he asked.

"Yup," said Banner. "Armed and set. Remote trigger. Pass me that screwdriver."

Hunt obliged.

Banner, who still had not looked up, took the tool and used the grip end to hammer off the wedged inspection plate.

Hunt could see that Banner was focused and intent. He could also see that the man was sweating. Agitated. Suddenly, Hunt realized he wasn't sure what he was more afraid of: the bomb or Banner.

"Do you know what you're doing?" he asked.

"I hope so. I ought to."

"Is there a schematic?"

"Plenty," said Banner. "But hardwiring of the trigger mechanism is pretty standard. Ah."

"Ah? Ah what?"

"There's the transceiver for the remote signal."

Banner reached in with pliers.

"Where's Wyndham?" Hunt asked.

"Gone. Just now. Teleported. I couldn't stop him."

"Damn," said Hunt.

"Hence the rush," said Banner. "He's intending to detonate this from his new location."

"It'll take out the island," said Hunt.

"Just for starters," Banner agreed.

He made a cut, and then pulled out a sheaf of wires.

"That's the remote trigger," he said, and breathed out.

He looked up at Hunt. Beads of perspiration had collected around the lower-inside rim of his spectacles.

"The bomb is still armed," he said. "We'll need to see about that. But the trigger's disabled."

"I'll get a disposal team in," said Hunt.

"Do it fast. I'm pretty sure there are no backup triggers, but Wyndham is smart. This thing needs to be taken apart, right down to its components. And it's dirty. Get your team suited."

Hunt made the call. Banner stood up.

"You okay?" Hunt asked.

Banner nodded.

"Doc? Doc?"

They turned. McHale was limping into the bomb chamber,

escorted by the tac team that had freed him from his cell.

He shook off their support and walked up to Banner. They stood face-to-face.

"You were playing him?" asked McHale. "Tell me I read that right. You were playing him?"

"Yes," said Banner. "I'm sorry about the—"

"Just tell me you were playing him."

"I was. I had to go along with him. I had to convince him I was sympathetic."

"I guess hitting me over the head was a pretty good demonstration," said McHale.

"Had to make it convincing," said Banner. "Sorry."

"My skull forgives you," said McHale.

"You played along with Wyndham to learn about the bomb?" asked Hunt.

"Yes, but more than that. The bomb was Wyndham's response to a threat—a threat that affects us all. But he wouldn't talk about it. I had to hang on until he was willing to tell me."

He looked back at McHale.

"If you'd sprung me when you had the chance, we'd have lost any opportunity to find out what he knew."

"There's a problem bigger than a gamma bomb?" asked Hunt.

Banner nodded.

"Much bigger," he said.

"Did you pull it off?" asked McHale. "Did you convince him to talk?"

"I ran out of time," said Banner.

"Dammit!" exclaimed McHale.

"So I forced him," Banner said. "I threatened him."

Hunt looked the scientist up and down.

"With what?" the British agent asked.

"Something even I'm afraid of," said Banner.

He took off his glasses and cleaned them on the front of his shirt.

"He talked," he said, "then he got the hell out."

Banner turned back to Hunt.

"I need to speak to the Avengers," he said. "Maximum priority."

"There's a problem," said Hunt. "Comms are dark. No one's talking to anyone."

WASHINGTON, D.C.
13.13 LOCAL, JUNE 13TH

STARK'S first blast of repulsors staggered Ultron, forcing it back a step or two.

The AI ramped up the shielding of its stolen armor and fired back, throwing Iron Man into the side of a munitions cart. Missiles rolled off onto the floor like bowling pins.

Ultron advanced, firing again. Stark took off, zooming across the vast interior space. Repulsor beams chased him, blowing out ducts, vent systems, and jet-blast screens.

Stark circled and fired back, ripping a deep gouge in the deck's surface and blasting Ultron up into the air.

Ultron adjusted its boot jets and flew at Stark. They clashed in midair, trading blows. Stark heard receptors whine as they strained to soak up the beating. He smashed his hand up under Ultron's chin, and fired his repulsor.

Ultron cartwheeled out of the air, trailing smoke, and knocked over a fuel pump. Relentless, Ultron rose up out of the mangled wreckage.

Stark was coming for him, head down, at high velocity.

Ultron fired the suit's unibeam and blew Stark out of the air, sending him back down the deck. Stark collided with a parked warplane, demolishing forty million dollars' worth of military hardware. The warplane exploded.

Ultron turned away.

"Next?" it said.

Automatic-weapon fire raked the captured Iron Man suit. Three S.H.I.E.L.D. security teams, in spread cover around the main deck access, unloaded with everything they had.

Ultron barely moved. Bullets spanked and pinged off the suit. Stark had built it well.

"Pathetic," said Ultron. It raised a hand to unleash repulsor energy.

The Vision came up out of the deck in front of Ultron, phasing directly through the metal. Instantly solidifying, the Vision threw a punch of vast, synthetic strength. Ultron reeled, its head smashed so hard it was facing the other way.

Ultron straightened up. Metal squealed and complained as it turned back its head. The neck of the Iron Man armor buckled and rebounded as nanites repaired the damage.

The Vision surged forward, fist drawn back. Ultron swung at him, but his blow passed straight through the phased Avenger's insubstantial form.

The Vision plunged his fist into Ultron's head.

"Since you last did that, I have learned," said Ultron, the Vision's arm extruding from its grinning faceplate.

Ultron sent feedback surging through the armor's shielding system. The Vision cried out in pain and staggered backwards, phasing in and out of solidity.

Ultron timed its punch for a moment when the Vision was tangible.

The impact hurled the synthetic Avenger across the deck.

Explosive rounds nailed Ultron and the deck around him. Flames licked out from each impact. Nick Fury stood on one of the deck's raised walkways, hosing the rogue AI with shots from a heavy-caliber machine gun.

"Pour it on!" he yelled.

The S.H.I.E.L.D. security squads resumed firing. Additional teams had arrived from other sides of the deck. Massive gunfire enveloped Ultron. From a service ramp, Valentina de la Fontaine blasted with a laser pistol.

Ultron staggered under the monumental onslaught, but did not drop. It turned toward Fury and fired off several repulsor bursts. The energy blasts blew out part of the walkway and its guard rail, and Fury had to dive out of the way. Ultron kept blasting until the entire walkway fell away from its support brackets. It crashed to the deck in a tangle of struts. Fury leapt clear as it fell, landed on top of a parked service truck, and jumped down into cover.

Ultron turned back and raked the security teams with its repulsors. S.H.I.E.L.D. troopers were thrown into the air and hurled into bulkheads.

"Ha ha ha," said Ultron.

Something blurred around Ultron. Quicksilver was barely visible, running between bullets and blasts in a display of astonishing speed and coordination. To Pietro Maximoff, the blizzard of slow-spinning rounds looked almost static in the air. He slid between them, circling Ultron.

Ultron had detected him. It swung punches, trying to swat the Avenger, but Pietro was moving too fast for even Stark-designed target predictors to catch. The lunging fists kept missing Pietro's blurred, whipping shape as he ducked and swerved in circles.

Ultron's nanites rebuilt the predictor systems rapidly, upgrading them to new levels. They quickly managed to log Pietro's track. Ultron swung another punch that would have killed Quicksilver had the Avenger not darted back.

Quicksilver slid across the deck and skidded to a halt, looking back.

"How pointless," remarked Ultron. "You run around me, but you present no harm to me. Did you even try to land a blow?"

"It's on," panted Quicksilver. He wasn't replying to Ultron.

Iron Man stepped out of the conflagration that had once been a S.H.I.E.L.D. warplane. The firelight reflected off his polished armor. Backlit by the fireball, he walked down the deck toward Ultron.

"I wish I had a button to press," he said sourly. "You know, something satisfying to click."

He didn't. The initializer was simply a pop-down menu option on his HUD.

He selected it anyway.

Ultron looked down, and saw the data-isolation unit that Quicksilver had magnetically clamped to its chest plate. The device was small, no bigger than a coffee cup.

"This is not acceptable," Ultron said, and tried to detach it.

"Tough," said Stark. He activated the initializer.

Ultron screamed. It shuddered as if it were being electrocuted and sank to its knees.

The isolation unit rapidly extracted Ultron's digital essence from the armor and the nanite swarm supporting it. It sucked Ultron's sentience into a tiny, field-insulated containment grid.

Ultron stopped twitching. The suit stayed upright on its knees, head tilted up, back hunched. Smoke from burned-out nanites billowed off the armor.

Stark walked up to the dead armor and unlocked the isolation unit. He held it up.

"A glass and a magazine," he announced. "Now let's find somewhere safe to put this. I'm thinking Pluto."

He looked around. Fury was rising from cover. De la Fontaine and other agents were tending to the fallen troopers. Pietro was helping the Vision to his feet.

"We can turn the world back on now," Stark said to Fury.

He looked back at the grinning, dead features of Ultron—features that the nanites had sculpted into the Iron Man faceplate.

"You can wipe that grin off my damned face," he said, and he vaporized the head of the kneeling suit with a blast of his repulsors.

TWENTY-FOUR

WASHINGTON, D.C.
14.07 LOCAL, JUNE 13TH

ACROSS the Helicarrier's main command deck, screens were flashing back into life. Systems were being reactivated and restarted. With the Ultron threat gone, locked-down networks could be restored safely.

"There's a lot of repair work still to do," said the Contessa. "The power and communications infrastructures have been seriously disrupted. But we can work on fixes now."

"How's the satellite coverage?" asked Stark. "Do we have anything on the Siberian incident?"

"Preliminary views look stable," said de la Fontaine. "There's a massive storm formation moving southwest, but the dimensional breach seems to have closed. The chunk of the continental structure that vanished is back."

"That's something," said Stark.

"Any word from Wanda or Thor?" asked the Vision.

"Is my sister alive?" Pietro demanded.

"There's been nothing," de la Fontaine replied. "But atmospherics are terrible in the region, and our network isn't fully up yet."

"But we have some comms?" asked Fury.

"We're rolling out the relinks," she replied. "As you might expect, there's a huge amount of traffic. Everybody's trying to talk at once."

"Triage it," said Stark.

"We are," said the Contessa. "Priority channels and emergency broadcasts first. S.H.I.E.L.D. links are going live globally. And we have an Avengers priority."

"Berlin?" asked Stark.

"Yes."

"Let's have it," said Fury.

They stood in front of a wall display. A section of the screen plate fizzled, and then became an open window. G.W. Bridge appeared.

"Director," he said.

"What's the story, Bridge?" asked Fury.

"Hydra threat is contained," said Bridge. "Touch and go for a while there, but the situation is now safe. We're downscaling from Alpha. How about you?"

"We're through the worst," said Fury. "I'll catch you up later. Right now, I'd like to speak to Cap."

On screen, Bridge moved aside, and the camera settled on Captain America.

"Did you fight World War II *again*?" asked Stark. He was standing beside Fury, his arms folded, his faceplate retracted.

"Feels like it," replied Cap. "Listen, I don't want to waste time. I know things have been pretty hairy for you, too. There's another potential Alpha."

"What have you got?" asked Stark. "Is this Siberia?"

"I don't think so," replied Cap. "I was going to ask you about that. What's the sitrep?"

"Unclear, but it looks like the worst of that may be over," said Stark. "So what are *you* talking about?"

"Strucker told me he was acting in response to an ultimatum," said Cap. "Basically, if Hydra didn't make good on its threats to move in and control the world, someone else was going to."

"He say who?" asked Fury.

"Of course not."

"But you hit him a lot and repeated the question, right?" asked Stark.

"He's not talking," Cap said. "But the threat's real. The fact that Hydra took it so seriously gives it genuine credibility."

"Supports our theory," Fury said to Stark.

"Yeah, unless Ultron was the instigator," agreed Stark.

"You've had Ultron on your plate?" asked Cap.

"It's been a day," said Stark. "What can I tell you?"

"Avengers priority signal!" called de la Fontaine. "Routing from McMurdo Sound, Antarctica."

"On screen," said Fury.

"Stay on the line, Cap," said Stark.

Cap nodded. A second window appeared. They could see Black Widow and Hawkeye in the cockpit of an unidentified craft.

"Helicarrier?" called Widow.

"Receiving you, Natasha," said Fury.

"You guys never pick up the phone these days," said Hawkeye.

"I'm hoping you can tell us that the A.I.M. thing has been put to bed," said Fury.

On-screen, Widow and Hawkeye exchanged looks. She scowled. He looked uncomfortable.

"Kinda," said Hawkeye.

"We're not at home to 'kinda,'" warned Fury.

"A.I.M. is out of action here," Widow said. "But we're concerned there may be some nanotech contamination in the area."

"Dammit," said Stark. He sighed. "Gotta say, I've had my fill of nanites today. No pun intended."

"Good news is, we snagged the A.I.M. guy who helped build the stuff," said Hawkeye, "We got a full technical rundown out of him."

"I can squirt that now," said Widow, leaning forward to operate a control. "Data package sent."

"Stuff's pretty inert in itself," said Hawkeye. "From my understanding, anyway. But if it gets in our DNA, it gives M.O.D.O.K. a foothold. Mind-control stuff."

"How'd you get the A.I.M. guy to talk?" asked Fury.

"Arrows are pointy," replied Hawkeye.

"I'll scramble a nano-tainment task force," said Fury. "They can—"

"No need," said the Vision.

He was reviewing the data that Widow had sent.

"We can shortcut a solution to the spill," he said, "using Ultron's nanites. They are dormant now, but the swarm remains, and Ultron no longer controls them. It would be a straightforward task to reprogram them, and set them to target and destroy the A.I.M. nanotechnology."

"Oh, there's sweet justice in that," said Stark. "Dog eat dog. Ultron will hate the idea that its tech is being used for cleanup."

"There's something else," said Widow. "Thewell, the A.I.M. agent, was pretty talkative. I think he's hoping for some immunity.

He made it clear that A.I.M.'s operation was a response to some external threat. M.O.D.O.K. had fast-tracked its operation to secure world domination before somebody else could step in."

"We're hearing that a lot today," said Stark. "He give you anything useful?"

"No," said Hawkeye. "He doesn't know details. We're—"

"We're on it," said Fury.

"A threat big enough to provoke Hydra and A.I.M. has got to be big," said Cap. "It has to be hidden. Well hidden."

"I know where it is," said Stark. He looked at Fury. "Get your specialists to look at Wanda's message again."

"A mathematical expression of our universe and the other dimension..." the Vision began.

"Plus a separate little side-pocket of reality," agreed Stark, "right in our world. A bubble of counter-dimensional energy. Like a cloaking device. Wanda didn't know what she was showing us, but she mapped everything."

"Find out where it is," Fury said to de la Fontaine. She nodded and hurried away.

"We need to—" Stark started to say.

"Incoming," said Fury, reaching for the console. "A third Avengers priority."

Another comm window opened. Thor and the Scarlet Witch were sitting in a Quinjet. The image was unstable.

"—you hear us?" Wanda called.

"We can, Wanda," replied the Vision.

"Ah, we see you!" Thor declared, pointing at the screen.

"Sister! Where are you?" asked Quicksilver.

"Inbound out of Siberia," replied Wanda.

"It's good to see you," said Pietro.

"You too, brother."

"I heard you. I heard you in the darkness."

"My message got through?" she asked in surprise.

"Big time," said Stark.

"I thought I'd failed," she said.

"There has been much tumult," said Thor. "The Dread Dormammu—"

"Dormammu?" exclaimed Fury. "Geez, I hate magic stuff."

"His threat is ended," said Thor. "The battle was hard-fought. His dimensional rift has been closed and Earth restored, but the aftershocks are still coming."

"We're riding out a storm you wouldn't believe," said Wanda. "We barely got out of the void alive."

"We're glad you did," said Stark. "Hit the juice. We're going to need you back here."

"Aye," said Thor with a nod. "But surely we must discuss—"

"There is another priority," interrupted the Vision, "routing via S.H.I.E.L.D. channels in the Far East."

"Take it," said Stark.

A fourth window opened. Bruce Banner appeared on-screen. He looked surprised.

"Oh," he said. "It worked. They told me the links were screwed."

"We see you, Doctor," said Fury.

"Lot of people there," said Banner, peering into the camera.

"How you doing, Bruce?" asked Stark.

"Good, Tony, thanks. Well, all right. There's been a lot happening."

"Is there a situation there, Doctor?" asked Fury.

"Not anymore," Banner said. "But there's another problem."

"Keep it short," said Fury.

"I was going to," replied Banner calmly. "There's a threat. A hidden threat. No one knows about it, but—"

"We know about it," said Stark.

"You do?" asked Banner. He looked crestfallen. "Well, okay, then. Good. That's good. I was worried. It's pretty big."

"We're on it, Doctor," said Fury. "Just get yourself to somewhere secure. And quiet. Looks like you've had a long day."

"I'm fine," said Banner. "But thank you for your concern."

"We're handling the threat, Bruce," said Stark. "Just identifying it now."

"You don't know what it is?" asked Banner.

"No, but we will very soon," said Stark. "Until then—"

"I can tell you what it is," Banner said. "I know."

Stark, Fury, and the Vision looked at each other.

"Good for you, Doc," said Fury. "One step ahead."

"Just trying to help out," said Banner.

"Appreciate that," said Stark. "And this is confirmed?"

"By the highest authority," said Banner.

"Okay," said Stark. "Let's do this. We're all ears, Bruce. Give us the lowdown. Oh, just before you start—"

He looked up at the screen image of Cap.

"You want to do this or shall I?" he asked.

"Be my guest," said Cap.

"I think it's your turn," said Stark.

"Just do it," Cap said.

"It should come from you," said Stark. "It sounds better coming from you."

"Gentlemen…" growled Fury.

Stark smiled and nodded to Cap.

"Okay," said Captain America. "Avengers…assemble."

25

PINE BARRENS, NEW JERSEY
06.31 LOCAL, JUNE 14TH

FROM above, there was nothing to see. Just the expanse of dense forest, thick and dark in the early morning air.

"Time to target, four minutes," Iron Man said from the helm of the Quinjet. They were coming in low and fast. The sky was hard blue above them, and the ocean of emerald trees below rushed past perilously close. The wake of the speeding Quinjet scored a rippling line across the treetops.

"Nothing on visual," reported Hawkeye. "We sure this is right?"

"There's definitely something there," said the Scarlet Witch, turning her hands in front of her face and staring at her fingers

"You can feel it?" asked Quicksilver.

"Now that we're close, yes," she replied. "Vast, yet invisible. It's as though I can touch it."

"S.H.I.E.L.D. reports in position," said Widow. "Full mobilization at your discretion."

"Let's see if we can handle this," said Cap. He adjusted his shield and glanced at the others.

"I am eager to," said Thor.

"Three minutes," said Iron Man. "Vision? You're up."

The Vision nodded and rose to his feet.

"See you inside," he said, and he phased down through the deck of the speeding craft.

Outside, he turned and accelerated like a missile, flying alongside the Quinjet as it ripped across the tree-cover. Then he began to pull away. He turned sideways in a graceful arc and descended toward the heart of the forest.

The cloaking shield was advanced and sophisticated, but Stark had analyzed the data in advance and identified the harmonic values. Phasing, the Vision flew into the trees and began to pulse his molecular structure to the correct harmonic frequency. It was a delicate, subtle manipulation of his synth-organic system.

He plunged into the invisible cloak.

There was a shimmer.

Its pattern disrupted, the cloaking field failed and collapsed.

The forest glimmered away, revealing a depression in the trees eight miles in diameter. The trees had been removed with surgical precision by fusion beamers, and the cloak had simply reproduced their appearance, matching itself to the surrounding forest.

Now, daylight revealed what the cloak had been hiding.

It was vast, monolithic. A vehicle. A starship.

The starship was circular, a huge disk of gleaming green-and-white alloy, with architectural structures extending from the center of the top surface. It looked too big to be real, like some strange city seen from a distance.

"I think I see it now," Hawkeye murmured.

"No kidding," replied Iron Man. "Superclass dreadnought.

That's a ship of the line."

"Size of that thing," muttered Quicksilver.

Iron Man banked the Quinjet and decelerated hard. Vector nozzles turned and fired.

"They'll have seen us," said the Scarlet Witch.

"Even with stealth mode engaged, they'll have seen us from a hundred miles out," replied Iron Man. "You know what? I no longer care."

"Why aren't they shooting at us?" asked Widow. "Why no countermeasures?"

"Maybe they don't want a fight," replied Hawkeye.

"They're going to be disappointed," said Cap.

Cap opened the Quinjet's deck hatch. Iron Man put the craft into a steady VTOL hover and slaved the controls remotely to his suit. They were in among the trees, twenty feet above the forest floor and about six hundred yards from the edge of the vast ship.

"Go!" cried Cap.

Thor led the way, followed by Iron Man, his boot jets firing. Quicksilver came out of the Quinjet like a shaft of blue light, a dazzling trail that dropped to the ground and snaked between the trees toward the ship.

CAP jumped, landing on his feet. The others dropped by fast rope.

Airborne and running, they tracked through the trees toward the immense structure.

"Oh, they just realized we're worth their attention," said Iron Man. "Shields are coming on. Watch for defense systems."

Automated gun turrets extruded from recesses along the rim of the ship's hull. Beam emitters opened their apertures and began to spit sizzling darts of fusion energy, decimating trees and throwing up geysers of soil. Quicksilver zagged between the explosions. Cap leapt to avoid being crushed by a toppling pine. Hawkeye flinched as a blast ripped up the ground close to him, showering him with dirt. He kept running.

"They're not employing their main arsenal," said Widow, vaulting a tree trunk. "This is just to discourage us from getting closer. They're relying on their shields."

"Which I'm about to jam," reported Iron Man, banking aside to avoid fusion bolts. He was flying between the treetops.

"You confident you can?" replied Cap over the link. He was running hard, shield on his arm.

"We know their tech," said Iron Man. "I've been working on a few things in case we ever had to face them again."

His unibeam pulsed, and the energy fields around the hull shivered and burst. The starship's shields—built for sustained, deep-void combat with rival superclass vessels—suffered an immediate and catastrophic failure. They all felt the pop of the air-pressure changing. There was a stink of ozone and pine sap.

The automated turrets immediately started to fire at a heavier rate. Fusion bolts rained into the treeline, turning tall trees into wooden shrapnel, torching others, and ripping up the soil.

"Okay, now they're mad," snapped Hawkeye, diving for cover. He rolled, raising his bow.

He shot blast arrows at the gun turrets in rapid succession. He was aiming directly at the pulsing apertures of the turrets' emitter modules. Adamantium-tipped arrowheads pierced the modules deeply and precisely, and the charges did the rest.

The gun turrets exploded along the saucer rim in a series of flurrying blasts. Power-feed subsystems inside the hull-skin fed back and blew out, shredding sections of the hull. Debris rained down, and smoke gusted into the blue sky.

A broad section of the starship's anti-personnel net was crippled. The Avengers had a clear and unopposed line of approach. They left the burning forest and rushed the ship.

"Thor? Vision? Get the door," ordered Iron Man.

Synthetic human and Asgardian flew in side-by-side. Thor delivered a huge blow to the hull with Mjolnir, smashing a hole through it. He and the Vision grabbed the edges of the puncture and hauled in opposite directions.

They tore the hull section wide open.

Iron Man flew straight in through the yawning gap, followed by Quicksilver, who had converted his acceleration into a flying leap. Cap stormed in a moment later, followed by Black Widow, the Scarlet Witch, and Hawkeye. Vision melted in through the hull, and Thor smashed open yet another entry point.

Inside the cool, high-ceilinged hallways of the craft, warriors of the Kree Stellar Empire scrambled to meet them.

The Kree were an ancient and highly advanced race, and their civilization had long dominated galactic affairs. They had built a star-spanning culture, preserved their dynastic purity, and achieved great feats of cosmic engineering and science.

None of which had been accomplished without ruthless military zeal. They had fought off rival empires. They had conquered worlds.

They were not afraid of conflict or bloodshed.

Hundreds of Kree warriors rushed to repel the invaders. Their green-and-white battle armor and crested helms were menacing and sinister. Their discipline and fire-team order were immaculately controlled.

Within seconds, they started to fall.

Iron Man strafed them, raking the hallway with repulsor fire, mowing down the Kree and casting bodies into the air. Thor thundered in behind him, unleashing hammer blows of Asgardian rage that crushed the Kree battlefield elite.

Kree blasters fired. The air filled with a criss-cross of dazzling bolts and beams. Cap's shield deflected shots as he charged into the opposition ranks, punching and kicking troopers aside. Each blow was perfectly timed and perfectly aimed. There was no waste of effort. Kree warriors toppled and collapsed, overwhelmed by the intensity of Cap's expert assault. Cap barely lost any momentum. He plowed into their formations.

Quicksilver raced ahead of him, zipping through the warriors and dropping them with rapid punches while dodging every blaster shot. Hawkeye hung back, using the mangled cover of the breach-point, and took down officers with pinpoint accuracy. He spotted groups of Kree on an upper level, crews who were trying to set up heavy blasters on tripods. He spun up more blast arrows and blew the walkway out from under them. Flailing Kree warriors fell, along with sections of walkway and burning weapon mounts.

Widow moved up alongside Cap, spin-kicking and shooting as she came, covering Cap's flank to prevent the increasingly frantic Kree from closing in around him. Her nines roared, firing Stark-built penetrator rounds that could punch through just about any-thing—including the Kree's advanced battle-plate.

Broken green-and-white armored bodies began to litter the deck.

The Vision rose through the deck like a ghost, solidified, and slammed together the heads of two firing Kree warriors. He turned and laid out another with a straight punch. Several more warriors blasted at him, but their beams passed straight through him and knocked down Kree troopers behind him. The Vision reached down, ripped out the deck, and sent a dozen warriors flying as though a carpet had been yanked out under them.

Support squads poured into the hallways, rushing to engage. The Scarlet Witch, tall and elegant, calmly strode along the corridor behind the main assault as if oblivious to the mayhem. She had woven a hex around herself that deflected energy fire like rain. At the sight of the reinforcements, she raised her hands and conjured a wave of misfortune.

Multiple and simultaneous weapons malfunctions swept through the ranks. Some guns exploded in the hands of the warriors trying to fire them. Some were suddenly drained of their energy charges. Others simply refused to fire; the baffled warriors wielding them quickly fell before Cap's fists, Widow's bullets, Hawkeye's arrows, and the Vision's disorienting alterations of solidity.

Iron Man, Quicksilver, and Thor broke through, entering a huge internal gallery.

"Power levels are rising," said Iron Man, firing his repulsors at the Kree defenders. "I think our visitors are trying to light the engines and get the hell out of here."

"Too late," remarked Thor.

"I don't think they're happy to be having this confrontation," said Pietro. He was moving so fast that light was distorting in his wake.

Dozens of warriors kept appearing, sprawled and unconscious, on the deck where he had passed.

"Too late," Thor repeated, and drove his hammer through a bulkhead. He smashed his way into an engineering space, ripped a massive power hub off the deck, and hurled it. It crashed through a chamber wall and exploded in the next compartment.

Eerie damage sirens sounded. The air was full of smoke.

"Central command?" Iron Man requested over the comlink.

"Two levels below you," replied the Scarlet Witch, locating it with a complex conjuration.

"Thank you," said Iron Man. "That matches the energy profiles I'm reading."

Iron Man banked and executed a power dive into a main, through-deck shaft, firing his repulsors ahead of him and exploding down through the levels. The Vision, Thor, and Quicksilver followed him, lancing through the air. Cap vaulted a handrail and dropped after them. The Widow emptied her clips into approaching warriors, and then followed suit. Hawkeye glanced at the drop— and the burning path his fellow Avengers were cutting into the heart of the ship.

"Guess I'll be climbing, then," he said, wheeling around to bury an arrow in an attacking Kree warrior.

"Allow me," said the Scarlet Witch, casting a hex that lifted both her and Hawkeye into midair and lowered them gracefully down the through-deck space.

Thor and Iron Man took out the huge blast doors protecting the central-command space. Debris flew in all directions. Three Kree officers opened fire, but a flying shield smacked them off their feet.

Iron Man came in to land and walked forward, leading the Avengers into the chamber. Another Kree officer grabbed a weapon, and Widow turned to blast him with her Bite—but Hawkeye had already pinned his arm to a console with an arrow.

Iron Man looked up at the giant life-support tank in front of them. Its sides were transparent. From the energized liquid within, a huge, distorted face gazed down at them. Its features were solemn and sad. Fiber-cable links connected its cranium to the tank's framework.

"This will be your only warning, Avengers," said the Supreme Intelligence of the Kree Stellar Empire. "You are not welcome here."

"Uh-uh," said Iron Man. "You've got some 'splainin' to do."

"This is an act of war," the Intelligence declared.

"This is an act of sovereign defense," replied Cap. "You have assaulted our planet."

"We have not," replied the Intelligence. "We have merely observed."

"You've meddled," said Cap. "You've provoked. We know about the ultimatum. Thanks to you, five serious threats have arisen. Threats that could have destroyed our world or changed it forever."

"That was to be wished," said the Intelligence.

"You admit it?" asked Thor.

"The Earth is dangerous. It cannot be allowed to continue on its present course."

"So you'd place its fate in the hands of terrorists and monsters?" asked Cap.

"The Earth must be tamed," said the Supreme Intelligence. "For the galactic good. Your criminal elements and insurgents have long sought world domination, each in their various ways. They were offered the chance to make good on their designs."

"Are you serious?" asked the Scarlet Witch.

"Each one has the means," said the Supreme Intelligence. "The means and the desire to control your world. To impose a new order. To curb the wayward nature of humanity."

"Because they're psychopaths," said Hawkeye. "Their idea of curbing is…dictatorship. The loss of freedom, the—"

"They would dominate and control," said the Supreme Intelligence. "They would diligently administrate this world, and prevent it from polluting the galaxy."

"Or reduce us to the Stone Age," said Cap.

"That, too, would have been an acceptable solution," answered the Intelligence.

"So you just wanted others to do your dirty work and cripple the world?" asked Widow.

"The Earth must be tamed."

"It's more than that," said Stark. "The galactic authorities have declared Earth off-limits. If the Kree staged an intervention or an invasion, they would have found themselves at war with the other powers of the cosmos. But if Earth collapsed because of an indigenous threat, that would be okay. Predictable. That's dirty pool, Supremor."

"It is a method."

"And you guys could have stepped in, taken over, apparently peacekeeping and cleaning up the mess," said Stark. "Looking after a wounded neighbor. Apparently humanitarian and caring. Invasion by proxy."

Cap stepped forward beside Iron Man and looked up at the vast tank.

"Why are you so scared of us?" he asked.

"Behold, human, how you have bludgeoned your way into my presence," said the Supreme Intelligence.

"This is self-defense," Cap repeated. "A response to your threat. I meant, why are you so afraid of Earth?"

For a moment, the Supreme Intelligence did not answer.

"You are a child race," it said at last. "Newcomers to the galactic community. In the few short years we have been aware of you, we have become horrified by your propensities. Your technologies escalate at a pace that even you don't understand. You breed meta-beings at a rate unmatched by any other world, and those meta-beings live without control or limitation, yet many of them possess the power to damage or destroy worlds—or even destabilize the galaxy as a whole.

"Hunger and disease riddle your world," the Supreme Intelligence continued, "and there is no unification of political agenda. Yet you actively enmesh yourselves in the business of other cultures. Earth is a dangerous planet. It is a danger to itself and a danger to other worlds. You have no maturity or wisdom. You have great power but no responsibility. You are reckless and emotional. You are imperfect and lacking unity. You are headstrong and do not know your own strength.

"While Earth exists in its present, volatile state, no culture in space is safe. And the Kree Stellar Empire is not about to be brought down by a selfish, too-powerful infant species."

"You really think we're a threat to you?" asked Iron Man.

"In time, you will be," replied the Supreme Intelligence. "You will turn your sights upon the stars and envy what others have. Until then, you are a threat without even meaning to be. One rogue meta-being, one uncontrollable disease, one technological mishap. You could end galactic culture by mistake and misadventure."

"So you wanted to stop us?" asked Cap. "To curb us and contain us?"

"Yes," said the Supreme Intelligence. "Any one of the parties we encouraged would have been capable of taking control of the Earth, and ruling it. They would have tamed your wild nature and made humankind subservient. The victorious party would have been in fealty to the Kree, and the Kree would have ruled through them. This, they all saw, was preferable to the destruction of their world and their ambitions."

"You reckoned without us," said Cap. "You underestimated our ability to police ourselves. To stop the threats and to see your hand in them. Doesn't that prove we are far more than the children you believe us to be?"

"The threat remains," said the Supreme Intelligence. "You are defiant and willful. The galaxy would be better rid of you."

"I suggest," said Iron Man, "you activate auto-repair, fix your ship, and get the hell off our planet. You'll never be permitted to do this again. Take that message back to your people."

"No," said the Supreme Intelligence. "This attempt to pacify the Earth has failed. The Kree are reluctant to move against you directly, for fear of censure, but we always knew we would act ourselves if our hand was forced. With regret, that is now our only option. You have resisted change. Change will now be obligatory."

Hatches opened along the walls of the control chamber. In the huge compartment beyond, the Avengers could see ranks of massive, silent android figures: Kree Sentries, implacable robotic war-machines of extraordinary power.

"The Sentries will be activated," announced the Supreme Intelligence. "Earth will be crushed. And you meta-beings will be the first to be eliminated."

PINE BARRENS, NEW JERSEY
07.09 LOCAL, JUNE 14TH

CAN we get any closer?" asked Banner.

"They told you to hold off, Doc," replied McHale.

Banner fidgeted with the harness that held him in the flight seat. The S.H.I.E.L.D. transport was circling the target site at high altitude, part of the task force waiting for word from the Avengers.

"I wanted to be there," said Banner.

He was fretting. Since retrieval in Madripoor, S.H.I.E.L.D. had insisted on feeding him sedatives. He felt woozy. He felt too calm. He hated the lethargy, but he knew it was necessary. He thought about Wyndham's offer, a final solution for his curse. It had been so tempting. And if anyone could ever cure his condition, it would be the High Evolutionary.

But some things were more important. Like being true to your friends. And yourself. Whoever and whatever you were.

"I think the Avengers can handle things," McHale replied.

"They've fought against the Kree before," said Banner. "But the Kree are powerful. Really powerful. I—"

"Just relax and enjoy the view, Doc. It's going to be fine."

Banner sat back and looked out the window port. Far below, he could see the vast, gleaming expanse of the revealed starship.

Banner and McHale heard voices from the deck forward of them. Nick Fury was at the comms station. They heard him curse.

"Director?" McHale called.

"Something's wrong," said Fury. "I just lost contact with Stark. We're registering an energy buildup, serious levels, from inside that ship. I don't think the Kree are backing down."

"Should I order our teams in?" asked Valentina de la Fontaine.

"If the Avengers can't handle it, there's not a lot our fire-teams are gonna be able to do," snapped Fury. "I knew we should've just bombed the site. The nuclear option—"

"There's more than one nuclear option, Fury."

They looked around. Banner had unstrapped his harness and was on his feet.

"Banner?"

"I said there's more than one," said Banner. He moved toward the side hatch. The sedatives made him a little unsteady on his feet. They made him punch-drunk, too. They made him uninhibited.

"Doctor Banner, sit the hell down!" yelled Fury.

Banner hauled the hatch open. Freezing air howled in. Banner looked at McHale.

"Doc?" McHale asked, wide-eyed. He moved toward Banner.

"Your turn, McHale," Banner said.

"What?"

Banner smiled and pointed to his own chin.

"Seems only fair," he said. "Make it a good one."

"Are you crazy?" McHale asked.

"One thing everyone seems to forget, McHale," said Banner, with a sad smile. "Part of me is an Avenger, too."

McHale looked at him for a moment. Then he smiled and shook his head.

"Goddamn it, Doc," he said.

He threw a punch.

Banner's head snapped back, and he flew backwards out of the hatch.

IT WAS a hell of a drop.

Falling, Banner knew he was plunging to his death at terminal velocity. The fall was going to kill him.

The fall was absolutely, definitely, going to kill Bruce Banner.

He knew he ought to be anxious, frantic, screaming. He ought to be smarting and angry from the punch. But those damned sedatives...

He closed his eyes. He thought about the impending impact. He concentrated on it.

His pulse rate rose. It started racing. The reality of the fall began to penetrate the haze of the sedative shots. It scared the hell out of him.

He focused on that, on the fear. He tried to clear his foggy head. He stopped trying to remain calm about anything.

His adrenaline levels began to spike.

PINE BARRENS, NEW JERSEY
07.11 LOCAL, JUNE 14TH

THE KREE warship shook as something struck its upper hull and tore down through its superstructure. Inner partitions failed. Bulkheads ruptured. Decks caved in.

The Hulk landed in the middle of the immense Sentry compartment. The impact of his gigantic frame buckled the deck and disintegrated several of the robot units.

Hulk roared. He reached out with his massive hands, grabbing and ripping at the Sentries that were waking around him. Arms as thick as tree trunks drove fists the size of wrecking balls into Kree-built war-machine technology.

Hulk smashed.

From the adjacent control center, the Avengers looked on in shock. The Hulk's arrival had caused a shockwave that had thrown all of them to the deck, along with all the Kree warriors present. They struggled to their feet.

"Oh my god!" the Scarlet Witch cried, gazing into the Sentry compartment at the Hulk's feral rampage.

"What is this?" asked the Supreme Intelligence. "What is this?"

Kree Warriors fired through the hatchway at the Hulk and from overhead walkways in the Sentry compartment. Iron Man knocked down the nearest ones with a blast of his repulsors.

"What part of this is a good idea?" asked Iron Man.

"The part where we win," replied Thor.

The Hulk plowed through the Sentry units, hurling broken and twisted fragments of them up into the air. Devastating green fists shredded the robots, row after row. Support and power cables snapped. Flames surged up.

The Sentries had brought star systems to their knees.

But the Hulk...was the Hulk.

Thor ducked as a dismembered Sentry unit flew into the central-command space and tumbled across the deck. Then he grinned and hefted Mjolnir.

"I am with the green one," he said. "Who's with me?"

Iron Man looked at Cap.

"Avengers?" he asked.

"I think we're assembled," replied Cap.

He raised his shield.

In response, the heroes rushed into the fight together, smashing through the Kree ranks. Together, they combined magic, technology, speed, marksmanship, and unrivalled combat skills.

They moved as one. One team. Earth's Mightiest.

PINE BARRENS, NEW JERSEY
07.30 LOCAL, JUNE 14TH

A MONUMENTAL plume of black smoke rose from the burning ruin of the starship into the New Jersey sky.

"Is it confirmed?" asked Cap, walking into the treeline to join the others.

Iron Man nodded.

"That pod we saw lift off was some kind of hyper-shuttle, " he said. "The Supreme Intelligence making his escape. S.W.O.R.D. monitors picked it up entering high warp just outside the orbit of the Moon."

"S.H.I.E.L.D. teams are moving in to secure the wreck," said the Vision.

"How about...?" Cap asked.

Iron Man jerked his thumb.

Thirty yards away, the brooding mass of the Hulk stood beside a shattered tree, hunched and panting. The Widow stood in front of Hulk, staring up at him.

"What's she doing?" asked Cap.

"Talking to him," said Iron Man.

"It's over," she said softly. "Do you understand? It's over now. You can calm down."

"Hulk does not want to be calm," Hulk growled.

"You must be," she said. "It's time to be."

The others slowly approached.

"Another fight?" Hulk snarled. "More things for Hulk to smash?"

"No, no," the Widow assured him. "Just friends, Hulk. Just Avengers."

"Hulk?" asked Iron Man. "Bruce?"

"No Bruce. Hulk hate Bruce. Just Hulk."

"Hulk," said Iron Man. "It's okay."

"Tin Man want to fight Hulk. Tin Man want to hurt Hulk."

"No," said Iron Man. "Tin Man just wants to say…thank you."

Hulk grunted. He did not reply.

They moved back to give him some space. Hulk sat down and gazed at the smoke for a while.

"You know," said Iron Man quietly to Cap, "there's one thing that kind of bugs me."

"What?" asked Cap.

"Look what we did, Steve."

They looked at the burning starship. Iron Man retracted his faceplate.

"We saved the world," said Cap firmly.

"Yeah, we did," said Stark. "And we had good cause. We took care of a threat that could have ended the human race. But do you see how we did it?"

Captain America glanced at the Hulk, alone and brooding.

"He's only human," said Cap.

"Yeah," said Stark. "And so are you, and so am I. Only human."

"What are you saying, Tony?"

"I'm saying," said Stark, "I'm saying, in some ways, maybe the Kree had a point."

Cap didn't respond. He stared at the ground.

"That's all we ever can be," he said at last. "Human. Let's keep making sure it's enough."

Nick Fury approached, making his way up the bank.

"Hey," he said.

"Everything okay?" asked Cap.

Fury shrugged.

"Not sure," he said. "Plenty here that needs sorting out. Look, I hate to mention it, but the S.H.I.E.L.D. station in LA just squirted me. Every clock in California just got set back by three hundred minutes. There are reports of a tachyon flare around the San Diego area."

"Temporal disruption?" asked Cap. "Someone screwing with time?"

"Could be Kang," said Stark. "Kang, or Immortus. Or the other guy. The one with the headdress."

"Could be anything," said Fury.

Cap and Iron Man looked at each other.

"Your turn," said Iron Man.

"I did it last time."

Tony Stark sighed.

"Okay," he said. He turned toward the others.

"Avengers?" he called. "Guess what I'm going to say next."

Special Excerpt

Marvel Super Heroes Secret Wars

by Alex Irvine

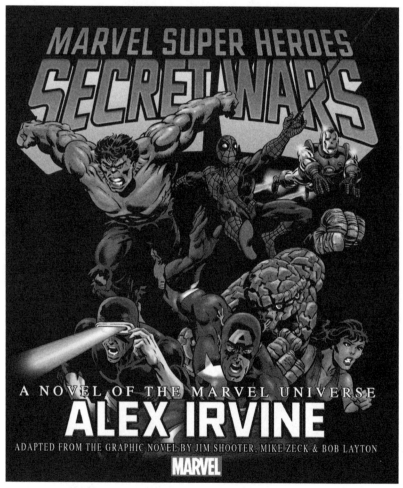

On Sale Now

ONE

STEVE ROGERS knew he was in a spaceship of some kind. He stood in the middle of an open floor underneath a transparent dome through which he could see a field of stars. He was still wearing his Captain America uniform, and he clutched his shield at his side.

But there the familiar ended. A moment before, Steve had been conducting a training exercise for new S.H.I.E.L.D. recruits at Nick Fury's intake facility on Long Island. A bright flash had blinded him and he'd flinched, thinking something had gone wrong with the training equipment.

Then, suddenly, he just wasn't on Long Island anymore.

Steve turned in a complete circle, taking in and analyzing his surroundings. The ship was huge—at least the size of a S.H.I.E.L.D. Helicarrier. The open area where Steve had appeared was ringed with banks of monitors and consoles, none of which looked anything like current S.H.I.E.L.D. or Stark technology. Steve looked up through the dome again and saw the dissipating traces of some huge release of celestial energy—multicolored, overpowering. He blinked hard.

The stars above weren't familiar, and he didn't see any nearby planets. By the looks of things, he was in the middle of galactic nowhere.

And he wasn't alone. Other heroes had appeared all around him—all just as confused, by the looks of things. Automatically, Steve performed a head count and updated his threat assessment.

Three of the Fantastic Four were present: Mister Fantastic, the Human Torch, and the Thing. Where was the Invisible Woman? Steve made a mental note to ask later. Spider-Man looked around warily—his thin, costumed frame crouched next to the Thing's orange, rocky bulk. Several of Steve's fellow Avengers were also there: Hawkeye, She-Hulk, Iron Man, Thor, Wasp, Hulk, and Spectrum. That was good news. He knew his people, and he knew he could count on them.

From the X-Men, there was Nightcrawler, Colossus, Kitty Pryde's pet dragon Lockheed, Wolverine, Rogue, Cyclops, Storm, and Charles Xavier. Another note went into Steve's mental situation file: After assessing the threat level, ask Xavier what he knows about this. In addition to being a telepath, Xavier was often in the know about global-level threats before anyone at S.H.I.E.L.D. had an inkling of their existence.

Steve completed his circle and noticed one person who stood out like a sore thumb: Magneto, the X-Men's mortal adversary—also in full costume. Steve almost flattened Magneto with his shield, just on general principle, but it wasn't in Steve's nature to hit a man without provocation.

Magneto was the only visible enemy, and he looked as thunderstruck and confused as the rest of them. Steve left him alone and started looking for any potential point within view from which an attack might come. There were plenty of ways out of the room, and therefore plenty of ways an enemy might enter—but he saw no immediate threats.

After the first few seconds, when everyone else was doing more or less what Steve was doing, the questions started to come.

"How did we—?"

"Where are we?"

"Ooh, I got it!" Spider-Man said, raising his hand. "We're on some kind of giant ship in outer space." He shot out a web to an overhead girder and swung up to stick himself to the transparent dome. He couldn't just stand around like a normal guy, Steve thought. But hey, he was younger than the rest of them—or at least that's how he always acted, with the wisecracks and showing off.

Mister Fantastic—Reed Richards—seemed to be assessing the situation like it was a puzzle just for him to solve. That's how he saw everything, Steve figured. With his graying temples and thoughtful approach—not to mention a vocabulary full of what used to be called fifty-cent words—Richards was almost the stereotypical nutty professor. Except, of course, for his powers, which he was exhibiting now. He stretched his head and one arm over to the closest instrument panel and examined it. The rest of his body—and the rest of his suit, with its white, circled "4" logo—didn't move. For the millionth time, Steve wondered how the blue fabric of his suit handled all the stretching. Reed could have made a killing if he'd patented that. "No identifiable origin," he said. "These gauges look like Kree, Shi'ar...I'll have a handle on it soon."

"Brain trust?" Steve said. "Xavier? Banner? Any idea how we got here?"

He was looking at the Hulk when he finished asking the question. It was difficult for Steve to reconcile the presence of Banner's mind trapped in a body full of the Hulk's primitive rage. In any case, Reed was the first one to try to answer. "Teleportation, some kind of dimensional breach...hard to tell," Reed said.

"That's obvious, Richards," spat the Hulk.

Noting the edge in Banner's voice, Steve looked to Iron Man next. "Tony?"

"Um, no idea," Iron Man said, shifting from side to side as he glanced away. "Reed's the expert."

Steve cocked an eyebrow. It was unlike Tony Stark to admit anyone else was more of an expert on anything.

"Let's set some groups and start exploring," he said. "If this is a ship, we better find out how it works. We'll break it up into territories for each team."

"Hold on," Spider-Man said. "We weren't together on Earth. Why are we all in the same place now? Did we all get picked for some kind of galactic dodgeball game? I mean, I was getting a sandwich."

"We were all in the Baxter Building," Reed said. He looked around. "Where's Susan?"

Steve took note: Even Reed didn't know why his wife—Sue Richards, the Invisible Woman—wasn't there.

"Typical Reed—only just now noticing my sister is missing," said Johnny Storm, the Human Torch.

"We're all missing some members," Cyclops said. "Not all of the X-Men are here—or the Avengers, either."

"Ahem," said Spider-Man. "Some of us aren't part of your fancy teams."

"Nothing fancy about the X-Men, bub," Wolverine said. He and the rest of the mutants were in their uniforms, too, like they'd been ready for a fight. Cyclops always wore his ruby-quartz visor to control his optic force blasts, but some of the other X-Men would have been pretty easy to mistake for normal people. Colossus, when he wasn't organic steel, just looked like the big Russian farm boy he was. Storm might easily have been mistaken for a down-and-out musician or artist, with her leather clothes and white mohawk. Wolverine had itinerant drifter written all over him, except when he showed his claws.

And then there was Nightcrawler. It was pretty hard not to stand out in a crowd when you had blue skin, three prehensile toes on each foot, the same number of fingers, and a pointed tail. And the purple dragon—Lockheed—what was he doing there? He was bonded to Kitty Pryde, and she wasn't around.

"We're here," Wolverine said. "Let's figure it out. What I want to know is, what's he doing here?"

He pointed at Magneto.

Steve took a step closer to Wolverine in case he had to stop a fight from breaking out. Then movement outside, against the field of distant stars, caught his attention.

"Heads up," Steve said. "Four o'clock high. Another ship."

Xavier frowned and said, "I sense other humans there...our enemies."

"Who?" Steve asked, peering up at the other ship as it drifted closer. It too was domed in glass, but Steve couldn't identify the figures within.

"Kang the Conqueror. The Wrecking Crew. Absorbing Man. Doctor Octopus. Molecule Man. The Lizard. Doctor Doom." Xavier spoke slowly as he focused his telepathic powers. "Another... perhaps several others. Something—another mind—is shielding them against my psionic investigation."

"Pretty random," Spider-Man commented. "Just like us. Only mean and ugly. Hey, Spectrum, maybe you can do your light-speed thing—zip over there and back before they notice you?"

"Hold on," Steve said. "Don't go off half-cocked. We don't want to start a fight before we understand what's going on here."

"Speaking of fights," the Thing said, "I'm with Wolverine. What's this mook doing here instead of joining his buddies up there?" He pointed a finger at Magneto, who stood apart from the rest. Ben Grimm's rocky frame was poised for a fight, and Steve knew even Magneto might have trouble against the Thing.

"I might as justifiably ask why I am cast among such as you," Magneto shot back.

"Gang, we've got a bigger problem. Literally," Spider-Man said. "See?"

He pointed, and now they were all close enough to see that the other spaceship didn't just contain a motley assortment of their human enemies.

It also held Galactus. He loomed over the rest of the forms in the vessel. This was a whole new category of danger. Galactus was as old as the universe, and as powerful as any ancient civilization had imagined its gods to be. He wandered the universe in search of planets he could consume, always searching for a way to sate his uncontrollable hunger. No one in the group of heroes could match that kind of power. If they had to fight the occupants of the other ship, and Galactus took their side, it was going to be a very short fight.

"Bigger problem," said Ben. "Ha. Ha. Ha."

CHARLES XAVIER

His mind touched another. Not one of his allies, not one of his enemies. An ambient consciousness, a field of thought and desire, infusing the space around him with knowledge of its presence. Xavier had never felt anything like it. Ripped from his Westchester home, dropped on a strange ship in deep space, he felt no fear. Instead, he felt a sense of destiny like a physical pressure, a weight on his mind and soul. The X-Men were here for a reason. They would discover it in time.

He reached out and touched, ever so lightly, some of the other minds around him. They were feeling it, too, though he sensed them grasping to understand. Not all of them were even conscious of it.

Xavier was. He felt unbounded, as if the very air he breathed were a message saying: Yes. Yes. Yes. He was conscious of possibility, that things were possible here that none of them could have dreamed of back on Earth. It was not some hypnotic suggestion from the consciousness he touched. Xavier was in full possession of his faculties.

It was a greeting.

It struck him that he could be something new here. Something more than the instructor, bound as he was to his wheelchair.

He could act. Rules here were different. All of them. He had no idea in what way they would be different, or who had caused them to be so, but that difference was part and parcel of the way his mind experienced the reality of this place.

Things seemed possible here that had not been possible before. That which had been taken away from him might be granted again.

And if it could not, what would be lost in the attempt?

Around him, the X-Men were talking. The Avengers were talking. Three of the Fantastic Four were talking. All of them talked and talked, and Xavier fell deeply into himself and reached a point at which he knew that anything he wanted powerfully enough, he could achieve.

Xavier gave in to his fondest desire.

He stood.